D1328542

Financial Policy Decisions

Financial Policy Decisions

Harold Bierman, Jr.

CONTRIBUTIONS BY

WARREN H. HAUSMAN, SEYMOUR SMIDT, RICHARD R. WEST

The Macmillan Company / Collier-Macmillan Limited, London

First Printing

Library of Congress catalog card number: 70–93285

THE MACMILLAN COMPANY
866 THIRD AVENUE, NEW YORK, NEW YORK 10022

COLLIER-MACMILLAN CANADA, LTD., TORONTO, ONTARIO

Printed in the United States of America

Acknowledgments

A large portion of this book was written in conjunction with other colleagues and has appeared in print as journal articles. I wish to thank the editors of these journals and the following co-authors for their assistance and for allowing me to use the results of their research and writing efforts in this publication:

Alan McAdams, Chapter 1 (decisions involving cash)
Warren H. Hausman, Chapters 3 (credit decisions) and 17 (convertible bonds)
Richard West, Chapters 8 (dividends) and 9 (reacquisition of shares)
Seymour Smidt, Chapters 11 (measuring debt) and 12 (subordination and the cost of debt)
Bowman Brown, Chapter 13 (income bonds)

I also owe a debt to stimulating co-workers for ideas developed in other portions of the book. Among these are Richard Schramm and Jerome Hass. Several students who helped contribute to my understanding are acknowledged in the text, but I also wish to thank the many others not mentioned by name. Stewart C. Myers reviewed an earlier draft of the manuscript and offered many useful suggestions.

H. B.

Preface

In recent years the literature on business decision making has shifted from a more or less intuitive qualitative approach to a much more analytical and mathematical approach. This book is an attempt to extend analytical methods to a variety of decisions that may be classified as financial policy decisions.[1]

An analytical approach to financial policy decisions is useful for two important reasons:

1. The use of analysis (including a mathematical model) may give us a specific optimum answer.
2. It may not be possible to apply the model and obtain a specific answer, but the use of the model may lead to a better understanding of the decision process, which in turn may lead to better decisions.

Mathematical models of financial decisions do not replace judgment but rather they apply the judgment and experience of the decision maker more effectively to the problem being studied. Many of the situations with which we will be dealing are decisions made under uncertainty; thus the decision indicated by the model may, after the event has occurred, turn out to be a less desirable alternative than others that were available. This is, of course, a characteristic of decision making under uncertainty. When there is uncertainty there is generally a probability that an event may occur for which there is a better action than the action chosen.

Many of the decisions considered in this book lead to mathematical models. I have placed complex mathematics or mathematical manipulations in appendixes to the chapters whenever this is possible. Thus a person with no interest in the mathematical derivations may read the chapter, and the person who is interested in the derivations may go on and read the appendixes to the

---

[1] For other efforts along this line see A. A. Robichek and S. C. Myers, *Optimal Financing Decisions* (Prentice-Hall, Englewood Cliffs, N.J., 1965); W. Beranek, *Analysis for Financial Decisions* (Irwin, Homewood, Ill., 1963); M. J. Gordon, *The Investment, Financing, and Valuation of the Corporation* (Irwin, Homewood, Ill., 1962); and Ezra Solomon, *The Theory of Financial Management* (Columbia University Press, New York, 1963).

chapter. Obviously, it is to a person's advantage to be able to check the origin (and implicit assumptions) of the formulas that are scattered throughout the book. I have tried to make the assumptions clear in the text of the chapters but there is no satisfactory substitute for the inspection of the derivations.

It is a characteristic of written material in the area of finance that it becomes obsolete the day of publication. This is a price we pay for progress. It would be foolish to predict that this book will stand the test of time; a much safer prediction is that one can expect to see more and more analysis (similar to that presented here) in the area of finance and less and less acceptance of reasons without reasoning.

H. B.

Contents

D ecisions Involving Liquid Assets

Part I of this book deals with decisions involving cash, marketable securities, and accounts receivable (the granting of credit). We find that the decisions affecting cash are tied to decisions involving the issue of securities and, as is to be expected, decisions affecting accounts receivable directly affect income.

SYMBOLS

K_s the fixed transactions cost of selling securities

D the expected demand for cash per year

r_L the rate that can be earned by lending funds short term

C the optimum amount of cash obtained by selling securities currently held

TC the total cost of a policy

CHAPTER 1

Decisions Affecting Cash and Marketable Securities

Decisions affecting cash and short-term marketable securities are influenced by an interesting mixture of facts and subjective judgments. The treasurer of a corporation may have some of the facts of the cost of borrowing from a bank but these facts (the explicit terms of the loan) are only part of the information that he requires. There are also the implicit costs associated with issuing more debt and there are subjective benefits arising from having more cash on deposit in the bank (thus being in a safer position). The treasurer may decide to buy some insurance against financial illiquidity by arranging and paying for a credit agreement committing a bank to lend up to an agreed upon sum. The value of this insurance is difficult to measure since the benefit consists of a change in the probability of being able to obtain the needed funds from some high probability to a still higher probability. What would be the cost to the firm if the funds were not obtained? This may be difficult to measure.

The decisions affecting cash and readily marketable securities may be classified as follows:

1. Bank relation decisions
2. Cash decisions (the term cash includes demand deposits)
3. Marketable security (near-cash) decisions

Bank Relation Decisions

Terminology used in discussing the arrangements between borrower and bank for future borrowings are confusing. Among the terms encountered are "line of credit," "credit agreement," and "committed line of credit." We will define a line of credit to be an arrangement whereby the bank agrees to consider in a friendly manner a loan application but does not make a firm commitment to lend the funds. The company may pay for the line of credit by agreeing to leave compensating balances (idle deposits) in the bank. If the financial affairs of the firm deteriorate, or if the bank does not have the lending capacity, the bank may refuse to lend, but it certainly would make efforts to act in a manner consistent with the credit agreement. The firm benefits from a credit agreement by having established preliminary relations with the bank and indicating an intention to borrow in the near future. A sudden attempt to borrow might be unsettling to the banker. He might think the borrowing was being made from a situation of weakness. The bank benefits by having a customer indicate a desire to borrow (this increases the probability that the borrower will obtain the funds from the bank) and the information will help the bank's planning.

A "credit agreement" or a "committed line of credit" implies a firm commitment by the bank to lend the funds. This commitment cannot be dropped by the bank just because the financial affairs of the corporation seeking to borrow are not as good as the bank would like. To obtain this firm commitment the corporation will have to pay either by keeping larger compensating balances or by paying an explicit dollar amount. The amount paid may be a percentage of the total commitment which has not yet been taken down (borrowed) by the firm.

The terms of loan are not necessarily affected by the presence or absence of an agreement between the corporation and the bank. Generally the terms of the loan will be established at the time of the borrowing, but this can be modified by agreement between the parties.

How much should a corporation be willing to pay for more easily accessible (more certain) credit? Imagine a demand curve sloping downward to the right reflecting the willingness of a corporation to pay a reasonably large amount for the insurance that guarantees the ability to borrow the minimum amount necessary to maintain continued existence. As we increase the amount of the funds to be borrowed and decrease their importance to the firm, the willingness to pay (per dollar of commitment) will decrease.

In making the credit-agreement decision the corporation cannot be sure of:

1. How much it will want to borrow.
2. Whether it could have obtained the funds anyway, thus did not need a formal agreement with the bank.

Thus we have all the elements of decision making under uncertainty. We do not know which state of nature will prevail. (How much will be needed and could it be obtained without an agreement?) In addition we do not know for sure the consequences of not being able to obtain the funds when they are needed. In fact we may find it difficult to determine the costs of a particular agreement if the agreement is paid for by leaving more funds on deposit. (The compensating balances may be paying for more than one bank service and the valid measure of the cost is a difficult to measure opportunity cost.)

Cash Decisions

The basic cash decisions made by a corporation are:

1. Determining when cash should be obtained and how much new cash should be obtained from sources outside the firm.
2. Determining whether marketable securities should be purchased or sold.

A corporation will hold cash for three reasons:

1. To conform with the bank's request that balances be carried. These compensating balances serve to pay the bank for account activity, services, a line of credit, bank loans outstanding, and in compensation for the float arising from the corporation's account. (The bank has credited the account for a deposited check but has not yet collected from the party paying the check.)
2. To finance transactions involving normal operations or capital asset acquisitions.
3. In anticipation of contingencies.

The amount to be held to satisfy the banks with which the company does business is determined either by meeting all the requests of the bank, since they seem fair, or by negotiating with the bank. The corporation will attempt to minimize the amount sitting idle in the banks but must recognize that the bank's desire to be compensated for its services is natural.

Assuming the firm is reasonably large (dealing on a daily basis with multi-millions of dollars) with a low cost of transactions involving marketable securities, the amount of cash held to provide for transactions should be no more than the amount necessary to pay tomorrow's bills (assuming today's bills are already paid). The remainder of the near-cash assets should be in the form of interest-earning, readily marketable securities. A firm can enter and leave the marketable security market with great ease and low cost. An assistant treasurer can be given the task of selling the amount of securities necessary to meet the day's bills or investing the amount of excess cash, and it will take a small percentage of his time.

Some firms will leave the excess cash in its bank to compensate the bank for its services. This is reasonable *if* the bank considers the average balance in the account in computing the profitability of the account, and in effect gives the corporation "credit" for its policy. One suspects that banks have not always exploited the possibilities for inducing firms to leave excess cash on deposit.[1]

The third reason offered for holding cash is to anticipate an unusual undesirable event. We argue that a firm should not hold cash for contingencies.

---

[1] Statutory limitations have also prevented banks from competing more effectively for short-term funds of corporation. For example, there are maximum interest rates on time deposits and no interest is paid on demand deposits.

It may want to hold some marketable securities (or investment-type securities) for minor difficulties that may arise. It is more difficult for a corporation to provide for major problems by holding liquid assets. For example, corporations would find it difficult to hold enough liquid assets to provide for the survival of the firm during a major depression or war. The amount of liquid assets held for minor difficulties will depend on the desires of the owners and managers to be safe compared with their desire to invest the funds in higher earning but less liquid assets.

We conclude that a firm should hold cash to satisfy its banks (the amount may be determined in negotiation with the bank) and for transactions (an amount equal to the most immediate payments coming due). Excess cash should be invested in marketable securities until it can be used to finance operations or the acquisition of long-lived assets. The desire for liquidity should lead to the holding of marketable securities; it should not lead to the holding of cash.

Decisions Affecting Marketable Securities

The previous section has suggested that a corporation will want to purchase marketable securities when it has excess cash. The decisions that will be encountered by a firm willing to invest in marketable securities (rather than leaving the cash in the bank) are:

1. The amount of cash to be invested in securities.
2. The types of securities to be purchased (nature of the issuing body, and the characteristics of the securities and their maturity).
3. The timing of security purchases.

The amount of cash to be invested has already been discussed. Essentially the purchase of securities is a residual decision resulting from previous decisions that brought the cash into the firm and resulted in excess cash being available.

Corporations have a wide range of securities they can purchase. These include:

1. Short-term federal government securities (the certainty of payment and short maturity combine to minimize risk).
2. Repurchase agreements with dealers (the firm "purchases" the security with their being an agreement with a security dealer that the dealer will repurchase the security in a short period of time, say a day, at a set price).
3. Negotiable commercial paper issued by corporations.
4. Certificates of deposit issued by banks.
5. Securities issued by government agencies.

6. Securities issued by foreign governments and other foreign organizations.
7. Securities issued by tax-exempt governmental bodies.
8. Long-term securities issued by any of the above.

The securities described can have a wide range of risk. The risk is apt to be increased as we increase the maturity term beyond the date when the funds are expected to be used. In like manner the risk may be increased by moving from securities issued by the federal government to securities issued by organizations where there is a risk of default. The treasurer must balance the possibility for a likely higher return with the risk associated with that return.

Tax-exempt securities have the advantage of offering higher after-tax returns due to their tax exemption status (the before-tax return is generally lower than securities with comparable risk). However, there are regulations that prevent a corporation from exploiting the full possibility of investment in these securities (temporary excess cash may be so invested but funds cannot be obtained for the purpose of investing in tax-exempt securities). There are times where it is institutionally feasible for a corporation to buy these securities, but a corporation should check the current treasury regulations before doing so.

The timing of purchase of securities is not an important consideration. Securities should be purchased as soon as the excess cash is on hand. The timing aspect might seem to be important since we could conclude that a firm expecting interest rates to increase should postpone investment. We would answer this by suggesting that investment should still be made, but the expectation of higher interest rates should lead a firm to invest in short-term securities so that the firm will be in cash or near-cash when the interest-rate change takes place. Thus rather than facing a timing-of-purchase problem, a firm has a maturity-determination problem. There is no question that a firm investing its excess cash in marketable securities has an opportunity to speculate and profit from prospective interest-rate changes. (It can also lose from changes that are not anticipated.)

The safest procedure is for the firm to invest in securities that mature when the cash is needed, since this will result in the firm having an amount of cash equal to the amount invested plus the interest expected to be earned. In any other investment policy, there is a possibility that the amount of cash held at the time of need will be different than the amount expected to be held.

Converting Marketable Securities to Cash

Let us assume that a firm currently holding marketable securities faces a net need for cash (in excess of the cash flows generated) of D per year. The marketable securities are earning r_L per year. Every time securities are sold there is a fixed transactions cost of K_s. How many securities should be sold when there is a need for cash? Let C be the optimum amount of securities converted into cash. There are two costs:

$K_s \dfrac{D}{C}$ The fixed costs of a transaction times the number of transactions

$r_L \dfrac{C}{2}$ The interest lost by converting from earning assets into cash times the average amount of cash

The total cost (TC) is

$$TC = K_s \frac{D}{C} + r_L \frac{C}{2}$$

The optimum amount of cash obtained at one time is[2]

$$C = \sqrt{\frac{2 K_s D}{r_L}}$$

This is the familiar economic order quantity (EOQ) model of inventory theory.

EXAMPLE

$D = \$1,000,000$ per year $= 10^6$

$r_L = .04$

$K_s = \$50$

$C = \sqrt{\dfrac{2 \times 50 \times 10^6}{.04}} = \sqrt{25 \times 10^8} = \$50,000$

Multiplying C/D by 365 we obtain the number of days supply of cash obtained by the sale of securities;

$$\frac{C}{D} \times 365 = \frac{50,000}{1,000,000} \times 365 = 18 \text{ days of cash.}$$

Now let $D = \$100,000,000$ (or 10^8), we obtain a new C:

$$C = \sqrt{\frac{2 \times 50 \times 10^8}{.04}} = \$500,000$$

or

$$\frac{C}{D} \times 365 = \frac{500,000}{100,000,000} \times 365 = 1.8 \text{ days of cash.}$$

---

[2] The first derivative of TC with respect to C is

$$\frac{dTC}{dC} = -K_s \frac{D}{C^2} + \frac{r_L}{2}.$$

Solving for C we obtain:

$$C = \sqrt{\frac{2 K_s D}{r_L}}.$$

Conclusions

This chapter has introduced the decisions encountered by a corporation treasurer in administering his cash and near-cash assets. He must first decide on the nature of his relationships with his banks and may attempt to formalize these relationships by establishing lines of credit (the banks are not committed to make a loan) or a credit agreement (a bank commits itself to lend up to a set amount). The next decision is to determine the amount of cash that will be held. We have not yet discussed one of the more important aspects of the cash decision: How much cash should be obtained from sources external to the firm? This question will be considered in the next chapter. Once the cash has been obtained and the corporation finds it has excess cash, the firm is then faced with decisions involving marketable securities. These decisions involve determination of the nature of securities (type and maturity), the amount to be purchased, and the timing of purchase.

A manager of cash may be able to hide his inability to administer liquid resources efficiently behind a policy of having a large amount of excess cash on deposit (thus satisfying the banker and insuring no difficulty in paying bills), and investing only in very safe government securities maturing when the cash is needed (thus insuring that there is no risk of default or loss arising from fluctuating interest rates). This set of policies will tend to bypass most of the controls established to indicate inefficiency. There will be no complaints from bankers or other creditors, and there is little or no risk that a security that is purchased will default or that less cash will be obtained from the sale of the security than was invested. However, the failure of the system to report the opportunities that are lost should not prevent us from realizing that such opportunities exist. In the management of cash and near cash there are opportunities for taking risk, for being efficient, and for increasing the profit of the firm. In the next chapter, we consider the possibility of increasing profit by using a quantitative decision model when it is appropriate to obtain additional capital.

PROBLEMS

1. What managerial decisions deal with the amount of cash on hand or the amount of cash available?
2. Why might a corporation be willing to pay something for the right to borrow from a bank (the right to call on the bank for a loan)? What factors might influence this decision?
3. Why does a corporation hold funds on demand deposit with a bank?

4. A compensating balance is a method of paying a bank for services rendered. What services does a commercial bank offer its depositors?

5. What types of decisions involving short-term marketable securities are faced by corporate management?

6. Does the recognition that there is uncertainty about the future affect the amount of cash held or the amount of marketable securities held?

7. Is there a cost involved in a situation where the corporation finds it is short of cash?

8. A corporation follows the policy of not investing in marketable securities unless it is sure the funds would not be needed. Discuss this policy.

9. If you were a corporate treasurer would you wait until interest rates were "right" before investing your excess funds?

10. As a corporate officer would you prefer for a bank to require compensating balances or charge a direct fee? What would be your preference as a bank officer?

11. The ABC Company must make a decision relative to the amount of credit agreement it carries with its bank. The cost of the credit agreement is .005 of the unused credit. There is an implicit psychological cost of $9000 per million dollars for funds needed in excess of the credit agreement.

To simplify the computations assume that if the money is borrowed at all, it is borrowed immediately for the entire period. Management has determined the following probabilities of possible events:

EVENT: THE DEMAND FOR CASH IS		PROBABILITY OF EVENT
0	Millions of dollars	.20
1	Millions of dollars	.30
2	Millions of dollars	.40
3	Millions of dollars	.10
4	Millions of dollars	.00
		1.00

Required: Determine the size of the credit agreement the ABC Company should establish.

12. The CDE Company must make a decision relative to the amount of credit agreement it carries with its bank. The cost of the credit agreement is .005 of the unused credit. Management has determined the following probabilities of possible events:

EVENT: THE DEMAND FOR CASH IS		PROBABILITY OF EVENT
0	Millions of dollars	.20
1	Millions of dollars	.30
2	Millions of dollars	.40
3	Millions of dollars	.10
4	Millions of dollars	.00
		1.00

In addition, management has determined the following schedule of "costs" of having to arrange loans on a short notice (i.e., costs of demand being in excess of the credit).

MILLIONS OF DOLLARS (DEMAND IN EXCESS OF THE CREDIT)	COST OF EVENT
0	0
1	9,000
2	20,000
3	40,000

Required: Determine the size of the credit agreement which the CDE Company should establish.

13. The FGH Company must make a decision relative to the amount of cash credit agreement it carries with its bank. The cost of the credit agreement is .004 of the credit. Management has determined the following probabilities of possible events:

EVENT: THE DEMAND FOR CASH IS		PROBABILITY OF EVENT
0	Millions of dollars	.20
1	Millions of dollars	.50
2	Millions of dollars	.30

There is a $10,000 cost of being short per million dollars of shortage. If there is no credit agreement the firm has a .6 probability of being able to successfully arrange the financing.

Required: Determine the size of the credit agreement the FGH Company should establish.

14. The GHI Company had invested $10,000,000 excess funds in long-term

government bonds yielding .04 and selling at par at the time of purchase. The company needs the funds for operating purposes when the current yield of the bonds is .06 and the bonds have ten years until maturity. The bonds pay interest annually.

Required: (a) How much will the firm realize from the sale of the $10,000,000 of bonds?

(b) Assuming the bonds had been held for two years, how much did the firm receive in total?

15. If a company paying a borrowing rate of .06 maintains a minimum compensating balance of $10,000,000 to reward the bank, which has lent it $80,000,000 in total, what is the effective interest rate on the loan?
16. The GHI Company currently has $100,000,000 invested in marketable securities that are earning .04. The firm expects to use the $100,000,000 over the coming twelve months to finance an expansion program. The fixed costs associated with a security transaction are estimated to be $50 per transaction.

Required: (a) Assuming the cash will be needed evenly throughout the year, at what rate should the securities be sold?

(b) How many days supply of cash will be obtained each time a batch of securities is sold?

REFERENCES

Anderson, P. F., and Harman, R. D. B. "The Management of Excess Corporate Cash," *Financial Executive* (October), 1964.

Baumol, W. J. "The Transactions Demand for Cash: An Inventory Theoretic Approach," *Quarterly Journal of Economics* (November), 1952.

Bierman, H., Jr., and McAdams, A. K. *Management Decisions for Cash and Marketable Securities* (Cornell Studies in Policy and Administration, Cornell University, Ithaca, N.Y., 1962).

Brunner, K., and Meltzer, A. H. "Economies of Scale in Cash Balances Reconsidered, *The Quarterly Journal of Economics* (August), 1967.

Jacobs, Donald P. "The Marketable Security Portfolios of Non-Financial Corporations, Investment Practices and Trends," *Journal of Finance* (September), 1960.

Johnson, R. W. *Financial Management* (Allyn & Bacon, Boston, 1966), pp. 98–116.

National Industrial Conference Board, *Managing Corporate Cash* (Studies in Business Policy, No. 99: New York, 1961).

Van Horne, J. C. *Financial Management and Policy* (Prentice-Hall, Englewood Cliffs, N.J., 1968), pp. 355–358.

CHAPTER 2

The Bond Issue Size Decision[1]

SYMBOLS

K incremental cost of issuing securities where the cost is not a function of the size of issue

D the expected demand in dollars per unit time

k the net cost per year per dollar (associated with long-term debt) of carrying the inventory of cash rising from the issue of the long-term debt (net of any interest that can be earned by investing the funds)

Q the optimum amount of cash to be obtained by the issue of long-term debt

S the amount left from a security issue after the repayment of bank debt

$Q - S$ the amount of bank debt

k_s the net cost per year per dollar of borrowing from the bank (net of any interest that can be earned using the idle funds)

TC the total cost of a policy

k_0 the difference between the bank borrowing rate and long-term borrowing rate if an overdraft system is being used. It is the net cost of going to the bank compared with borrowing long term:
$$k_0 = k_s - k$$

V_n the net financing cost of obtaining cash at time n

r_i the market rate of interest if long-term debt is issued at time i (let r be equivalent to r_0)

$a_{r \rceil n}$ the present value of an annuity of n periods with an interest rate r

a_i the time-value factor: $a_i = (1 + r)^{-i}$

r_L the rate that can be earned by lending funds short term
$$k = r - r_L$$

r_b the bank borrowing rate
$$k_s = r_b - r_L$$
$$k_0 = k_s - k = r_b - r$$

The highly quantitative bond issue size decision is generally made in a somewhat qualitative manner. The subjective opinions of brokers and intuitive rules of thumb of financial officers are rarely, if ever, compared to the optimum issue size resulting from calculations incorporating the costs of issuing

[1] Portions of this chapter were previously published as an article in the *Journal of Financial and Quantitative Analysis* (December, 1966) and introduced in Chapter 1.

bonds, and the costs of carrying extra cash. Unfortunately performance measurement in this area is very difficult, thus both good and bad decision processes tend to go unnoticed. It is possible to look at a financial decision which has been made, and, with the aid of hindsight, conclude it was a bad decision, but this proves very little. Some financial officers have done very well administering the financial affairs of their corporations, but this does not indicate that the decision process cannot be improved.

In Chapter 1 the necessity of determining the optimum amount of cash was introduced.[2] However, we have not yet considered the questions of how much cash should be obtained from external sources, and the possibility of borrowing in sequence using banks (or other financial institutional sources of short-term money) and bonds. In addition we should also attempt to incorporate projected interest rate changes into the analysis.

For some corporations these complications do not affect the decision since these firms do not borrow from banks and do not attempt to out-guess the money market's projection of interest-rate changes. On the other hand, where a corporation is willing to borrow from banks or to project future interest rates, these considerations affect the amount of bonds it should issue in the market at a given moment in time. In this chapter the possibility of borrowing from banks will be incorporated into a model, and the effect of interest-rate change expectations will be considered.

Bank Borrowing and Bond Issue Size

There are two basic problems to be solved in the following sections. If funds are needed, how much should be borrowed from the banks before going to the bond market, and how much should be borrowed at one time from the bond market? If we assume all the facts are known, we need not be concerned with any elements of uncertainty in this initial model. Also, we assume that no interest-rate changes are projected by management.

In practice, the problem described is generally solved by rules of thumb or intuition. The models that will be developed are not substitutes for experience and institutional knowledge, but rather they are possible aids to the business decision maker. In view of the large amount of information available pertaining to bank borrowing and long-term debt issue decisions, it would seem reasonable to make computations that indicate the decisions leading to the minimum total borrowing cost. We may ultimately want to make other decisions, but we should know what the difference in decisions is expected to cost.

[2] See "Financial Decisions and New Decision Tools," *The Financial Executive* (May, 1964), pp. 23–30, co-authored by Alan K. McAdams and the present author. Also, *Management Decisions for Cash and Marketable Securities,* by the same authors (Graduate School of Business and Public Administration, Cornell University, 1962).

Assume a situation when a corporation forecasts cash needs of $180,000,000 a year for the foreseeable future (let D represent the expected demand). It is currently paying .05 per year for long-term debt and can earn .04 on the funds by investing in short-term securities. The net cost of carrying the inventory of cash (k) is .01. The fixed incremental cost of floating a bond issue (K) is $100,000. The basic optimum-order size formula leads to the following calculations, where Q is the optimum amount of debt to be issued each time the firm goes to the market.[3]

$$K = \$100,000 = 10^5,$$

$$D = 180,000,000 = 1.8 \times 10^8,$$

$$k = .01,$$

$$Q = \left(\frac{2KD}{k}\right)^{1/2} = \left(\frac{2 \times 10^5 \times 1.8 \times 10^8}{.01}\right)^{1/2} =$$

$$(36 \times 10^{14})^{1/2} = \$60,000,000.$$

The calculations indicate the firm should go to the market three times in the coming year and obtain $60,000,000 each time.

The total cost of this policy for one year is equal to the cost of ordering ($D/Q \times K$) plus the cost of carrying the average inventory of cash ($Q/2 \times k$).

$$\text{Total Cost} = \left(\frac{D}{Q}\right)K + \left(\frac{Q}{2}\right)k$$

$$= \frac{180,000,000}{60,000,000} \times 100,000 + \frac{60,000,000}{2} \times .01$$

$$= 300,000 + 300,000 = \$600,000.$$

If the entire $180,000,000 were obtained immediately the total cost would be

$$\text{Total Cost} = 100,000 + \left(\frac{180,000,000}{2}\right) \times .01$$

$$= 100,000 + 900,000 = \$1,000,000.$$

Assume that instead of borrowing $60,000,000 we had borrowed $20,000,000 at a time (and borrowed three times as frequently). The total cost for one year would again have been $400,000 more than the cost associated with the optimum decision.

$$\text{Total Cost} = \left(\frac{180,000,000}{20,000,000}\right) \times 100,000 + \frac{20,000,000}{2} \times .01$$

$$= 900,000 + 100,000 = \$1,000,000.$$

[3] See Appendix 1 of this chapter for the derivation. This is the familiar EOQ (Economic Order Quantity) model used in inventory control and introduced in Chapter 1.

It becomes apparent that borrowing too much or too little at once may result in unnecessary costs of debt (including the costs of issuing debt). There is only one amount of debt for the situation described that will lead to a minimization of the total costs.

Figure 2–1 is a representation of the costs of carrying the inventory of cash.

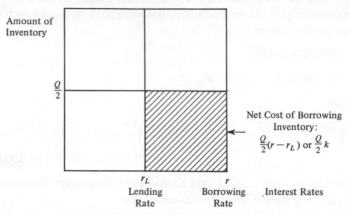

FIGURE 2–1

Bank Borrowing: Lump Sum

Now assume that the firm may borrow from its bank at an effective cost of .06. The terms of the loan are that the funds will be borrowed from the bank in a lump sum and the entire amount may be used as it is needed. Figure 2–2 shows the situation that has been described. The lending rate is .04.

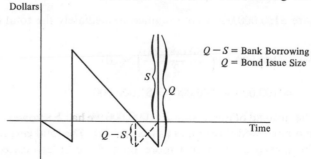

FIGURE 2–2

Define k_s to be the *net* carrying cost of borrowing from the bank $1 per unit of time. In the example, $k_s = .06 - .04 = .02.$[4] The formulas we need

---

[4] We are assuming that funds borrowed from the bank may be invested to earn .04. If the agreement with the bank restricts the withdrawal of the funds the value of k_s may be increased. See Appendix 2 of this chapter for the derivation of the formulas.

are

$$Q = \left(\frac{2KD}{k}\right)^{1/2} \times \left(\frac{k_s}{k_s - k/2}\right)^{1/2},$$

$$S = \left(\frac{2KD}{k}\right)^{1/2} \times \left(\frac{k_s - k/2}{k_s}\right)^{1/2} = Q\left(\frac{k_s - k/2}{k_s}\right).$$

Q is the amount obtained each time that long-term debt is issued. $Q - S$ is the bank borrowing and S is the amount left from Q each cycle after the bank is repaid. The above two formulas are based on the fact that the entire amount borrowed from the bank during the borrowing period bears a cost of $k_s - k$; that is, bank borrowing costs exceed long-term debt costs by $k_s - k$. In addition, there is a carrying cost of k per dollar per unit time associated with having the borrowed funds wait for the long-term investments.[5]

Inserting the given data in the above equations and solving for Q and S, we obtain:

$$Q = 60,000,000 \left(\frac{.02}{.02 - .005}\right)^{1/2}$$

$$= 60,000,000 \ (1.333)^{1/2}$$

$$= 60,000,000 \times 1.154 = \$69,200,000.$$

$$S = 60,000,000 \times \frac{1}{1.154} = \$51,900,000.$$

The firm will now borrow $17,300,000 from the bank (that is $Q - S$). At the appropriate time it will issue $69,200,000 of bonds, repay the bank and temporarily invest the surplus cash until it is needed. The firm can make use of the banks to reduce the number of visits to the bond market as well as to give more flexibility to the timing of the bond issues.

The total cost for the policy is

$$TC = \left(\frac{S^2}{2Q}\right)k + \frac{(Q - S)^2}{Q}\ (k_s - k/2) + K\frac{D}{Q},$$

$$= \frac{(51,900,000)^2}{2 \times 69,200,000} \times .01 + \frac{(17,300,000)^2}{69,200,000} \times (.02 - .005) +$$

$$100,000 \times \frac{180}{69.2}$$

$$= 195,000 + 50,000 + 260,000$$

$$= \$505,000.$$

---

[5] The use of the formula requires that $k_s > k/2$. If $k_s = k/2$ we have a situation where Q is not defined, since we are dividing by zero. If k_s were less than $k/2$, Q would be an imaginary number using the above formula, which is not a feasible solution. See Appendix 2 to this chapter for the derivation of the formulas.

In this example, the net cost of financing has been reduced to $505,000 by using bank borrowing, compared to $600,000 following the best policy with no bank borrowing, and $1,000,000 with one issue for the year. It becomes apparent that management should be aware that the total cost of financing will be a function of the size of issue and the utilization of bank borrowing, and that this total cost can be minimized.

Bank Borrowing: Overdrafts Allowed

The previous model assumed that the entire amount borrowed from the bank was immediately obtained and withdrawn to be invested in short-term securities. Now assume that the funds are only obtained as they are needed. We call this system the "overdraft situation." It is not necessary that an actual overdraft system be used since we could also approximate an overdraft with a line of credit that allowed the firm to borrow in small pieces.

We will use the symbol k_0 to represent the net bank cost with an overdraft system. Since we only borrow when we need the fund, there is never any excess cash invested in short-term investments. The cost k_0 is equal to the difference between the bank borrowing rate and the long-term borrowing rate. We are assuming that the bank rate is larger than the long-term bond rate; if it were less we would borrow from the banks until the bank made us seek long term financing.

The formulas for Q and S are now[6]

$$Q = \left(\frac{2KD}{k}\right)^{1/2} \times \left(\frac{k + k_0}{k_0}\right)^{1/2}$$

$$S = Q \times \left(\frac{k_0}{k_0 + k}\right) = \left(\frac{2KD}{k}\right)^{1/2}\left(\frac{k_0}{k + k_0}\right)^{1/2}.$$

Continuing the example where the bank borrowing rate is .06 and the bond rate is .05, we have

$$k_0 = .06 - .05 = .01.$$

$$Q = 60,000,000 \left(\frac{.01 + .01}{.01}\right)^{1/2} = 60,000,000 \ (2)^{1/2}$$

$$= 60,000,000 \times 1.41 = \$84,000,000.$$

$$S = 84,000,000 \times \tfrac{1}{2} = 42,000,000.$$

---

[6] See Appendix 3 of this chapter for the derivation of the formulas.

The total cost of this policy is

$$TC = \frac{S^2}{2Q} k + \frac{(Q - S)^2}{2Q} k_0 + K \frac{D}{Q}$$

$$= \frac{(42,000,000)^2}{2(84,000,000)} \times .01 + \frac{(42,000,000)^2}{2(84,000,000)} \times .01 + 100,000 \times \frac{180}{84}$$

$$= \frac{42,000,000 \times .01}{4} + \frac{42,000,000 \times .01}{4} + 214,000$$

$$= 210,000 + 214,000 = \$424,000.$$

The ability to borrow as needed compared to borrowing a lump sum saves $81,000 in this situation (505,000 − 424,000).

Interest-Rate Changes

In some situations management may expect that interest rates will increase in the near future. They may hold this belief so strongly that, for purposes of this discussion, we may say that they "know" that the interest rates will increase. In other situations they may "know" that rates are going down in the future. When management has definite opinions about future interest rates it is to be expected that it would want this information incorporated into the model.

We shall make several assumptions that will simplify the formulas. Among the initial assumptions are

1. It has been decided not to issue bonds more frequently than once a year, and management has forecasted interest rates and cash needs for two years.
2. Funds can be obtained from the bank at a carrying cost equal to the carrying cost k that occurs if funds are obtained immediately from the issuance of bonds.
3. We will test the cost of issuing the bonds, now and one year from now.
4. The amount of funds Q that will be obtained is equal to the amount of funds needed for the entire period of two years.
5. We shall ignore the time-value factor associated with the fact that the costs associated with issue will be incurred in different time periods.

We shall first assume that the entire amount is borrowed immediately. Thus Q, the issue size, is equal to D, the expected usage. There will be one cost of issue (K). The inventory of cash at time zero is Q and at time 1 is $Q/2$. The average inventory of cash the first year is $(Q + Q/2)/2$, and this is multiplied by k to find the first year's carrying cost. The average inventory of cash the second year is $(Q/2)/2$ and again we multiply by k. The net financing cost (V_0) of obtaining the cash immediately is

$$V_0 = \left[K + \frac{Q + Q/2}{2} k + \frac{Q/2 + 0}{2} k \right],$$

$$= K + \frac{3Qk}{4} + \frac{Qk}{4} = K + Qk.$$

Now, assume that we expect an increase in interest costs, and we want to know the cost of obtaining the two-year supply of cash after one year. Assume further that the first year's usage of cash is equal to $Q/2$ and the funds are borrowed from the bank as needed (an average loan of $Q/4$ is outstanding) at a net cost of k per year. Let r_i be the market interest rate if debt is issued in time i. The cost of borrowing the needed funds at time 1 is V_1.

Cost of bank borrowing	Cost of carrying cash	Present value of increased interest costs
↓	↓	↓

$$V_1 = \frac{Q}{4} k \quad + \quad \left[K + \frac{Q}{4} k \right] \quad + \quad Q(r_1 - r_0)a_{r_1 \rceil t} $$

The symbol $a_{r_1 \rceil t}$ represents the present value of an annuity of \$1 per period of t years duration (the life of the bond issue) with an interest rate r_1 (the forecasted interest rate). A more exact formulation would use the projected interest rates of each time period in computing the present value of the increased interest costs, $Q(r_1 - r_0)$.

We want to compare V_0 and V_1, and choose the decision that leads to the lower cost.

$$V_1 - V_0 = \frac{Q}{4} k + \left[K + \frac{Q}{4} k + Q(r_1 - r_0)a_{r_1 \rceil t} \right] - K - Qk,$$

$$= Q(r_1 - r_0)a_{r_1 \rceil t} - \frac{Q}{2} k = Q \left[(r_1 - r_0) a_{r_1 \rceil t} - \frac{k}{2} \right].$$

If the value of $\left[(r_1 - r_0)a_{r_1 \rceil t} - \frac{k}{2} \right]$ is positive we should wait one time

period or, equivalently, we should wait if

$$r_1 - r_0 > \frac{k}{2a_{r_1 \rceil t}}.$$

If $r_1 - r_0$ is less than the right-hand side of the equation, then borrow at the end of the year.

Assume the bonds are to be issued for twenty years and $a_{.04 \rceil 20} = \$13$.

Then, $k = .01, r_0 = .0395, r_1 = .0400, K = \$100,000$, and $D = \$200,000,000$ (the present value of cash needs). The break-even interest increase is

$$r_1 - r_0 = \frac{k}{2a_{r_1 \rceil t}} = \frac{.01}{2 \times 13} = \frac{.01}{26} \approx .0004.$$

According to these calculations, a projected increase of .0004 or more in interest rates makes it desirable to issue the securities immediately. The expected increase for the next period is .0005, therefore we should issue the debt now and not wait for the higher rates. A smaller increase, or the slightest decrease in interest costs, would result in the computations indicating that the bonds should be issued later. Thus, with the given model, when there are projected interest-rate changes, the bond issue decision hinges heavily on the direction of the change. Effectively the model indicates that if interest rates are expected to increase, this information tends to overpower other considerations. A large amount of debt should be issued now.

An Improved Model

The following model assumes the carrying cost of bank debt (k_s) is different than the carrying cost of bonds (k). Previously, k_s was assumed to be equal to k. Also, we will take the timing of the costs into consideration. Let a_i be the time factor $(1 + r)^{-i}$, then

$$V_0 = \left[K + \frac{Q + Q/2}{2}k + \frac{Q/2 + 0}{2}ka_1\right],$$

$$= K + \frac{3Qk}{4} + \frac{Qka_1}{4},$$

$$= K + \frac{Qk}{4}(3 + a_1)$$

where V_0 is the cost of following a policy of obtaining the cash immediately.

Assume that k_s is greater than k and an amount equal to $Q/2$ is borrowed from the bank (an average amount of $(Q/2 + 0)/2$ is unused). Then $Qk/4$ is the basic carrying cost of $Q/2$ dollars from the bank, and $Q/2(k_s - k)$ is the cost of obtaining the funds from the bank, rather than long-term bonds. Adding the two costs we obtain

$$\frac{Qk}{4} + \frac{Q(k_s - k)}{2} = \frac{Q(2k_s - k)}{4}.$$

V_1, the cost of waiting one year, is

$$V_1 = \frac{Q(2k_s - k)}{4} + \left[K + \frac{Qk}{4} + Q(r_1 - r_0)a_{r_1 \rceil t}\right]a_1.$$

Let $V_0 = V_1$, and solve for $r_1 - r_0$:

$$K + \frac{3Qk}{4} + \frac{a_1 Qk}{4} = \frac{Q(2k_s - k)}{4} + a_1 K + \frac{a_1 Qk}{4} + a_1 Q (r_1 - r_0)a_{r_1 \eta t};$$

$$a_1 Q (r_1 - r_0)a_{r_1 \eta t} = K(1 - a_1) - \frac{2Qk_s}{4} + \frac{Qk}{4} (3 + a_1 - a_1 + 1);$$

and

$$r_1 - r_0 = \frac{K(1 - a_1)}{a_1 Q a_{r_1 \eta t}} - \frac{k_s}{2a_1 a_{r_1 \eta t}} + \frac{4k}{4a_1 a_{r_1 \eta t}}.$$

If Q is very large, then $K(1 - a_1)/(a_1 Q a_{r_1 \eta t})$ becomes small, and

$$r_1 - r_0 = \frac{2k - k_s}{2a_1 a_{r_1 \eta t}} = \frac{(2k - k_s)(1 + r)}{2a_{r_1 \eta t}}.$$

Returning to the example and letting $k_s = .02$:

$$r_1 - r_0 = \frac{(2 \times .01 - .02)(1 + .04)}{2 \times 13} = \frac{0}{26} = 0.$$

In this example, if the interest is expected to stay constant or increase by any amount, we should issue the bonds now.

Conclusions

There are a great number of simplifying assumptions in the models discussed in this chapter. It is not too difficult to prepare more sophisticated mathematical descriptions of the debt-issue size decision, but obtaining solutions to the more complex equations would be more difficult. In view of the amount of uncertainty associated with the inputs (especially the projected interest-rate changes), it would seem that there is need for a technique that is usable and understandable, even if it is some-what inexact. The above models at least attempt to bring opinions relative to future interest rates into the decision. If management prefers not to project future interest rates (the market projections are already incorporated in the present long-term market rates), then the basic inventory model of the first half of this chapter may be used. In the presence of interest-rate change projections, the present value of the interest savings (or costs) tends to overwhelm the bond issue costs and carrying costs. With a $100,000,000 bond issue the costs of issue varying with the number of orders is apt to be of the order of $100,000. The additional cost of a .001 increase in interest rates is the present value of $100,000 per year. Management should know the optimum bond-issue size and bank-borrowing policy and the cost of diverging from the optimum.

Appendix 1

Derivation of Basic Certainty Model

We want to show that

$$Q = \left(\frac{2DK}{k}\right)^{1/2}.$$

Let TC = total cost

D = the total amount of funds needed for the period in excess of the cash that will be generated internally

K = fixed cost of each issue of securities (the costs are unaffected by the size of the issue but the number of issues affects the total amount of cost)

Q = the amount of funds received from each issue of securities (D/Q is the number of orders during the period)

$Q/2$ = the average amount of funds on hand during the period (assuming the funds are used at a uniform rate during the period)

k = the average net cost per period of borrowing $1 and having it invested in short-term securities.

The total cost for one period is

$$TC = K\left(\frac{Q}{D}\right) + k\left(\frac{Q}{2}\right).$$

The total cost is equal to the cost of ordering times the numbers of orders plus the cost of carrying $1 per period times the average inventory of cash.

To minimize the total cost we take the first derivative of TC with respect to Q and set it equal to zero:

$$\frac{dTC}{dQ} = -\frac{KD}{Q^2} + \frac{k}{2} = 0.$$

Solving this expression for Q we obtain

$$Q = \left(\frac{2DK}{k}\right)^{1/2}.$$

Appendix 2

Derivation of Formulas

Bank Borrowing: Lump Sum

We want to show that

$$Q = \left(\frac{2KD}{k}\right)^{1/2} \times \left(\frac{k_s}{k_s - k/2}\right)^{1/2}$$

and

$$S = \left(\frac{2KD}{k}\right)^{1/2} \times \left(\frac{k_s - k/2}{k_s}\right)^{1/2}.$$

Assume a firm can borrow at a bank. Figure 2–3 shows the situation where Q dollars of bonds are issued at time t_0 and $Q - S$ or b dollars are borrowed at the bank. The length of a complete borrowing cycle is t_s.

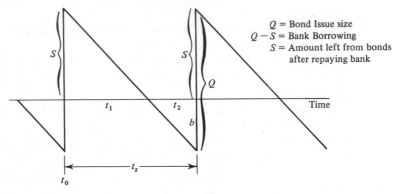

Q = Bond Issue size
$Q - S$ = Bank Borrowing
S = Amount left from bonds after repaying bank

FIGURE 2–3

By basic plain geometry, we have

$$\frac{t_1}{S} = \frac{t_s}{S + b} = \frac{t_s}{Q},$$

$$t_1 = \frac{S}{Q} t_s,$$

$$t_2 = \frac{Q - S}{Q} t_s.$$

During time period t_1 there are $S/2$ units in inventory. The carrying cost per inventory cycle is $(S/2)kt_1$, where k is the difference in the long-term borrowing rate and the rate at which funds can be invested for the short term, t_1 is the length of time idle funds are held and k is the net carrying cost.

Let k_s be the difference in the bank borrowing rate and the short-term lending rate. Then, during time period t_2, the company has a cost because it borrowed from the bank rather than used long-term debt. This cost is

$$(Q - S)(k_s - k)t_2.$$

In addition, during time period t_2, the average excess cash is $\dfrac{Q - S}{2}$.

The carrying cost per borrowing cycle is $\dfrac{Q - S}{2} kt_2$.

Adding these last two costs:

$$(Q - S)(k_s - k)t_2 + \frac{(Q - S)}{2} kt_2,$$

or

$$(Q - S)k_s t_2 - \frac{(Q - S)}{2} kt_2 = (Q - S)t_2 \left(k_s - \frac{k}{2}\right).$$

There is also an issue cost per borrowing cycle of K. The total cost (TC) for D/Q number of cycles is

$$TC = \left[\frac{S}{2} kt_1 + (Q - S)t_2 \left(k_s - \frac{k}{2}\right) + K\right] \frac{D}{Q}.$$

Substituting for t_1 and t_2, using the relationships

$$t_1 = \frac{S}{Q} t_s \text{ and } t_2 = \frac{Q - S}{Q} t_s;$$

$$TC = \left[\frac{S^2}{2Q} kt_s + \frac{(Q - S)^2}{Q} t_s \left(k_s - \frac{k}{2}\right) + K\right] \frac{D}{Q}.$$

We have $T = (D/Q)t_s$ or $t_s = (Q/D)T$. If T is equal to 1, then $t_s = Q/D$; $TC = (S^2/2Q)k + (Q - S)^2/Q(k_s - k/2) + KD/Q$.

Taking the partial derivative with respect to S and setting it equal to zero:

$$\frac{\partial TC}{\partial S} = \frac{S}{Q} k + \frac{2(Q - S)(-1)}{Q} \left(k_s - \frac{k}{2}\right) = 0,$$

$$Sk = 2(Q - S) \left(k_s - \frac{k}{2}\right),$$

$$S = \frac{2Q(k_s - k/2)}{k + 2(k_s - k/2)} = \frac{Q(k_s - k/2)}{k_s}.$$

Taking the partial derivative of the total cost equation with respect to Q and setting it equal to zero:

$$\frac{\partial TC}{\partial Q} = -\frac{S^2}{2Q^2} k + \frac{Q[2(Q - S)] - (Q - S)^2}{Q^2} \left(k - \frac{k}{2}\right) - \frac{KD}{Q^2};$$

$$-\frac{S^2}{2} k + (Q^2 - S^2)\left(k_s - \frac{k}{2}\right) - KD = 0;$$

$$Q^2 \left(k_s - \frac{k}{2}\right) - S^2 k_s - KD = 0.$$

Substituting for S

$$Q^2 \left(k_s - \frac{k}{2}\right) - Q^2 \frac{(k_s - k/2)^2}{k_s^2} k_s - KD = 0$$

$$Q^2 \left(\frac{k_s^2 - kk_s/2 - k_s^2 + kk_s - k^2/4}{k_s} \right) = KD$$

$$Q^2 \left(\frac{kk_s/2 - k^2/4}{k_s} \right) = KD$$

$$Q^2 = \frac{2KD}{k} \times \frac{k_s}{k_s - k/2}$$

$$Q = \left(\frac{2KD}{k} \right)^{1/2} \times \left(\frac{k_s}{k_s - k/2} \right)^{1/2}$$

$$S = Q \frac{(k_s - k/2)}{k_s} = \left(\frac{2KD}{k} \right)^{1/2} \times \left(\frac{k_s}{k_s - k/2} \right)^{1/2} \times \frac{k_s - k/2}{k_s}$$

$$= \left(\frac{2KD}{k} \right)^{1/2} \times \left(\frac{k_s - k/2}{k_s} \right)^{1/2}.$$

Second-order tests may be applied to insure that we have obtained a minimum cost.

The portion of the total cost equation relating to the cost of carrying an inventory of cash and using banks $(S/2kt_1 + (Q - S)t_2(k_s - k/2)$ is explained in Figs. 2–4 and 2–5. Since $r - r_L = k$ and $r_b - r = k_0$, we have $(Q - S)t_2 (k_0 + k/2)$ or equivalently, since $k_0 = k_s - k$, we have $(Q - S) t_2(k_s - k/2)$.

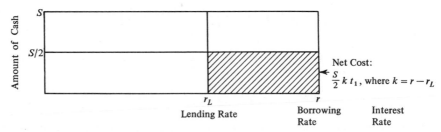

FIGURE 2–4   Cost of carrying inventory of cash.

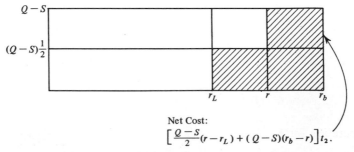

FIGURE 2–5   Cost of borrowing from bank compared to borrowing using bond plus cost of carrying $(Q - S)/2$ of cash inventory.

Appendix 3

Bank Borrowing: Overdrafts

Assume a firm can borrow from the bank at a cost that is k_0 higher than the long-term bond rate. Figure 2–6 shows the situation where Q dollars are obtained by issuing bonds at time t_0 and $Q - S$ units are borrowed from the bank.

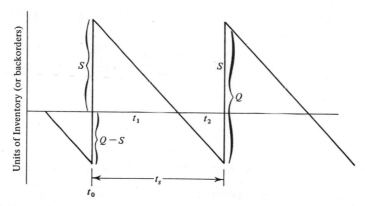

FIGURE 2–6

By simple geometry, we have

$$\frac{t_1}{S} = \frac{t_s}{S + (Q - S)} = \frac{t_s}{Q},$$

$$t_1 = \frac{S}{Q} t_s,$$

$$t_2 = \frac{Q - S}{Q} t_s.$$

During time period t_1 there are on the average $S/2$ dollars on hand. The carrying cost per cycle is

$$\frac{S}{2} kt_1.$$

During time period t_2 the average bank borrowing is $(Q - S)/2$. The borrowing cost per inventory cycle is $[(Q - S)/2]k_0t_2$.

There are D/Q cycles per planning period. The total cost is

$$TC = \left(\frac{S}{2} kt_1 + \frac{Q - S}{2} k_0t_2 + K \right) \frac{D}{Q}.$$

Substituting for t_1 and t_2

$$TC = \left(\frac{S^2}{2Q} kt_s + \frac{(Q - S)^2}{2Q} k_0 t_s + K \right) \frac{D}{Q}.$$

Let $t_s(D/Q) = T$ or $t_s = (Q/D)T$, where T is the length of the planning period (the same time dimension as D, the demand), and simplify:

$$TC = \frac{S^2}{2Q} kT + \frac{(Q - S)^2}{2Q} k_0 T + K \frac{D}{Q}.$$

Taking the partial derivative of the total cost equation with respect to S and setting it equal to zero:

$$\frac{\partial TC}{\partial S} = \frac{S}{Q} kT - \frac{(Q - S)}{Q} k_0 T = 0,$$

$$Sk = (Q - S)k_0,$$

$$S = Q \frac{k_0}{k + k_0}.$$

Taking the partial derivative with respect to Q and setting it equal to zero:

$$\frac{\partial TC}{\partial Q} = - \frac{S^2 kT}{2Q^2} + \frac{4Q(Q - S) - 2(Q - S)^2}{4Q^2} k_0 T - \frac{KD}{Q^2} = 0$$

$$- 2S^2 k + [4Q(Q - S) - 2(Q - S)^2]k_0 - \frac{4KD}{T} = 0$$

$$- 2S^2 k + [(Q - S)(4Q - 2Q + 2S)]k_0 = \frac{4KD}{T}$$

$$- 2S^2 k + [2(Q^2 - S^2)]k_0 = \frac{4KD}{T}$$

$$Q^2 k_0 - S^2(k_0 + k) = \frac{2KD}{T}.$$

Substituting for S^2,

$$Q^2 k_0 - Q^2 \frac{k^2}{(k + k_0)^2} \times (k + k_0) = \frac{2KD}{T}.$$

$$Q^2 \left(\frac{k_0 k + k_0^2 - k_0^2}{k + k_0} \right) = \frac{2KD}{T},$$

$$Q = \sqrt{\frac{2KD}{Tk}} \times \frac{k + k_0}{k_0} = \sqrt{\frac{2KD}{Tk}} \times \sqrt{\frac{k + k_0}{k_0}}$$

If $T = 1$, we then have

$$Q = \sqrt{\frac{2KD}{k}} \times \sqrt{\frac{k + k_0}{k_0}}$$

$$S = Q \times \frac{k_0}{k_0 + k}.$$

The portion of the total cost equation relating to the cost of carrying an inventory of cash and using banks:

$$\frac{S}{2} k t_1 + \frac{Q - S}{2} k_0 t_2$$

can be explained using the following two figures:

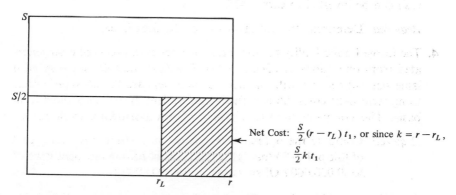

FIGURE 2-7   Cost of carrying inventory of cash arising from issue of bonds.

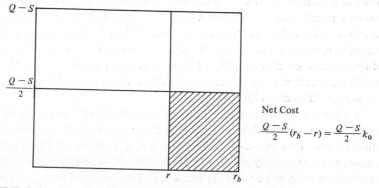

FIGURE 2-8   Cost of using bank credit instead of bonds.

PROBLEMS

1. The ABC Company has decided it needs additional cash resources. The fixed costs connected with marketing a debt issue are $80,000. The expected demand for cash in the next year is $4,000,000. The securities can be issued at a yield rate of .05; excess cash can be invested to earn .04 in riskless short-term securities.

   Required: Determine the optimum size of the debt issue.

2. Assume the situation is the same as in Problem 1 except that the expected demand for cash in the next year is $16,000,000.

   Required: Determine the optimum size of the debt issue.

3. Assume the situation is the same as in Problem 1 except that the excess cash can be invested to earn .0475.

   Required: Determine the optimum size of the debt issue.

4. The Large Public Utility has expected cash needs in excess of cash generated from operations of $360,000,000. The costs that do not vary with issue size but do vary with the number of orders are $200,000 per order. Long-term debt costs .06 and funds can be lent at .05 on a short-term basis. The company follows a policy of not borrowing from banks.

   Required: Compute the optimum debt issue size. What is the total cost of this policy? What is the total cost of having one debt issue of $360,000,000? Of six issues of $60,000,000?

5. As of January 1968, Arbor Chemical Corporation expected cash needs for a period of two years to be approximately $250 million (usage was expected to be at a constant rate over the period).

   The treasurer makes estimates each year of the unused debt capacity that is available to the corporation. The unused capacity is based on certain rough rules of thumb about a desirable debt-equity ratio. The maximum debt that the treasurer's office feels a corporation of this type should have, in light of the reactions of financial institutions to such debt, is between 20 and 30% of total sources of capital. After the $250 million debenture issue, it was estimated that there was still a large amount of unused debt capacity.

   In addition to the outlay of dollars associated with the issue of debt, there is also a good deal of time and effort involved in preparing for a public issue. This was considered to be a major factor for the treasurer's department, especially since the public issue of securities was an unusual occurrence with Arbor and the treasurer's organization took it on as one further task without the addition of new staff. In assessing these costs the treasurer estimated the incremental fixed cost of an issue to be $100,000, an amount which excluded the strain on the staff (though it did include an allocation of costs for the time regular employees spent on the issue).

The financial managers as well as the staff economists and other informed persons of the organization anticipated that there would be relatively stable interest rates in the foreseeable future.

The basic question the treasurer faced late in 1967 was how much new money should be sought in the market in early 1968. It was hoped that it would obtain the funds in the market at about .0615. The company could invest money not used during the year in short-term investments to return about .055. It was thought that before the end of 1968, the company would need $125 million of outside financing. Bank financing could be obtained at a cost of .07 if the debenture issue was delayed.

Principal costs of issuing $250,000,000 of debentures:

1. Fixed and variable

S.E.C. Registration Fee[a]	$24,000
Fees and Disbursements of Trustee[a]	44,000
Printing and Engraving of Debentures[a]	92,000
Printing Registration Statement, Prospectus, Indentures and Other Documents	33,000
Accountant's Fees (Estimate)	25,000
Federal Original Issue Taxes—Debentures[a]	260,000
N.Y. Stock Exchange Listing Fees[a]	28,000
Miscellaneous (to date)	1,000
	507,000
Underwriters Fee[a]	2,188,000
Total	$2,695,000

2. Out-of-pocket or incremental with decision: $2000 (overtime) Accounting
3. Nonincremental (allocations):

(1) Treasurer's	$15,000
(2) Office of General Counsel	8,000
(3) Comptroller	30,000
(4) Secretary	7,000
	$60,000

[a] Signifies costs which are variable with size of issue.

Required: How much debt should Arbor Chemical issue in 1968?

6. The treasurer of the Bi-State Gas and Electric Company had to decide on the size of a new issue of debentures that would be marketed in the near future. The usual considerations that influenced the size of such an issue by the firm were several.

1. The projection of cash needed over the next several years.
2. The limitations on capital structure proportions desired by management.
3. The general state of the securities market.
4. The potential reaction of the financial community to the particular type of security.
5. Interest costs.
6. The limitations on borrowing put into effect by various indentures of previous bonds and of the preferred stock.
7. The expected reaction of regulatory bodies.

The pattern of Bi-State's cash generation was seasonal, influenced quite heavily by residential sales of gas for space heating purposes. Heavy cash outflow resulted from the firm's construction activities, which were normally carried out during the summer and fall months. The recent rate of construction had been at about $30 million a year, two-thirds of which was being supplied from internal sources. The sum of depreciation charges and income in excess of dividends in a normal year were about $20 million. The usual financial pattern was to meet cash needs from internal sources to the degree possible and then borrow from banks the amount necessary to finance construction. Well before the firm had borrowed to the limits on its unsecured credit, it would go to the market for permanent financing to repay the bank credit and to finance further construction needs. It would seek permanent financing before it exhausted its bank credit so that it would retain flexibility in timing its issue of securities. When the company did go to the market for funds, it usually borrowed an amount large enough to carry it for about one year. The total sum borrowed would always include funds for the repayment of bank loans and sufficient funds in addition to carry the company through the rest of the year. On the average, financing took place in the capital markets at slightly more than annual intervals.

There were several reasons for this timing pattern. In the first place regulatory agencies tend to frown on excessive idle cash held by a utility, thus the issue was not made larger. It was not smaller than a year's needs since there was a general feeling in the treasurer's office that the market would look askance at a company that had not planned ahead sufficiently to get enough funds for a full year when it went to the market, and had to return to the market within twelve months. The specific timing of a security issue was dependent upon the calendar of marketings by corporations published by an investment banking house, the interest rates which were effective in the market, and the degree to which the company had flexibility in relation to the limitations set by indentures, bank loans, etc. Another important factor was the demand for the particular securities of the company. It often became known to the corporation through various informal communication channels that specific large investors were interested in an offering by Bi-State. This information could often influence the timing of the issue.

The company has an excellent reputation in the financial community and the history of recent offerings has been that they have "gone out the window" within a few hours of the offering. This reputation is highly valued by financial executives of the company.

The company policy is to make its offerings to the public through competitive bidding. The corporation itself selects the attorney for the offering (whose fees are paid by the low bidding syndicate). There are a number of fixed charges to a security offering, which must be assumed by the seller. The major expenses are:

1. Cost of legal fees (exclusive of the fees described above).
2. Cost of printing of the security issue itself and all the documents which accompany it (the Trust Indenture Act, applicable SEC regulations for public offerings, and the requirements of the State Public Service Commission and the Federal Power Commission are the major causes for the extensive documentation).
3. Various taxes: state mortgage tax and federal original issue tax.

The treasurer and one man in his office plus three or four people from the controller's office are ordinarily tied up extensively for a period of approximately sixty days from the time of the decision to make an offering, until the offering has been completed in the market. There is a considerable investment of management time, energy, and emotions in this activity. This results in a considerable aversion to the possibility of frequent offerings in the security market.

The usual types of securities that the corporation offers are unsecured debentures, secured first mortgage bonds, preferred stock, and common stock. The company attempts to maintain a predetermined "target" proportion of these types of securities. The rule of thumb that is ordinarily applied is that the mortgage bonds will not be more than 50% of the total value of the property of the firm. The common stock is kept somewhere between 35 and 40% of total capital and the preferred stock is usually somewhere around 10%. There is an upper limit (60% of the value of its property) on the amount of the mortgage bonds that the company can issue. The limit is an enforceable requirement of the trust indenture.

The treasurer states that the general order of desirability of sources of financing is (1) moderate short-term bank borrowings; (2) mortgage bonds; (3) debenture bonds, and (4) common stock issues. Preferred stock is regarded as something of a costly hybrid and is generally not offered except under unusual circumstances (the fact that insurance companies like preferred stock influences the thinking of the treasurer). The bonds of the corporation are usually rated AA. The market has come to expect high quality in the securities of Bi-State, an expectation the company has tried to live up to.

In its dealings with its banks the company likes to have a margin of safety; it does not want to be "under the gun" by being very near its unsecured financing limit when borrowing from the banks. If the company allowed itself to be put in this position, it would also find itself at a disadvantage in the competitive bidding of various investment bankers when it went to the market to refund the bank financing. The margin of safety between the maximum bank indebtedness limit and the amount that the company has borrowed from the banks insures it a reasonable bargaining position with the banks and gives the firm the ability to turn down all bids on a security offering if they are deemed to be unsatisfactory.

A limit on total borrowings is placed on the company by the indenture covering two series of debentures (totalling $26,800,000) which includes a clause binding the company on the amount of interest that may be paid during a twelve month period. The annual earnings before taxes of the company must be at least twice all annual interest charges and long-term rental payments (on leases of five or more years) before additional long-term indebtedness (over one year) of any type may be incurred.

Annual interest charges at this time are about $7,800,000 and long-term rental obligations are $51,000; the total is $7,851,000. Annual earnings must be at least $15,702,000 before new debt can be issued. Earnings available for fixed charges are currently $37,600,000, which will support more than twice the amount of debt currently outstanding.

In a recent issue of $25 million of Mortgage Bonds, the total recorded out-of-pocket expenses came to about $230,000. Of this amount, $125,000 was the fifty-cents-per-hundred mortgage tax and the remainder was made up of printing costs, legal, and accounting fees, etc.

The company has banking activities in three major New York City banks plus ninety-seven other banks that are mainly depositories in the various communities in which the company operates. The usual low level for working funds is considered to be about $4.5 million, the range in a recent cash forecast was from $4 to about $8.5. Within this range it appears that marketable securities are not purchased. The Public Service Commission does not allow investments in securities with funds derived from operations unless its consent and approval are first obtained. When excessive funds are on hand from a major financing operation, marketable securities are then purchased.

Eighteen months ago $25 million of mortgage bonds were issued, $12.5 was used to repay banks, and $10 was then used for construction. As of January 1 of this year approximately $4 million of excess cash was on hand. There were no bank loans outstanding.

Required: Assuming the firm can legally issue $32,500,000 of unsecured debt, prepare a report indicating the amount of debentures which should be issued in January. The current interest rate on comparable debentures is .045 and short term marketable securities are yielding .03. Short-term funds can be obtained from the banks at a cost of .055 per year.

REFERENCES

See also References for Chapter 1.

Beranek, W. *Analysis for Financial Decisions* (Irwin, Homewood, Ill., 1963), Chapter 11.

Bierman, H., Jr., Bonini, Charles, and Hausman, Warren. *Quantitative Analysis for Business Decisions* (Irwin, Homewood, Ill., 1969), Chapters 10–11.

Fetter, R. B., and Dallack, W. C. *Decision Models for Inventory Management* (Irwin, Homewood, Ill., 1961).

Lindsay, J. R., and Sametz, A. W. *Financial Management* (Irwin, Homewood, Ill., 1967).

Miller, M. H., and Orr, D. "A Model of the Demand for Money by Firms," *Quarterly Journal of Economics* (August), 1966.

Tobin, J. "The Interest Elasticity of Transactions Demand for Cash," *Review of Economics and Statistics* (August), 1956.

CHAPTER 3

The Credit Decision[1]

SYMBOLS

p	the probability of collection	a	the time value factor equal to $1/(1+k)$
R	the revenue per unit (price)	$D_i(r, n)$	the optimal action to take at stage i
C	the incremental cost per unit	K_1	the gain that results if credit is given and collection occurs
$f_\beta(p\|r, n)$	a beta probability distribution		
r, n	the parameters of the beta distribution	K_2	the loss that results if credit occurs and no collections occur
	r is the number of successes (number of collections)		
	n is the number of trials (times credit is offered)	I	the number of periods in the future when the process stops
	Without a prime we have the prior estimates, with a prime r and n represent the new evidence and with a double prime they are the revised values	B_i	the break-even ratio of r_i/n_i for the ith period
		Y	a multiple of the standard amount of credit
EMV	expected monetary value	$P(Y)$	probability of collection for Y credit (collection of full amount of credit; it is assumed that partial collections cannot be made)
k	the discount rate		
t	the number of time periods		
$f_i(r, n)$	maximum discounted expected payoff from stage i to ∞ assuming optimal decisions are made from now on	Q	the dollar amount of credit
		α	is a scale factor to convert Q into Y: $Q = \alpha Y$ or $Y = Q/\alpha$

[1] Portions of this chapter were previously published as an article in *Management Science* (April 1970). The article was co-authored by Warren Hausman.

The credit-granting policy of a firm is an important decision area. Too restrictive a credit granting policy will reduce sales and profits, whereas an overly permissive credit policy which does not distinguish between good and bad risks will result in excessive uncollectable accounts.

Previous work related to this decision has been largely concerned with methods of discriminating between "good" credit risks and "poor" ones, often without taking the relevant costs and revenues into account. Of the research which has gone further, the work by Beranek builds on a Markovian model, originally set forth by Cyert, Davidson, and Thompson, that assumes the customers move among various credit states (paid-up, one-month old, etc.) through a stationary transition probability matrix. Beranek has added to this model the option of varying the credit policy of a firm and using the various steady-state probabilities to compute expected profits, thereby obtaining the credit policy "... which maximizes expected long-run profits per period."[2] His model does not specify precisely the relationship between credit policy and the transition probabilities, nor does it provide for any way of incorporating additional information (such as collections) which may become available through time. Moreover, there is no way of using initial, prior estimates of the probability of collection for a new customer.

Smith, in a model involving the probability of collection, does make provision for prior probability assessments. He suggests using discriminant analysis on a number of traits or characteristics associated with credit-worthiness, and develops a so-called risk index, defined as the sum of the posterior probabilities of default obtained from each of the various traits.[3] However, as pointed out by Cohen and Hammer in a comment on Smith's paper, Smith's computation of probabilities of default is erroneous, and the assumption that each trait is equally important has not been appropriately justified.[4] Again, no provision is made for the incorporation of additional information in the model.

Cohen and Hammer present a one-period formulation of the credit-granting decision.[5] In their model the amount of credit to offer is the decision variable, and the probability of collection is exponentially related to the amount of credit offered. The deficiency of the one-period model is that it ignores important future benefits from a customer who has repaid his debt.

[2] W. Beranek, *Analysis for Financial Decisions* (Richard D. Irwin, Homewood, Ill., 1963), p. 320; R. M. Cyert, H. J. Davidson, and G. L. Thompson, "Estimation of the Allowance for Doubtful Accounts by Markov Chains," *Management Science* (April, 1962), pp. 287–303; and J. H. Myers and E. W. Forgy, "The Development of Numerical Credit Evaluation Systems," *American Statistical Association Journal* (September, 1963), pp. 799–806.

[3] P. F. Smith, "Measuring Risk on Consumer Installment Credit," *Management Science* (November 1964), pp. 327–340.

[4] K. J. Cohen and F. S. Hammer, "Critical Comments on 'Measuring Risk on Consumer Instalment Credit' by Paul F. Smith," *Management Science* (May 1966), pp. 743–744.

[5] K. J. Cohen and F. S. Hammer, *Analytical Methods in Banking* (Richard D. Irwin, Homewood, Ill., 1966), (see Appendix to Chapter 6).

Greer presents a model that includes the estimation of future benefits associated with credit customers accepted in the current period.[6] He focuses on the number of credit applicants accepted and implicitly assumes that a ranking of customers from good risks to bad risks is available. In that sense Greer's model allows for incorporation of initial estimates of the probability of repayment for a new customer, but the model does not allow for additional information to be incorporated.

In an extension of his model, Greer provides a framework for measuring the value of initial information (i.e., information from a credit application form or from a credit bureau report).[7] However, this model again does not allow for additional information (such as collections) to be incorporated.

The incorporation of additional information has been emphasized here because it is the only way in which a customer can change from one credit-risk category to another based on his current credit behavior. None of the models cited above allows customers to move among risk categories; this is a serious shortcoming of the models in light of the imperfections contained in current methods of initial categorization.

In this chapter we shall develop procedures for incorporating initial, prior estimates of the probability of collection for a new customer and then revising these probabilities as new information is obtained (such as collection). Most important, the probabilities are used with the possible gains and losses to establish an optimal credit-granting policy.[8]

Because we will be dealing with subjective probabilities it is well to keep in mind an important benefit of the suggested procedures. Even if the information for any one customer is not perfect, the procedures implicitly weight the desirabilities of different customers, and as additional information is obtained (either collections or defaults) these weightings will change. There is no pretense of pinpoint accuracy; rather, an attempt is made to incorporate the attitudes of the decision maker so that they may be brought to bear on a difficult decision in order for that decision to be consistent with his opinions about the likelihood of collection. We assume it is appropriate to use expected monetary value to make credit decisions.

Single-Period, Two-Action Problem

We will introduce the problem with a series of simple models and gradually proceed to make the models more complex and realistic.

[6] C. C. Greer, "The Optimal Credit Acceptance Policy," *Journal of Financial and Quantitative Analysis* (December, 1967), pp. 399–415.
[7] C. C. Greer, "Measuring the Value of Information in Consumer Credit Screening," *Management Services* (May–June, 1967), pp. 44–54.
[8] Throughout this chapter we assume that a constant collection policy and a constant policy of credit terms holds. We are ignoring the possibility of charging interest on the credit accounts.

Suppose a product sells for a price of R and the incremental cost of producing, selling, and shipping a unit is C. We assume that the account is either collected in full or not collected at all, so we have a Bernoulli trial with some underlying probability of collection. Let p be our estimate of the probability of collection. Then, using expected monetary value as the guide to action, credit should be extended whenever the incremental expected return (pR) exceeds the incremental cost (C):

$$pR \geq C \quad \text{or} \quad p \geq C/R.$$

For example, suppose a product sells for $100 per unit, and incremental costs are $60. If we consider only a single period, then credit should be offered as long as the estimated probability of collection is greater than .6.

$$p \geq C/R = 60/100 = .6.$$

Subsequent Time Periods: Revision of Collection Probability

Up to this point we have only considered the expected profits resulting from one credit decision and one period of operation. Now we make the model more realistic by recognizing that the firm does not stop operating after one time period. Our estimate of the probability of collection will change after each time period, based on the collection experience.[9] For example, if we start with an estimated probability of collecton of .6, a favorable experience will lead us to increase our estimate of the probability of collecting from that customer for the next time period. Now instead of having only a point estimate of the probability of collection (e.g., .6), suppose we consider a prior distribution on p, the estimated probability of collection. Specifically, suppose we assume that a beta prior distribution on p exists:

$$f_\beta(p \mid r, n) = \frac{(n-1)!}{(r-1)!(n-r-1)!} p^{r-1}(1-p)^{n-r-1}, \quad 0 \leq p \leq 1, n > r > 0$$

$$= \frac{\Gamma(n)}{\Gamma(r)\Gamma(n-r)} p^{r-1}(1-p)^{n-r-1}.$$

The choice of the beta-distribution for a prior distribution on p is somewhat arbitrary but it does have the important advantage of revising very simply, and in a manner that is intuitively appealing.

---

[9] Throughout this model it is assumed that the underlying (unknown) probability of collection for a customer remains stationary.

If credit is extended n' times and r' collections are observed, the parameters of the posterior distribution (r'', n'') are calculated as follows:[10]

$$r'' = r + r',$$
$$n'' = n + n',$$

and

$$E(p \mid r'', n'') = \frac{r''}{n''}.$$

In this relationship r' and n' should both be expressed in terms of units of credit. For example, suppose credit sales of $10,000 is defined as one unit; then $30,000 of credit sales and collections would increase both r and n by 3 units. Assume the prior distribution on p has parameters $(r = 3, n = 5)$. The expected probability of collection is $r/n = 3/5 = .6$. Assume that the selling price R equals $10,000, and the incremental cost is $7000 per unit. Under these conditions, the expected monetary value for one period is $-$1000, and based on our first model, we would reject the sale. Now let us consider the credit decision for four time periods, where we expect credit sales of $10,000 per period. In this model it is assumed that once a failure to collect occurs, no further credit is extended. The expected probabilities of collection for subsequent time periods are as follows:

PERIOD	EXPECTED PROBABILITY OF COLLECTION, ASSUMING COLLECTIONS IN ALL PREVIOUS PERIODS	EXPECTED PROBABILITY OF REACHING THE PERIOD AND COLLECTING WITHOUT A FAILURE TO COLLECT	
1	$\frac{3}{5}$	$\frac{3}{5} =$	.6
2	$\frac{4}{6}$	$\frac{3}{5} \times \frac{4}{6} =$	.4
3	$\frac{5}{7}$	$\frac{3}{5} \times \frac{4}{6} \times \frac{5}{7} =$	.286
4	$\frac{6}{8}$	$\frac{3}{5} \times \frac{4}{6} \times \frac{5}{7} \times \frac{6}{8} =$	.214
			1.500

---

[10] H. Raiffa and R. Schlaifer, *Applied Statistical Decision Theory*, Division of Research, Graduate School of Business Administration, Harvard University. Boston, 1961, pp. 50–51.

The expected probabilities of not collecting (suffering a $7000 loss) are as follows:

PERIOD	EXPECTED PROBABILITY OF NO COLLECTION, ASSUMING COLLECTIONS IN ALL PREVIOUS PERIODS	EXPECTED PROBABILITY OF COLLECTING IN EVERY PERIOD EXCEPT THE LAST PERIOD	
1	$\dfrac{2}{5}$	$\dfrac{2}{5} =$	.4
2	$\dfrac{2}{6}$	$\dfrac{3}{5} \times \dfrac{2}{6} =$	.2
3	$\dfrac{2}{7}$	$\dfrac{3}{5} \times \dfrac{4}{6} \times \dfrac{2}{7} =$	.114
4	$\dfrac{2}{8}$	$\dfrac{3}{5} \times \dfrac{4}{6} \times \dfrac{5}{7} \times \dfrac{2}{8} =$	.071
			.785

For two periods, the decision tree is illustrated in Fig. 3–1.

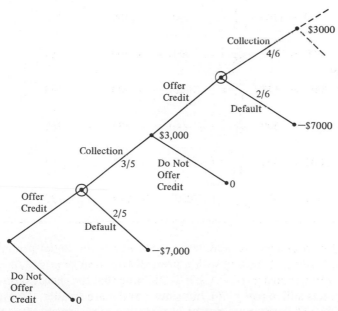

FIGURE 3–1 Decision Tree, Multiple-Period Problem (Stochastic branches are indicated by circles).

Ignoring the time value of money for the present, the expected monetary value of the decision to offer credit is:

$$EMV = .6 \times 3000 + .4 \times 3000 + .286 \times 3000 + .214 \times 3000$$
$$- .4 \times 7000 - .2 \times 7000 - .114286 \times 7000 - .071426 \times 7000$$
$$= 3000(1.5) - 7000(.785715)$$
$$= 4500 - 5,500 = -1000.$$

The expected monetary value is still -1000; however, consider the profit contributions of seven periods instead of one. We move from an expected loss of $1000 to an expected loss of $507. If the process continues for an infinite amount of time the expected gain is $2000.

PERIOD n	EXPECTED PROFIT (OR LOSS): ASSUMING COLLECTION	ASSUMING NO COLLECTION	EXPECTED NET PROFIT OF PERIOD	CUMULATIVE NET PROFIT
1	$\frac{3}{5} \times 3000 = 1800$	$\frac{2}{5} \times (-7000) = -2800$	-1000	-1000
2	$\frac{2}{5} \times 3000 = 1200$	$\frac{1}{5} \times (-7000) = -1400$	-200	-1200
3	$\frac{2}{7} \times 3000 = 857$	$\frac{4}{35} \times (-7000) = -800$	57	-1143
4	$\frac{3}{14} \times 3000 = 643$	$\frac{1}{14} \times (-7000) = -500$	143	-1000
5	$\frac{1}{6} \times 3000 = 500$	$\frac{1}{21} \times (-7000) = -333$	167	-833
6	$\frac{2}{15} \times 3000 = 400$	$\frac{1}{30} \times (-7000) = -233$	167	-666
7	$\frac{6}{55} \times 3000 = 327$	$\frac{4}{165} \times (-7000) = -170$	157	-507

We will now assume we were less certain about the initial probability of collection. Instead of starting with a prior distribution of ($r = 3$, $n = 5$), we will start with parameters ($r = 1.2$, $n = 2$). Note that the expected probability of collection is still .6 ($r/n = .6$), but since r and n are smaller, the experience of collection will carry more weight in updating our estimate of p. Now the expected probabilities of collecting in each time period are:

PERIOD	EXPECTED PROBABILITY OF REACHING THE PERIOD AND COLLECTING WITHOUT A FAILURE TO COLLECT	
1	$\dfrac{1.2}{2} =$	.6
2	$\dfrac{1.2}{2} \times \dfrac{2.2}{3} =$	.44
3	$\dfrac{1.2}{2} \times \dfrac{2.2}{3} \times \dfrac{3.2}{4} =$	.352
4	$\dfrac{1.2}{2} \times \dfrac{2.2}{3} \times \dfrac{3.2}{4} \times \dfrac{4.2}{5} =$ .296	
		1.688

The expected probabilities of not collecting in the final period are:

PERIOD	EXPECTED PROBABILITY OF COLLECTING IN EVERY PERIOD EXCEPT THE LAST PERIOD	
1	$\dfrac{.8}{2} =$	.40
2	$\dfrac{1.2}{2} \times \dfrac{.8}{3} =$	.16
3	$\dfrac{1.2}{2} \times \dfrac{2.2}{3} \times \dfrac{.8}{4} =$	.088
4	$\dfrac{1.2}{2} \times \dfrac{2.2}{3} \times \dfrac{3.2}{4} \times \dfrac{.8}{5} =$ $\begin{array}{c}.0563\\ \hline .7043\end{array}$	

The expected value of offering credit is:

$$EMV = 3000(1.688) - 7000(.7043)$$
$$= 5064 - 4930$$
$$= 134.$$

The solution, starting with considerably more uncertainty, indicates we should offer credit. Since the customer might stay with us longer than four periods the argument in favor of offering credit is even stronger than indicated (assuming no change in sales price or expenses associated with the sale). The example illustrates the importance of considering more than one time period, as well as the effect that the choice of the prior probability distribution has on the credit granting decision.

It is interesting to inspect the profit contribution of each of six periods as shown in the table on page 44.

PERIOD n	ASSUMING COLLECTION IN PERIOD n	ASSUMING NO COLLECTION IN PERIOD n	EXPECTED NET PROFIT	CUMULATIVE PROFIT
1	$\frac{1.2}{2} \times 3000 = 1800$	$\frac{.8}{2} \times (-7000) = -2800$	−1000	−1000
2	$\frac{1.2}{2} \times \frac{2.2}{3} \times 3000 = 1320$	$\frac{1.2}{2} \times \frac{8}{3}(-7000) = -1120$	200	−800
3	$\frac{1.2}{2} \times \frac{2.2}{3} \times \frac{3.2}{4} \times 3000 = 1056$	$\frac{1.2}{2} \times \frac{2.2}{3} \times \frac{.8}{4}(-7000) = -616$	440	−360
4	$\frac{1.2}{2} \times \frac{2.2}{3} \times \frac{3.2}{4} \times \frac{4.2}{5} \times 3000 = 888$	$\frac{1.2}{2} \times \frac{2.2}{3} \times \frac{3.2}{4} \times \frac{.8}{5}(-7000) = -394$	494	134
5	$.25625 \times 3000 = 769$	$.29568 \times \frac{.8}{6}(-7000) = -276$	493	627
6	$.22696 \times 3000 = 681$	$.25625 \times \frac{.8}{7}(-7000) = -205$	476	1103

It is apparent that as we consider more and more future periods we will add significant profits to the analysis; for example, the sixth period contributes $476 of expected profit. If we think that there is some probability that the customer will leave us, we can multiply each period's expected profits by the probability that the customer will initiate a change. This would be analogous to discounting for the time value of money.

The estimation of the prior parameters r and n can be a difficult task, and the sensitivity of the credit granting decision to these parameters is one of the prime weaknesses of the suggested procedure. However, the model could be used in reverse to find those values of r and n for which the decision maker is indifferent between granting credit and not granting credit with a four-period horizon (or any desired horizon), and then the decision maker only needs to decide whether the parameters appropriate to the particular credit customer are on one side of the break-even values or on the other.

Adding Discounting

The time value of money may easily be incorporated into the above analysis. The payoff in each future period t is simply multiplied by the appropriate discount factor $1/(1 + k)^t$ before the expected value calculation is performed. The addition of discounting will make subsequent periods somewhat less important than they were before, but it will still be true that inclusion of subsequent time periods may alter the optimal decision from "offer no credit" to "offer credit."

Dynamic Programming Model for Multiperiod, Two-Action Problem

The previous model omitted the possibility that credit might be extended when one "no-collection" period was experienced. Our previous model cannot incorporate this action, and we now present a dynamic programming model of the multiperiod, two-action problem which will be used subsequently to incorporate additional characteristics of the problem. The previous model set a minimum value for the expected profit which should be improved by the current model.

Assume a beta probability density function with parameters (r, n) represents the a priori probability density function on p, the estimated probability of collection of credit obligations, for a specific customer for the ith time period. Given that a gain of K_1 results if credit is given and collection occurs, while a loss of K_2 $(K_2 < 0)$ results if credit is given and a default occurs, how should the manager decide when to give credit and when not to give credit? Assume that if credit is given during the time period, then the manager faces a second problem (or opportunity) of giving credit again one period later; as long as credit is given, the problem recurs for subsequent periods, and future periods must be considered in solving the decision problem. Dynamic programming will be used to take into account the future effects of present actions.

Dynamic Programming Formulation: Credit Decision

Let (r, n) = state variable (a two-dimensional vector representing parameters of current beta probability density function on p at period i)

$f_i(r, n)$ = maximum discounted expected payoff from stage i to ∞, given the current state variable is (r, n) and that optimal decisions are made from now on (the return function)

$a = 1/(1 + \text{interest rate})$

Also let $D_i(r, n)$ = optimal action to take at stage i (a function of the state variable)

where $D_i(r, n) = \begin{cases} 1 \text{ implies } \textit{give credit} \\ 0 \text{ implies } \textit{do not give credit} \end{cases}$

Then the following general recurrence relation holds:

GIVE CREDIT

(collection)

$$f_i(r, n) = \max \{(r/n) [K_1 + af_{i+1}(r + 1, n + 1)]$$

(default)   DO NOT GIVE CREDIT

$$+ [1 - (r/n)][K_2 + af_{i+1}(r, n + 1)]; \qquad 0 \qquad \} \quad (3\text{-}1)$$
$$\text{for } i = 1, 2, \ldots.$$

The decision maker should choose that action (give credit or do not give credit) which results in the largest expected discounted payoff. The first two expressions in the brackets in Equation 3–1 represent the discounted expected payoff resulting from giving credit. In the first term, the expected probability of collection (r/n) is multiplied by the payoff which results if collection occurs: $[K_1 + af_{i+1}(r + 1, n + 1)]$. Note that this payoff is the sum of the immediate gain K_1 and the expected payoff from being in the situation that will exist one period from now, discounted back one period. The second term reflects the probability of no collection multiplied by the resulting payoff; in this case, there is an immediate loss of K_2 and a subsequent situation represented by $f_{i+1}(r, n + 1)$ which must be discounted back one period. If it is not optimal to extend credit to a customer who has defaulted once, then the term $f_{i+1}(r, n + 1)$ will be zero.[11] Finally, if credit is not extended, the situation in future time periods will be unchanged, and we therefore assume that credit will never be extended to this particular customer and the payoff of not extending credit is zero.

Solution: In order to solve the set of equations (3–1), we first assume that at some distant future period the process stops and the future value is zero. This approximation works because the discount rate makes future values less and less important in the decision process. Therefore for $I = 40$ periods away, say, set

$$f_I(r, n) = 0 \text{ for all } r \text{ and } n. \tag{3-2}$$

Now the set of equations (3–1) may be solved recursively, starting with the last equation ($i = 39$). We indicate the first few iterations:

GIVE CREDIT

(collection)

$$f_{39}(r, n) = \max \{(r/n[K_1 + af_{40}(r + 1, n + 1)] \tag{3-3}$$

DO NOT GIVE
CREDIT

(no collection)

$$+ [1 - (r/n)][K_2 + af_{40}(r, n + 1)]; \qquad 0\}$$

Since $f_{40}(r, n) = 0$,

$$f_{39}(r, n) = \max\{(r/n)K_1 + [1 - (r/n)]K_2; \qquad 0\}.$$

Let B_{39} equal the break-even ratio of (r/n) such that the decision maker is indifferent between giving credit and not giving credit in period 39.
Solving for the value of B_{39} at which both payoffs are equal,

$$B_{39}K_1 + (1 - B_{39})K_2 = 0 \tag{3-4}$$

or

$$B_{39} = -K_2/(K_1 - K_2). \tag{3-5}$$

Then Equation 3–3 may be stated more simply as

$$f_{39}(r, n) = \begin{cases} 0 & \text{if } (r/n) \le B_{39} \\ (r/n)K_1 + [1 - (r/n)]K_2 & \text{if } (r/n) > B_{39} \end{cases} \tag{3-6}$$

The optimal decision $D_{39}(r, n)$ in period 39 may be simply stated as "give

[11] Later in the chapter we argue that if no collection is made, the decision maker should investigate the situation and subjectively assign a new prior distribution on the probability of collection based on the new information.

credit ($D_{39} = 1$) if (r/n) exceeds B_{39}; otherwise, do not give credit ($D_{39} = 0$)."
Proceeding backward to stage 38, we write

GIVE CREDIT

(collection)

$$f_{38}(r, n) = \max\{(r/n)[K_1 + af_{39}(r + 1, n + 1)] \tag{3–7}$$

(no collection)   DO NOT GIVE CREDIT

$$+ [1 - (r/n)][K_2 + af_{39}(r, n + 1)]; \qquad 0 \qquad \}$$

where the term $f_{39}(\cdot)$ must be obtained from the previous solution of Equation 3–6. For a two-dimensional grid of possible values of r and n (say from 1 to 100 for each), we would tabulate $f_{39}(\cdot)$ and retain the table while solving Equation 3–7 for $f_{38}(\cdot)$.[12] Then after the maximization has been performed, we would again record the return function $f_{38}(r, n)$ in tabular form, working backward eventually to $f_1(r, n)$ and $D_1(r, n)$. While the procedure would take time on a large computer, it is feasible and would yield a set of optimal decision rules for the finite-horizon, two-action credit decision. The decision rule for the first stage $D_1(r, n)$ would be the appropriate one to follow initially for the problem in which a horizon of 40 periods exists: more importantly, it will typically be the optimal decision for problems with more than 40 periods, including problems with an infinite horizon.[13] The optimal decision rule $D_1(r, n)$ would be a two-dimensional table of r versus n, with the table entries being "1" where giving credit was optimal and "0" where not giving credit was optimal.

An illustration of the optimal decision table for values of r and n from 1 to 5 might be:

Optimal Decision Table 1 = grant credit 0 = do not grant credit

r \ n	1	2	3	4	5
1	1	0	0	0	0
2	X	1	0	0	0
3	X	X	1	0	0
4	X	X	X	1	1
5	X	X	X	X	1

[12] Note that for this period and succeeding periods, the optimal policy is not simply a function of the ratio r/n; thus the maximization must be performed by calculating each expected discounted payoff and choosing the larger of the two.

[13] As we work backward on this problem for a large number of periods, successive f tables will be identical and the decision rule will converge to a stationary decision rule (i.e., $D_i(r, n)$ and $D_{i-1}(r, n)$ will be identical). When this convergence occurs (e.g., after 40 periods) the resulting decision rule will be the optimal policy under an infinite horizon.

Since it makes no sense for r to be greater than n, an X has been placed in those entries in the table.

EXAMPLE: Consider an example where $r = 2$, $n = 3$. The choice of integer values for r and n simplifies the preparation of the cost tables by drastically reducing their size. The unit of credit is \$10,000 and incremental costs are \$7000 per unit of credit. We will do a four-period analysis where $f_4(r, n) = 0$ for all r and n. The rate of interest is zero.

$$K_1 = 10,000 - 7000 = 3000$$

$$K_2 = -7000$$

$$a = \frac{1}{1 + i} = 1$$

$$f_3(r, n) = \max \left\{ \frac{r}{n} [K_1 + f_4(r + 1, n + 1)] + \left(1 - \frac{r}{n}\right) [K_2 + f_4(r, n + 1); 0 \right.$$

$$= \max \left\{ \frac{r}{n} [K_1] + \left(1 - \frac{r}{n}\right) K_2; 0 \right\}.$$

Let B_3 be the break-even ratio of $\dfrac{r}{n}$:

$$B_3 K_1 + (1 - B_3)K_2 = 0$$

$$B_3 = \frac{K_2}{K_2 - K_1} = \frac{-7000}{-7000 - 3000} = \frac{7}{10}$$

If $\dfrac{r}{n} \leq \dfrac{7}{10}$ GIVE NO CREDIT

$\dfrac{r}{n} > \dfrac{7}{10}$ GIVE CREDIT.

The table for f_3 would be:

r \ n	1	2	$f_3(r, n)$ 3	4	5
1	3000	0	0	0	0
2	X	3000	0	0	0
3	X	X	3000	500[a]	0
4	X	X	X	3000	1000[b]
5	X	X	X	X	3000

[a] $.75 \times 3000 + .25(-7000) = 500$.
[b] $.8 \times 3000 + .2(-7000) = 1000$.

We now solve for $f_2(r, n)$:

$$f_2(r, n) = \max \left\{ \frac{r}{n} [3000 + f_3(r + 1, n + 1)] + \left(1 - \frac{r}{n}\right) [-7000 + f_3(r, n + 1)]; 0 \right\}.$$

r			$f_2(r, n)$	
n	1	2	3	4
1	6000	0	0	0
2	X	6000	0	0
3	X	X	6000	1250
4	X	X	X	6000

This table is derived as follows:

If $\begin{bmatrix} r = 1 \\ n = 1 \end{bmatrix}$ we will have $\begin{bmatrix} r + 1 = 2 \\ n + 1 = 2 \end{bmatrix}$ with probability 1;

$$f_2(1, 1) = \max\{1[3000 + 3000]; 0\} = 6000.$$

The same holds for $r = 2$, $n = 2$ and more generally whenever $r = n$.

If $\begin{bmatrix} r = 1 \\ n = 2 \end{bmatrix}$ we will have either $\begin{bmatrix} r + 1 = 2 \\ n = 3 \end{bmatrix}$ or $\begin{bmatrix} r = 1 \\ n = 3 \end{bmatrix}$;

$$f_2(1, 2) = \max \{\tfrac{1}{2}[3000 + f_3(2, 3)] + \tfrac{1}{2}[-7000 + f_3(1, 3)]; 0\}$$

$$= \max \{1500 - 3500; 0\} = 0$$

If $\begin{bmatrix} r = 2 \\ n = 3 \end{bmatrix}$ we will have either $\begin{bmatrix} 3 \\ 4 \end{bmatrix}$ or $\begin{bmatrix} 2 \\ 4 \end{bmatrix}$;

$$f_2(2, 3) = \max \{\tfrac{2}{3}[3000 + f_3(3, 4)] + \tfrac{1}{3}[-7000 + f_3(2, 4)]; 0\}$$

$$= \max \{\tfrac{2}{3}[3500] + \tfrac{1}{3}[-7000]; 0\} = 0.$$

If $\begin{bmatrix} r = 3 \\ n = 4 \end{bmatrix}$ we will have either $\begin{bmatrix} 4 \\ 5 \end{bmatrix}$ or $\begin{bmatrix} 3 \\ 5 \end{bmatrix}$;

$$f_2(3, 4) = \max \{\tfrac{3}{4}[3000 + f_3(4, 5)] + \tfrac{1}{4}[-7000 + f_3(3, 5)]; 0\}$$

$$= \max \{\tfrac{3}{4}[4000] + \tfrac{1}{4}[-7000]; 0\}$$

$$= 1250.$$

If $\begin{bmatrix} r = 2 \\ n = 4 \end{bmatrix}$ we will have either $\begin{bmatrix} 3 \\ 5 \end{bmatrix}$ or $\begin{bmatrix} 2 \\ 5 \end{bmatrix}$;

$$f_2(2, 4) = \max\{\tfrac{2}{4}[3000 + 0] + \tfrac{2}{4}[-7000]; 0\} = 0.$$

Other entries in the table are similarly computed.
The table for $f_1(r, n)$ is:

r \ n	1	$f_1(r, n)$ 2	3
1	9000	0	0
2	X	9000	500
3	X	X	9000

This table is derived as follows:

If $\begin{bmatrix} r = 1 \\ n = 2 \end{bmatrix}$ we will have either $\begin{bmatrix} r + 1 = 2 \\ n = 3 \end{bmatrix}$ or $\begin{bmatrix} r = 1 \\ n = 3 \end{bmatrix}$;

$$f_1(1, 2) = \max\{\tfrac{1}{2}[3000 + f_2(2, 3)] + \tfrac{1}{2}[-7000 + f_2(1, 3)]; 0\}$$
$$= \max\{\tfrac{1}{2}[3000 + 0] + \tfrac{1}{2}[-7000 + 0]; 0\} = 0.$$

If $\begin{bmatrix} r = 2 \\ n = 3 \end{bmatrix}$ we will have either $\begin{bmatrix} r + 1 = 3 \\ n = 4 \end{bmatrix}$ or $\begin{bmatrix} r = 2 \\ n = 4 \end{bmatrix}$;

$$f_1(2, 3) = \max\{\tfrac{2}{3}[3000 + 1250] + \tfrac{1}{3}[-7000 + 0]; 0\} = 500.$$

Inspection of table $f_1(r, n)$ indicates that with $r = 2$, $n = 3$, the expected profit is $500 and credit should be granted.

Let us now consider a situation where the time value of money per period is .10 and there is a .8 probability that the customer will leave in each period (there is a .2 probability that the customer will remain). We will multiply the value to be received one period from now by .2 (obtained by multiplying .9091 by .2 and rounding off). The table for $f_3(r, n)$ is unchanged since $f_4(r, n) = 0$ for all r and n. The table for $f_2(r, n)$ becomes:

r \ n	1	$f_2(r, n)$ 2	3	4
1	3600	0	0	0
2	X	3600	0	0
3	X	X	3600	650
4	X	X	X	3600

$$f_2(r, n) = \max \left\{ \frac{r}{n} [3000 + .2f_3(r + 1, n + 1)] \right.$$
$$\left. + \left(1 - \frac{r}{n}\right) [-7000 + .2f_3(r, n + 1)]; 0 \right\}.$$

If $r = n$ we have:

$$f_2(r, n) = \max \{\tfrac{2}{2}[3000 + .2 \times 3000]; 0\} = 3600.$$

If $\begin{bmatrix} r = 3 \\ n = 4 \end{bmatrix}$,

$$f_2(r, n) = \max \{\tfrac{3}{4}[3000 + .2 \times 1000] + \tfrac{1}{4}[-7000 + .2 \times 0]; 0\}$$
$$= \max \{2400 - 1750; 0\} = 650.$$

Assume the other entries in the table remain 0 since they are not improved by the use of the .2 risk-time discount factor.

The table for $f_1(r, n)$ becomes:

| | n | $f_1(r, n)$ | |
r	1	2	3
1	3720	0	0
2	X	3720	0
3	X	X	3720

For $r = n$, we have

$$f_1(r, n) = \max \{[3000 + .2 \times 3600]; 0\} = 3720.$$

For $r = 2, n = 3$

$$f_1(r, n) = \max \{\tfrac{2}{3}[3000 + .2 \times 650] + \tfrac{1}{3}[-7000]; 0\}$$
$$= \max \{[2087 - 2333; 0\} = 0.$$

The Amount-of-Credit Problem

Up to this point we have considered only the two-action problem, "give credit or do not give credit." In reality the problem is not that simple. The optimal amount of credit to be offered may be different for different customers. For many customers there is some relatively small amount of credit for which we would consider the probability of collection to be close to one. As the amount of credit is increased we would expect the customer to be placed under strain relative to his making the payment. Assume that we are selling to a retailer. As we increase our credit to him we can expect him to be accepting more and more higher-risk customers in order to increase his sales. How should the decision maker decide how much credit to offer a specific customer? In order to attack this problem we must specify some relationship between the amount of credit offered and the probability of collection.[14] Rather than estimating the relationship assume an exponentially declining relationship as illustrated in Fig. 3–2.

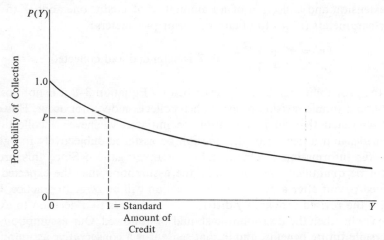

FIGURE 3–2 Probability of collection versus amount of credit. Y represents a multiple of the standard amount of credit.

Note that the amount of credit to be offered is measured in terms of a multiple of the standard amount. Thus $Y = .5$ would represent offering one-half of some standard amount of credit. The equation for the estimated probability of collection in Fig. 3–2 is:

$$\text{Prob(collection} \mid Y \text{ units of credit)} = p^Y \qquad (3\text{–}8)$$

where p represents the estimated probability of collecting the standard amount of credit.[15]

Revision of Probabilities

In order to incorporate the amount-of-credit decision problem into our dynamic programming framework, we must first demonstrate how a prior probability density function on p is revised after credit of amount Y is

[14] Here we assume that p represents the estimated probability of full collection of a standard amount and that partial collections are never made.

[15] If Q is the dollar amount of the credit, then we may write $Q = Y\alpha$, where α represents the standard amount of credit in dollars. Then the probability of collecting an amount Q is $p^{Q/\alpha} = p^Y$.

extended. Assume a beta prior with parameters (r, n) exists at time period i. Let $f_{i+1}(p \mid r, n; Y)$ represent the posterior probability density function after credit of amount Y is extended and collected in period i. Then by Bayes' theorem,[16]

$$f_{i+1}(p \mid r, n; Y) = f_{i+1}(p \mid r + Y, n + Y). \qquad (3\text{-}9)$$

That is, in order to revise the parameters of the beta prior distribution to reflect the extension and collection of an amount Y of credit, one adds Y to both prior parameters (r', n') to obtain posterior parameters:

$$\left\{ \begin{aligned} r'' &= r' + Y \\ n'' &= n' + Y \end{aligned} \right\} \quad \text{if } Y \text{ is extended and collected.}$$

For the probability relationship described by Equation 3–8 it is not possible to obtain a simple revision process when collection does not occur. However, it is suggested that an investigation be initiated whenever a collection is not made, and a new prior distribution be assigned subjectively in light of whatever information is obtained by the investigation. Since this process cannot be quantified, we now make the assumption that the expected discounted payoff after a period of no collection will be zero. In practice, however, if the revised probability distribution still leads to a decision to extend some credit, then the decision rule should be followed. Our assumption may understate future benefits, and in that sense it is a conservative assumption.

Dynamic Programming Formulation: Amount of Credit

Using previous notation, the following general recurrence relation may be written, assuming there is a future total payoff of zero if credit is offered but no collection occurs:

GIVE Y WORTH OF CREDIT	GIVE $Y = 0$
(collection)	(no collection)

$$f_i(r, n) = \max_{0 \le Y < \infty} \left\{ (r/n)^Y [K_1 Y + a f_{i+1}(r + Y, n + Y)] \right.$$
$$\left. + [1 - (r/n)^Y][K_2 Y]; 0 \right\} \qquad (3\text{-}10)$$

for $i = 1, 2, \ldots.$ and where the expected probability of collection is $(r/n)^Y = [E(p)]^Y$.

The method of solution of Equation 3–10 is as previously described: assume the process stops in some distant future period, form a two-dimensional

---

[16] See the Appendix to this chapter.

grid on r and n, and work backward, performing each required maximization by a search technique. In this case it would be necessary to interpolate on the grid for noninteger values of r and n.[17] As before, the decision rule for the first stage, $D_1(r, n)$, would be the appropriate one to follow for the infinite-horizon case. We want to find the value of Y that maximizes the value of $f(r, n)$.

Let the standard unit of credit (α) be $10,000. If we were considering giving $40,000 of credit ($Q = 40,000$) then Y would be

$$Y = \frac{Q}{\alpha} = \frac{40,000}{10,000} = 4$$

For each different value of Y that we want to consider we have to compute an expected monetary value table. The table for each Y would show for all values of r and n the expected payoffs. This set of tables could be used in the following manner. If a customer wanted $40,000 of credit we would go to the table for $Y = 4$ and base the decision on the r and n that we have for the customer (entering the table with that r and n).

An overall table showing the maximum Y to be granted for all combinations of r, n could also be prepared as well as a table showing the optimum amount of credit (based on the maximum expected values obtained from the Y tables).

Again assume $K_1 = 3000$ and $K_2 = -7000$.

If $Y = 1$ we have the same basic situation as has already been described. Let $Y = 2$. $P(\text{Collection} \mid Y = 2) = p^Y = p^2$.

The expected value of p is

$$E(p) = \frac{r}{n}.$$

If $a = 1$ the function to be maximized becomes

$$f_i(r, n) = \max \left\{ \left(\frac{r}{n}\right)^Y [K_1 Y + f_{i+1}(r + Y, n + Y)] \right.$$
$$\left. + \left[1 - \left(\frac{r}{n}\right)^Y\right] [K_2 Y + f_{i+1}(r, n + Y)]; 0 \right\}$$

If $f_{i+1}(r, n) = 0$ we have

$$f_i(r, n) = \max \left\{ \left(\frac{r}{n}\right)^Y [K_1 Y] + \left[1 - \left(\frac{r}{n}\right)^Y\right] [K_2 Y]; 0 \right\}.$$

If B is the break-even value of r/n:

$$B^Y K_1 Y + (1 - B^Y) K_2 Y = 0$$
$$B^Y K_1 + (1 - B^Y) K_2 = 0$$
$$B^Y (K_1 - K_2) = -K_2$$
$$B^Y = \frac{K_2}{K_2 - K_1}.$$

[17] The computational aspects of this method of solution are by no means trivial, although the required steps are well defined. See G. Hadley, *Nonlinear and Dynamic Programming* (Addison-Wesley, Reading, Mass., 1964), p. 425.

If $Y = 2$, we have

$$B^2 = \frac{K_2}{K_2 - K_1} = \frac{-7000}{-7000 - 3000} = .7$$

$$B = .836.$$

We can proceed to prepare the first table for $Y = 2$. For $Y = 3$ we would take the cube root of .7 to find the break-even value of r/n.

Problems in Application

The use of sales price and incremental costs implies that each product being sold having a different incremental profit per dollar of sales theoretically will require a different credit policy. This requirement may frequently be ignored in practice where the different products have very similar ratios of K_1 to K_2, but should be applied where the ratios are drastically different.

There is need for nearly instantaneous feedback in credit management. Having a credit limit is of little use if that limit is not applied at the point of sale. We should know when the customer is approaching his limit and he should be informed that he cannot expect more credit.

In many situations the customer will not borrow up to his limit. In fact, in most situations we would expect a customer to stop purchasing on credit while the probability of collection was still close to one.

The prior probability of collection should be adjusted whenever we obtain additional information. Prompt adjustment is desirable in order to avoid mounting losses. Any information about the financial affairs of the customer (or the customer's customers) may effect the probability of collection.

The suggestions made here lead to a control of the level of all receivables by controlling the individual accounts. We would not say that the total accounts receivable were too large if each individual account was at a proper level. Inspection of the total receivables may give a hint that control of the specific accounts has lapsed, but the total accounts receivable (even if related to sales) cannot be definitive evidence in judging how well credit is being managed.

Similarly, the amount of uncollectibles for the period, in total or as a percentage of receivables or sales, cannot be the sole criterion for judging the credit function. A smart credit manager can always reduce uncollectibles by increasing the quality of the customers being serviced, but this may have an undesirable effect on profits. One of the problems of credit management is to insure that the decision maker has the point of view of the firm rather than trying to make his operation "look good." In many situations there is a conflict in goals.

The degree of statistical independence of the economic affairs of the customers is a final consideration in evaluating the amount of risk associated with the outstanding credit. Our models have assumed independent behavior among customers. If the customers are separated geographically and involve relatively different types of industries then we can assume there is not a large amount of dependence, and relatively little risk. Selling exclusively to a housing project in Dearborn, Michigan, would be an example where there is a relatively large amount of dependence (Ford Motor Company contributes heavily to the economics of the area), and where there would be a relatively large amount of risk. If automobile production slacked off, a large percentage of the residents might find it difficult to pay their bills. The credit granting decision could be considered to be a "portfolio" type of investment problem. We have assumed that expected monetary value was a reasonable guide to action, thus we only had to determine the probability of collection for each customer. If we were to consider the portfolio effect we would have to determine how the probabilities of collection of the customers were related to each other (the covariances). This would have to be done if the utility function of the firm were not linear with respect to money.[18]

Conclusions

Credit management requires balancing the expected gains from sales against the possible loss if the amount receivable is not collected. A good credit policy will result in some uncollectible accounts, but it should also result in sales that increase profits despite the fact that the collection might be a risky operation. We have offered here a set of models that quantify the expected value of future credit extension opportunities, thereby reflecting an important factor in the credit decision. If credit is not granted today we not only lose this period's sales but also the sales of future periods.

Implicit in any credit decision is a probability of making the collection. We have suggested that it might be appropriate to use an *a priori* probability distribution on p, the estimated probability of collection, and then revise this distribution as new information about collections or defaults becomes available. Dynamic programming techniques can be used to prepare a set of decision rules on whether or not to offer credit to a customer.

While our *a priori* probabilities are subjective, we can use information regarding the financial affairs of the customer in selecting these probabilities.

[18] R. M. Cyert and G. L. Thompson, "Selecting a Portfolio of Credit Risks by Markov Chains," *Journal of Business* (January, 1968), pp. 39–46, includes one type of portfolio effect. They calculate the variance of the discounted net profit obtained from offering credit to any set of customers when each customer falls into a specific risk category with an associated transition probability matrix. However, in that model it is still assumed that each customer's behavior is statistically independent of that of the other customers; in our example of the housing project in Dearborn such an assumption would not be reasonable. In this sense the Cyert and Thompson model omits a portfolio effect which may be more important that the effect which they include.

The use of the method presented here could then alter the decision from being entirely subjective to one which effectively incorporates projections of the future and revises these projections as additional information concerning collections is obtained.

The analysis of this chapter has considered the possibility of changing the level of sales by influencing the credit-granting decision. A risk analysis has been made but it is only a partial analysis since no consideration has been given to the effect of the credit decision on other operating characteristics of the corporation. A global approach would consider the effect of a change in credit (say an easier credit policy) and the resulting change in sales on the cash position, the inventory needs, and the current liabilities. Before credit is actually given, these factors should be brought into the analysis. (The increase in cash and inventories less the increase in the current liabilities would be a cash flow deduction at the time of the sale if the credit is given.)

Appendix

Revision of Probabilities

Assume a beta prior probability density function with Y credit extended and collected in period i. Then by Bayes' theorem,

$$f_{i+1}(p \mid r, n; Y) = \frac{f_i(p \mid r, n) \cdot p^Y}{\int_0^1 p^Y \cdot f_i(p \mid r, n) \, dp}$$

$$= \frac{f_i(p \mid r, n) \cdot p^Y}{\frac{\Gamma(n)\Gamma(r + Y)\Gamma(n - r)}{\Gamma(r)\Gamma(n + Y)\Gamma(n - r)} \int_0^1 f_i(p \mid r + Y, n + Y) \, dp}$$

$$= \frac{\frac{\Gamma(n)}{\Gamma(r)} \Gamma(n - r) p^{r-1}(1 - p)^{n-r-1} p^Y}{\frac{\Gamma(n)\Gamma(r + Y)}{\Gamma(r)\Gamma(n + Y)}},$$

so

$$f_{i+1}(p \mid r, n; Y) = f_{i+1}(p \mid r + Y, n + Y).$$

PROBLEMS

1. Assume that a decision has to be made for a one-shot credit situation. The product sells for $1000 per unit. The average cost of the product is $800 and the incremental cost is $300. Analysis indicates that there is a .55 probability of collection.

Required: Should the credit be offered for the one unit assuming the plant has excess capacity? What would the probability of collection have to be to change your decision?

2. Continue Problem 1. Assume that the probability of collection is .25 but that if collection is made the probability of collection on a second sale is .6. If collection is not made the probability of collection is .1 on the second sale. Only two sales (in sequence) can be made.

Required: Should the credit be offered? Draw a decision tree illustrating the decision. Assume that if credit is offered the second sale is made after information is obtained about the first collection.

3. Continue Problem 1. Assume that the probability of collection is .25 and that we have a beta prior distribution with parameters r equal to 1 and n equal to 4. Ignore the time value of money.

Required: Prepare an analysis that shows how we might arrive at a decision assuming the period of analysis is:
   (a) One period
   (b) Two periods
   (c) Four periods

4. Continue Problem 3. Assume the time value of money is .04 and that each transaction will be separated by one time period.

Required: For the four period case, determine whether credit should be offered.

5. Assume the sale price of a product is $1000 and that the incremental costs associated with production and sale of the product are $300. Assume we can represent the probability of collecting Y units of credit for a customer as follows:

$$\text{Probability of collection} = .4^Y$$

Required: For a one period situation, how much credit should be offered if each unit of credit is $1,000,000?

REFERENCES

Berenek, W. *Analysis for Financial Decisions* (Irwin, Homewood, Ill., 1963), Chapter 10.

Cyert, R. M., and Thompson, G. L. "Selecting a Portfolio of Credit Risks by Markov Chains," *Journal of Business* (January), 1968.

———, Davidson, H. J. and Thompson, G. L. "Estimation of the Allowance for Doubtful Accounts by Markov Chains," *Management Science* (April), 1962.

Greer, C. C. "The Optimal Credit Acceptance Policy," *Journal of Financial and Quantitative Analysis* (December), 1967.

———. "Measuring the Value of Information in Consumer Credit Screening," *Management Science* (May–June), 1967.

Hadley, G. *Nonlinear and Dynamic Programming* (Addison–Wesley, Reading, Mass., 1964).

Johnson, R. W. *Financial Management* (Allyn & Bacon, Boston, 1966), Chapter 6.

McGrath, J. J. "Improved Credit Evaluation with a Weighted Application Blank," *Journal of Applied Psychology* (October), 1960.

Raiffa, H., and Schlaifer, R. *Applied Statistical Decision Theory* (Division of Research, Graduate School of Business Administration, Harvard University, Boston, 1961).

Smith, P. F. "Measuring Risk on Consumer Credit," *Management Science* (November), 1964.

PART II

The Cost of Capital and Capital Structure Decisions

Since 1958, the study of the cost of capital and capital structure has been greatly influenced by the Franco Modigliani and Merton Miller article, "The Cost of Capital, Corporation Finance, and the Theory of Investment."[1] This section considers the arguments offered by Modigliani and Miller in that article and suggests some modifications some of which have also been suggested by M–M that are more consistent with institutional realities.

Two basic operational questions are considered:

1. Can the value of a firm be increased by decisions affecting the capital structure?
2. What is the cost of the capital used by a firm, and what rate of discount should be used in evaluating investment opportunities?

---

[1] See *The American Economic Review* (June 1958), pp. 261–297. We shall refer to these authors as M-M.

CHAPTER 4

The Cost of Capital and Evaluation of Investments

SYMBOLS

K is the weighted average of discount rates being applied to the future cash flows by investors. It is the average cost of capital

X_i the cash flow of the ith period paid to the investors

D_i the dividend per share paid to stockholders in the ith time period

r is the cost of capital of common stockholders (cost of equity capital or the expected return)

$\dfrac{1}{r_k}$ factor of proportionality for any class of companies k

$\bar{X}_j$ the expected cash flow of the jth firm

P_j the value per share of the jth firm's stock (P will also be used for price per share)

The Financial officers of a firm are likely to be asked three questions involving capital structure:

1. How is the overall cost of capital of the firm changed by decisions affecting the capital structure?
2. How will the firm's value be affected?
3. What is the firm's cost of capital and what is its relevance to investment decisions?

Answers to the first two questions influence the types of securities that are issued to investors to finance expansion. The answer to the third question conventionally becomes the cut-off rate (or the rate of discount) for investments. The answers to these questions are not obvious, and it is likely that a businessman or student reading the literature pertaining to these questions will become confused. In Chapters 5, 6, and 7 we will consider how the overall cost of capital of the firm is affected by the issuance of debt. In this chapter we shall consider the question of the relevance of the cost of capital to investment decisions.

Definition of Cost of Capital

Define the cost of capital as the cost to the corporation of obtaining funds or, equivalently, as the average return that an investor in a corporation expects after having invested proportionately in all the securities of the corporation. To simplify the discussion, assume the rates at which the corporation can borrow and lend funds are equal. The above definition is appealingly simple, and leads to simple decision rules. If the cost of obtaining funds is K and if the corporation has an investment that yields more than K then it should accept the investment. Unfortunately the decision rule and the definition of cost of capital both gloss over considerations of uncertainty and risk preferences which we cannot ignore if we expect the decision rule to be operational in the real world.

Computation of the Cost of Capital

Consider the assumption that it is possible to compute the cost of capital with reasonable exactness and meaningfulness. It may be possible to take a stream of expected benefits in the future (say, the interest payments on debt and the dividends of a stock) and an outlay in the present (let X_i be the cash flow of period i) and find the constant K that causes Equation 4–1 to hold:

$$\sum_{i=0}^{\infty} (1 + K)^{-i} X_i = 0. \qquad (4\text{–}1)$$

Equation 4–1 is modified if we focus attention on the cost of common stock equity. Let D_i be the dividend paid to the stockholders in the ith time period. Consider Equation 4–2:

$$P = \sum_{i=0}^{\infty} (1 + r)^{-i} D_i, \qquad (4\text{–}2)$$

where P is the price of a share and r is the cost of capital of common stockholders and the D_i are the future dividends. It is naive to think that an investor explicitly applies Equation 4–2. It would also be incorrect to compute the expected value of a share of stock, and exclude risk considerations. There is little reason to think that Equation 4–2 offers a value for r that can be taken and used to make decisions in a different situation with a different timing of cash flows and different risk even where the same firm is involved.

Risk Classes, Factors of Proportionality, and the Cost of Capital

Modigliani and Miller assume that different risk classes of firms have different costs of capital.[1] If this is interpreted to mean that the larger the amount of risk, the higher the required return, the risk class concept is acceptable. However, an error would be introduced if it were assumed that it is appropriate to take the risk of an investment into account via the discounting (and compounding) procedure. There is no reason for assuming that risk is always compounded through time.

The problem which concerns us would not arise with firms in the same risk class if the cash flows of all investments were perpetuities. As defined by M–M the return on the unlevered shares issued by firms in the same risk class are perfectly correlated and differ at most by the scale factor.[2] The investments made by firms in the same risk class are being made using the same criterion.

Let the factor of proportionality for any class k be $1/r_k$, P the price per share, and $\bar{X}_j$ the expected return per share of the jth firm in class k, then we have[3]:

$$P_j = \frac{1}{r_k} \bar{X}_j,$$

$$r_k = \frac{\bar{X}_j}{P_j}.$$

It is then concluded that r_k is the expected rate of return of any share in class k, or the market rate of capitalization for the expected value of the uncertain streams generated by the kth class of firms.[4]

The above definitions or computations taken by themselves are correct. However, one should not assume that r_k is useful as a means of evaluating other streams of benefits to determine their desirability *vis-a-vis* the return requirements of the investors who have established r_k.[5] Here we have a measure that attempts to combine risk and time value into one computation, and there is no reason to conclude that it will always accomplish this objective. The following example illustrates a possible objection.

EXAMPLE: Make the assumption that we know investors' expectations. (M–M do not claim to have this ability, but even with it we soon get into

---

[1] See Franco Modigliani and Merton H. Miller, "The Cost of Capital, Corporation Finance, and the Theory of Investment," *The American Economic Review* (June, 1958), pp. 261–297; "The Cost of Capital, Corporation Finance, and the Theory of Investment: Reply," *The American Economic Review* (September, 1959), pp. 655–669; and "Taxes and the Cost of Capital: A Correction," *The American Economic Review* (June, 1963), pp. 433–443.

[2] *Ibid.*, (1958), p. 266.   [3] *Ibid.* p. 267.

[4] *Ibid.*, p. 267.   [5] *Ibid.*, p. 267.

difficulties.) Investors believe the Wildcat Corporation will pay $2200 yearly dividends per share for perpetuity starting one year from now. However, this is a risky enterprise and while there is a .5 probability of this event there is also .5 probability that the company will disappear with no return to the stockholders.

Assume the current market price is $2200 per share for the jth firm. The expected monetary return for the next period is $1100 and the desired return for the uncertain streams generated by this class of firms is .50. But how does the firm use this information? Assume it has an opportunity to make an investment that requires an outlay of $1000 and promises a certain return of $1200 one period hence. This return is .20 and this is significantly less than the required return of .50, thus we might reject. However, this investment would tend to improve the risk class of the firm and we are reasonably sure the investors who currently seem to be requiring a .50 return would be very pleased to have the firm accept the certain stream described. In fact M–M suggest that we use a different capitalization rate for sure streams rather than r_k.[6] However, assume there is added just a little risk to the return of $1200 (say there is 10^{-6} probability of $0). What interest rate do we now use? We can move the probability of $0 in small increments from 10^{-6} to 1. How much does the appropriate discount rate change with each increment? In fact, we can change the sample space of outcomes from two possible discrete outcomes to many outcomes, or an infinite number of outcomes. Is there to be a different r_k for each investment with different time value and risk characteristics? How do we make this operational?

Assume another investment is available that costs $1000 and promises to return either $2001 or $0, the events both having .5 probability. The events occur in time Δt, where Δt is very small. The expected yield is thus very large. While this investment is "obviously" acceptable using the criterion "accept when the expected return is greater than r_k," it is not all clear that investors who are currently expecting a return of .10 for a moderately risky firm would want this investment accepted.

In the real world the dividends of the future are not known with certainty and stockholders have in mind many possibilities that may occur (i.e., there is a probability distribution on the possible outcomes). If we take the mean values and find the rate of interest which equates the future dividends to the cost of stock we run into a difficulty since the investors are also incorporating their attitudes toward risk when they set a price.

Investors may prefer earning some return less than r_k in the jth firm even though they can earn r_k by investing in one of the other firms in the k class. Why are they willing to accept less than r_k? The answer lies in the fact that the return promised by the other firms all have a given risk characteristic and

[6] *Ibid.*, p. 268; also 1963, p. 435.

it is being suggested that the jth firm may have an investment opportunity with a lower expected return but a risk characteristic for a specific investment (such as a near certain return) which makes the investment desirable despite the lower expected return. The r_k cut-off can only be used if each and every investment of all the firms in the same risk class have exactly the same risk characteristics. This is, of course, not generally possible, and since it is not possible, r_k is not an operational tool.

The Time-Value Factor and Investment Evaluation

All investments have three basic elements that an investor is likely to take into account in some fashion.

1. The time value of money; funds at different times have different values.
2. The outcomes are uncertain; attitudes towards risk are relevant.
3. The value of the information; the uncertain flows are spread out through time and at present we do not have the information as to the outcome.

It is not surprising that there are markets that enable different individuals to attain their own preferences relative to the three elements listed. We may have a person whose near-term plans are completely independent of the actual outcomes of an investment, thus would pay nothing for information relative to the outcomes of an investment. Another person (say one planning the education of his children) may be very concerned with the fact that he will not know the outcome of his investment for a number of years. The same types of differences among individuals with respect to time value of money and risk lead to a conclusion that exchanges will take place if there is a market for such exchanges. Now we shall discuss the time value of money and how it should be incorporated into the evaluation of investments.

Time Value of Money

The conventional present value method of making capital budgeting decisions takes the time value of money into account using the firm's cost of capital as the discount rate. This might be called a risk-discount approach to the cost of capital. The essence of this approach is that the average cost of a particular source of capital is defined as the discount rate that makes the present value of the expected proceeds that will be received by the capital supplier equal to the market value of the securities representing that capital. With a business corporation, proceeds expected to be received by the capital supplier have some degree of uncertainty. This is clear in the case of equity capital; and so long as there is a probability of default, it is also true of debt. The excess of the cost of corporate capital sources over the discount rate that applies to default-free cash flows presumably reflects an adjustment for risk. Raising the discount rate to compute present values may not be an effective or useful way of allowing for risk. The use of a default-free rate of interest is not dependent on the cash flows of an investment being riskless. It may be used to accomplish discounting for time with uncertain flows, though the necessity of incorporating an adjustment for risk remains.

The Interest Rate

The classical approach to the description of the interest rate is to state that it is determined by the interaction of two forces which may be represented by schedules. On one hand is the schedule of consumption preferences through time for different rates of interest. On the other hand is the schedule of production opportunities which are acceptable for different rates of interest.[7]

A dollar available today for consumption or investment is more valuable than a dollar available one period from now assuming investment opportunities exist.

Assume we can exchange $1 now for $1.10 of purchasing power in the future, then we may exchange some consumption today for a higher level of consumption next period. If the return were higher than $1.10 we might defer (or save) an even larger amount. What determines the amount of future consumption which we can obtain for deferring present consumption? One factor is the productivity of capital (i.e., the expected return of invested funds). There are two primary reasons why capital can generate an interest return:

1. Some types of capital increase in value through time because of changes in physical characteristics, for example, cattle, wine, and timber.
2. There are many work processes where roundabout methods of production are desirable. If you are going to cut down a large tree it may be worth investing some time to sharpen your axe. If you are going to dig a hole you might want to build or buy a shovel, or even spend the time to manufacture a back-hoe.

These characteristics of capital lead to a situation in which business entities can pay interest for the use of money. If you invest $1 in an industrial firm the firm may be able to pay you $1 plus interest if your savings enabled the firm to use some roundabout method of production or to delay the sale of a product while it accreted in value. The interaction of the schedule of time

---

[7] For an indifference curve analysis of interest see J. Hirshleifer, "On the Theory of Optimal Investment Decision," *The Journal of Political Economy* (August, 1958), pp. 329–352.

consumption preferences and the productivity schedule (supply and demand for capital) help determine the interest rate.

This discussion ignores the fact that both the present outlays and the future benefits may not be certain. If an investor with reference to a specific uncertain investment indicates he requires a .20 return, this does not indicate that his time preference for money is .20 per year. It remains for us to decide how a firm should transform future benefits and outlays back to the present, collapsing all the cash flows to one measure.

It is interesting to note the effects of a corporation erring on the side of using too low a rate of discount (i.e., the estimate we use is less than the unknown "true" or appropriate rate of discount):

1. More investments are undertaken by the corporation than "should" be undertaken. This company grows faster than it would otherwise grow. The effects on the economy would depend on the number and scope of companies which used the "too-low" discount rate. Conceivably it could result in more total investment than would otherwise be undertaken; less immediate and more future consumption.
2. Less money is returned to the stockholders than should be returned (some stockholders in higher tax brackets will be pleased by not receiving the funds at this time).
3. Longer-lived investments (or investments with more cash flows in the future) have a better competitive position in the decision process compared with shorter-lived investments (or investments with more cash flows in the early years).

One would expect the price of such a stock to become depressed with the ultimate result that the present management would be replaced by a management willing to return excess funds to the owners of the firm.

The Discount Rate

The investor expects payment from a corporation for two factors:

1. The utilization of the funds through time.
2. The risk element associated with the possibility of the corporation failing to repay the investment or the interest on the investment.

The cost of capital combines these two factors into one measure, a percentage. This percentage is then used in a basic discounting formula. It is assumed that a stockholder should multiply a future cash flow D_i by $(1 + r)^{-n}$ to find the present value of D_i. The validity of this computation can be shown if r measures the time value of money. It has not be shown to be correct if r is a combination of two factors, a time value factor i and a risk factor j.

There are several ways in which we can show how a compounding formula applied to future cash flows fails to take risk effectively into consideration. For example:

1. Look at the effect of discounting $100 one period and 50 periods at two different rates. The effect is not easily forecasted.

TIME	INVESTMENT A .05	INVESTMENT B .20	RATIO OF COLUMN 1 TO COLUMN 2
1	95.24	83.33	1.1
50	8.72	.01	872

Does the risk of B increase relative to A the further the cash flows are from the present?

2. Consider the situation where the immediate outlay is uncertain but future flows are certain. Should we use a high discount rate? A variation of this situation occurs when all the events occur immediately (or in a very short time period). The use of a high discount rate will not affect the present value of the cash flows since $(1 + r)^{-t}$ equals 1 when $t = 0$.
3. It is possible to have a high expected present value and still not have a desirable investment. Increasing the discount rate may make the investment less desirable, but there is no reason to assume that it will effectively take risk into consideration.

The cost of capital implicitly incorporates a risk adjustment that is added to a time-value factor. When the cost of capital is inserted in the relationship to compute the present value of an investment this risk factor is then compounded. This may not be a correct way of incorporating risk considerations.

The rate of discount used in computing the present value of cash flows should not attempt to take into consideration risk preferences or aversions. It is appropriate that the time-value factor results in a compounding effect, it may not be appropriate to assume automatically that risk is the same type of compounding phenomena.

One possibility for the discount rate is the default free interest rate (say the appropriate rate on government securities). However, it can be shown that where the borrowing rate of the firm is higher than this rate, an investment with a yield less than the borrowing interest rate is not desirable if the cash flows of the investment are known with certainty, and if the funds have to be borrowed.

EXAMPLE: Assume the marginal borrowing rate of ABC Company is .06 and the rate on one-period governments is .04. Assume it has an investment that promises to yield with certainty the following cash flows:

$$\text{Period:} \quad \frac{0}{-1000} \quad \frac{1}{1050}.$$

The use of the default-free rate of .04 as the rate of discount would result in a positive present value, but a large number of these "desirable" investments financed at .06 could bankrupt the firm. Investments with certain cash flows and yields less than .06 should be rejected by the ABC Company if the funds have to be borrowed.[8] If the cash flows are not known with certainty, then risk characteristics, their effect on the risk characteristics of the current investments, and their effect on the cost of raising funds, must be considered.

A problem in using the interest rate on government securities as the rate of discount in making investment decisions is that we have to decide on the maturity of the debt used as our bench mark. The interest rate effective at any time is a function of the length of time until maturity. We could choose the interest rate of securities of the same duration as the life of the investment. Another possibility is to use the long-term debt interest rate.

Another problem with using interest rates on government securities is that they are greatly influenced by government-controlled (or government-inspired) actions. Thus, the interest rate on these securities may reflect bureaucratic decisions rather than consumption or production opportunities. This means that we cannot automatically accept the interest rate on government securities as a measure of the time value of money to the economy. From the point of view of the individual investor it does set an opportunity cost or minimum return he would require from other investments.

The Corporate Tax Consideration

Assume that we are dealing with a company that is paying no tax either because of the peculiarities of its business or because it is operating at a loss and expects to operate at a loss in the future. The government security interest rate is .06 and the firm can borrow funds at .06. The investment we are considering has certain cash flows. A correct decision rule would be to use the present value procedure accepting investments with a positive net present value using .06 as the rate of discount. If the firm accepted investments with a yield of less than .06 its investors would be worse off than if the firm returned the funds to the investors.

[8] If the funds are currently on hand, then this certain investment is better than certain investments available to the stockholder yielding .04.

Now we will assume that the firm is being taxed at a marginal rate of .4. How does this alter the decision process? It is commonly agreed that the cash flows used in the investment analysis should be on an after-tax basis. The corporation must be interested in what it has left after the tax bill is paid in order to compute the net benefit to the stockholders. With the cash flows on an after-tax basis, it is reasonable to assume that the discount rate should also be on an after-tax basis. If the company can borrow at a cost of .06, it can deduct the interest from its taxable income thus reducing its tax bill. With a .4 tax rate, the net interest cost to the corporation will be .6 of .06 or .036. The .036 assumes there is no possibility that the firm will have losses for a series of years and not be able to use the interest tax deduction.

EXAMPLE: Assume a certain investment promises the following before-tax cash flows:

$$\text{Period:} \qquad \frac{0}{-1000} \qquad \frac{1}{1080}.$$

The after-tax cash flows assuming a .4 tax rate are[9]

$$\text{Period:} \qquad \frac{0}{-1000} \qquad \frac{1}{1048}.$$

Using a .06 rate of discount the investment would be rejected. Using the after-tax borrowing rate of interest of .036 the investment has a net present value of $12:

$$-1000 + \frac{1048}{1.036} = \$12;$$

and the investment is judged to be acceptable. The stockholders are better off if the investment is undertaken than if the investment is rejected. The corporation's net income and asset position will be improved by accepting the investment. With certain cash flows the decision rule for an invest-borrow situation would be simple. "Use the after-tax cash flows and the after-tax interest rate cost to compute the net present value. Accept if the net present value is positive."

If the investment is to be financed by stock equity funds as well as debt we have a complication. The dividends paid to stockholders are not deductible for tax purposes. We would have to take a weighted average of the costs of the two sources.

EXAMPLE: Assume the time value of money of all capital contributions is .06 and that cost of both debt and stock equity funds is .06 before tax con-

[9] The tax on income of $80 is $32 and the net after-tax cash flow is $1,048.

siderations. The capital structure is .7 stock, .3 debt. The tax rate is .4. The after-tax cost would be:

	COST OF FUNDS	TAX FACTOR	AFTER-TAX COST	CAPITAL STRUCTURE	WEIGHTED AVERAGE
Stock	.06	1.0	.06	.7	.042
Debt	.06	.6	.036	.3	.0108
					.0528

If all capital structures are possible the after-tax cost can be as high as .06 and as low as .036 (with increasing risk to the stockholders).

EXAMPLE: Assume the borrowing rate is .06 and there is a .4 tax rate on corporate earnings. The firm can invest in a one period investment costing $2000 that will give cash flows in period 1 of $2120 before tax. The taxable income is $2120 − 2000 = $120. The net after tax is $72 and the cash flow is $2072. The following cash flows are after tax, but before financing cash flows.

0	1
− 2000	2072

If the firm can finance the investment entirely with .06 debt (as with a lease), the investment is marginally acceptable.[10] The financial type cash flows will be:

	0	1
Debt (principal)	+ 2000	− 2000
Interest		− 120
Tax Saving from Interest Deduction		48
Total	+ 2000	− 2072

The investment cash flows are just sufficient to repay the debt. The .036 is the minimum acceptable rate assuming 100% debt financing. Now assume the investment being discussed is financed 100% with common stock (the dividends are not deductible for tax purposes). The cash flows associated with

---

[10] The inclusion of interest in the cash flows is a form of double counting and may give incorrect results. However, it is possible to include all cash flows (including financial types of receipts and disbursements) and arrive at a comparable analysis.

the investment would result in $72 of additional cash being available for dividends. Assuming the investment is financed entirely with stock, the stockholders would receive a return of .036. This is not a satisfactory return to them since they could have earned .06 in bonds or stock of a comparable corporation. With 100% stock financing the rate of discount should be .06, the stockholders' time value of money (the opportunity cost to the stockholders).[11]

We will now incorporate in one example the two complexities that have been introduced (taxes and availability of cash). Assume the marginal borrowing rate is .06 and the rate on one period government securities subject to tax is .04. There is a .4 marginal tax rate. The following table shows the after-tax cost of obtaining new money and issuing stock at a before-tax cost of .06) or from bondholders (also at a before-tax cost of .06), assuming a capital structure having .3 debt.

	COST OF FUNDS	TAX FACTORS	AFTER-TAX COST	CAPITAL STRUCTURE	WEIGHTED AVERAGE
Stock	.06	1.0	.06	.7	.042
Debt	.06	.6	.036	.3	.0108
					.0528

Now assume that the firm is holding cash that is available for investment. The best certain return available to the investors is .04. Unless the firm can earn a certain return equal to or greater than .04, the funds should be returned to the investors.[12]

Assuming the investment being considered will give certain cash flows, the investment rule would be to invest if the net present value is positive using .0528 (assuming the funds have to be obtained from the market) or .04 (assuming the funds are currently being held by the corporation).

Time Preference and Uncertainty

Assume a normal investment situation where the cash flows of the future are not known with certainty, and that .05 is both an approximate measure of default free interest cost (as measured by government securities) and the

[11] This assumes either the stockholders are not subject to tax on the dividends they receive, or that the firm is using retained earnings.

[12] With debt outstanding the firm could retire the debt. This would be a .036 return after taxes, thus not as desirable a yield as returning the funds to the stockholders. However, it may still be a desirable action since it strengthens the capital structure giving management more flexibility.

minimum debt rate of interest (borrowing rate) for firms of this type. There are no taxes.

Let us inspect a tree diagram (Fig. 4–1) for two sequential lotteries (for each lottery there is a .5 probability of $0 and .5 probability of $1000). The first payoff is one period from the initial investment.

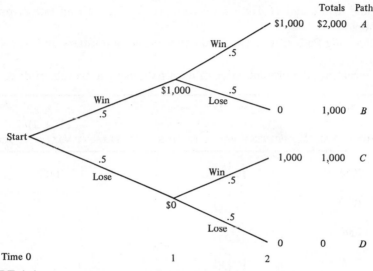

FIGURE 4–1.

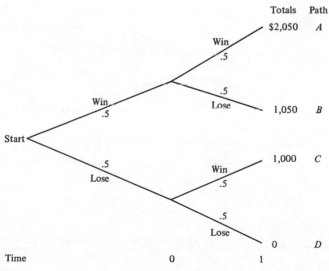

FIGURE 4–2.

Assume that we play the lotteries and nature decides that we follow Path *A*. We can borrow and lend at .05. See Fig. 4–2.

Following Path *A* we have an extra $1000 which we invest to earn $50 and at the end of Time 1 we can liquidate the investment to have $1050 (after winning the second $1000 we will have $2050).

Following Path *B* we again have $1000 available for investment to earn $50 and at the end of Time 1 we have $1050. The second lottery produces nothing.

Following Path *C* we have $1000 after the second lottery and $0 following Path *D*.

We can find the present value of each path using a .05 rate of discount.

| 1 | 2 | 3 |
| | | (1 × 2) |
TERMINAL VALUE	PRESENT VALUE FACTOR	PRESENT VALUE AT TIME 1
2050	$\left(\dfrac{1}{1.05}\right)^2$	1859
1050	$\left(\dfrac{1}{1.05}\right)^2$	952
1000	$\left(\dfrac{1}{1.05}\right)^2$	907
0	$\left(\dfrac{1}{1.05}\right)^2$	0

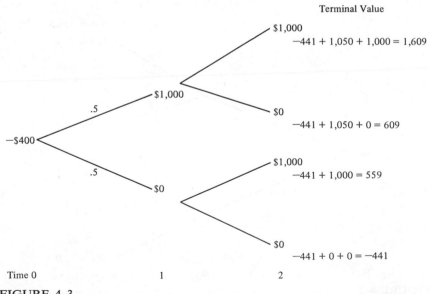

FIGURE 4–3

Note that the default-free rate of discount is being used to accomplish the transformation through time, but the risk attitudes will now have to be incorporated, possibly via a utility function, to find the certainty equivalent of the distribution of present values.

We are not assuming that each path is "certain." We do not know which path nature will dictate that we follow, but we can compute the present value equivalent of each path.

Now consider the tree diagram for the situation where there is a $400 outlay associated with playing the sequential lotteries. There is a cost of .05 for obtaining money to pay for the lottery, and available funds will earn .05 invested in other projects or invested outside the firm. Figure 4-3 shows the situation.

There are four paths, one of which leads to a loss of $441 (including interest on the outlay of $400). The present value of the outcomes of each path are as follows:

PATH	TERMINAL VALUES	PRESENT VALUES (DISCOUNTING FOR TWO PERIODS)
A	$1609	$1459
B	609	552
C	559	507
D	−441	−400

The decision maker can look at the collection of paths and decide subjectively whether this is a game he wants to play. Or, he can convert the outcomes to utility measures and determine whether the expected utility is equal to or greater than the utility of $0 (if so, he accepts).

We could compute a yield by equating the present value of the expected cash flows with the cost of the investment. This procedure automatically combines the time value for money preferences and the investor's attitudes toward risk in one master measure, and the individual effect of each is buried. If there were very little risk, the return demanded by stockholders would be approximately .05 (i.e., the return on default-free debt). As the risk increases, the necessary yield may be expected to increase, but this increase in required yield could be caused by attitudes to risky outcomes and not by an increase in the preference for immediate cash compared to future cash.

Referring to the sequential lottery with an immediate outlay of $400, assume that the investor would be willing to accept the investment, but considers this a marginal investment (i.e., he would not pay more). We can make the following computation of the expected rate of return.

PATH	OUTLAY	TIME 1	TIME 2	PROBABILITY OF EACH PATH
A	−400	1000	1000	.25
B	−400	1000	0	.25
C	−400	0	1000	.25
D	−400	0	0	.25
Expected cash flow	−400	500	500	
Rate of return =	90%			

The rate of return of this marginal investment using the mean values of the cash flows is 90%, but this does not measure the time value of money of the investor. Assume that a second investor would pay a maximum of $375 for the investment. This gives an indicated yield of 100%. It could be that this second investor has the same time value of money as the previous investor, but a different preference for the risks of this particular investment. To say that this investor requires a yield of 100% for all investments is not useful.

If we assume low-risk investment situations the investors will accept a return as low as that of minimum risk bonds. If we allow significant risk to enter the analysis the time preferences of the investors is apt to become confused with their attitudes toward risk.

With funds on hand, the suggested procedure is to accomplish the discounting for the time value of money by using a default-free return. The interest rate on government debt is an acceptable approximation to a default-free return. With funds that have to be obtained by borrowing, the after-tax borrowing cost should be used.

Assume the interest on government debt is found to be .05. In general, investors want a higher return than .05 for their investment commitment. How is this preference effectively implemented into the investment decision criterion? The use of .05 for taking into consideration the time value of money does not mean that this is the return that will be made by the investment.[13] Risk still has to be taken into consideration. The incorporation of attitudes toward risk can be accomplished in several ways. First, the entire investment data sheet can be reviewed, and a decision can be reached based on a feel for the investment and all its possible outcomes. Second, more formal methods of analysis may be applied including a utility analysis (assum-

[13] Since this is the minimum return required for acceptance, some of the investments will return higher than .05, thus the average return earned will be higher than .05 assuming all the expectations are realized.

ing we have determined the relevant utility function). Finally, the way in which the investment being considered will interact with other investments (the portfolio effect) must be considered.

The Value of Information

Discounting using a default-free cost of money (or borrowing rate) accomplishes the adjustment for time value, but several interesting problems remain. One is the question of the value of information.

Where we have to wait a period of time until the results are disclosed we have difficulty planning the consumption of the coming time periods. Thus two investments with the same present value and the same distribution of possible events may be worth different amounts depending on the timing of the disclosure of the outcomes of the investments. In addition to paying for the future cash flows we may be willing to pay some amount for information that will remove the uncertainty as to the actual outcomes; that is, we will pay if the results of the investment are disclosed immediately.

There is not a simple exact solution to the problem which has been posed. Assume we are willing to pay $100 for an investment that covers several time periods, but we will not know the actual cash flows of the time periods until the time periods actually occur. Now there is a second investment with exactly the same description of outcomes, except that we will know immediately what the results of the future time periods will be. For the second investment we would pay $100 plus X where X is the value of the additional information received immediately (X is zero or positive except for ostrich-like individuals who prefer ignorance to the possibility of learning bad news for which they might have to adjust their consumption plans).

A corollary to this is that one investment with a lower present value than a second investment might be more desirable because of the time shape of the cash flows. (We are implicitly assuming that we lack information about the actual outcomes and may not be able to borrow to balance off adverse outcomes.)

EXAMPLE: Assume there is an investment X that has different results for two different events A and B:

EVENT	PERIOD 1	PERIOD 2	PRESENT VALUE (USING .05)
A	− 10,000	100,000*	81,118
B	30,000	30,000	55,782

* An expectation with some probability of a loss.

A second investment *Y* will have the same outcome ($30,000 per period) with either event *A* or *B* (the outcome is known with certainty). Comparing the expected monetary value or the utilities of the investments (using the present value of each possible event) will lead to a conclusion that investment *X* is preferred to *Y*. It has a higher expected present value, and using present values as the basis of the expected utility computation, it would have a higher expected utility. However, consider the possibility of a negative $10,000 in Period 1. This may be a very undesirable event leading to extreme discomfort to the investor unless we can borrow on the prospect of $100,000 one period hence. Assuming that investors will not lend merely on the prospect of the $100,000 the investor may well prefer investment *Y* with its certain cash flows.

We conclude that it may not be sufficient to compute the present value of the outcome associated with each event and convert this present value to a utility measure. We must also consider the feasibility of moving back and forth through time by borrowing and lending. If it is not possible to borrow, then an investor may be willing to pay extra for stability of earnings or alternatively for information about future outcomes. Thus we should not mechanically convert the present value of a stream of cash flows associated with an event to a utility measure. It is also necessary to consider whether the shape of the cash flows is a plus or minus factor (i.e., whether it adds to or subtracts from the value stream).

Conclusions

This chapter has considered the question of the appropriate manner of incorporating time-value considerations in the evaluation of investments. The use of a default-free interest rate and the borrowing rate is suggested. However, it should be remembered that if the investment passes the time-value test it must still satisfy the risk criterion. We have considered the problem of adjusting for time value. In the next three chapters we shall look at the costs of the capital supplied. Each of the costs are expressed in one number (a percentage) and will include in that one number four factors:

1. The time-value consideration.
2. The expectation of the different events occurring.
3. The discounting for risk aversions (the investors require a risk premium for accepting more risk).
4. The value of information (or the cost of not having information).

Business decision making is constantly searching for rules that will lead to clearly defined accept or reject decisions. It is reassuring when we can direct our attention to one number and justify the decision using this number.

One could recommend taking the cost of capital and accepting only those independent investments that have positive net present values. Unfortunately this is an incorrect decision rule. We do not know that one should automatically reject investments that yield less than the estimated cost of capital; in fact stockholders may want firms to accept many such investments where the investments are relatively safe or where they have risk characteristics that reduce the overall risk of the firm. In like manner many investments yielding more than the cost of capital should be rejected because of their risk characteristics.

PROBLEMS

1. The cash flows of an investment are expected to be $10,000 in Period 0 and:

$$10,000 \left(\frac{1.10}{1.05}\right)^i \text{ or } 10,000 \ (1.0476)^i$$

in Period i.

The firm uses a .10 time-discount rate. Assume the investment has a perpetual life.

Required: Compute the present value of the investment.

2. The cash flows of an investment are expected to be $10,000 in Period 0 and $10,000 \ (1.05)^i$ in Period i.

The firm uses a .05 time-discount factor. Because of increasing risk through time the firm multiplies the cash flow of each time period by a risk factor $(1.10)^{-i}$. Assume the investment has a perpetual life.

Required: Compute the present value of the investment.

3. Assume a firm can borrow funds at .06 and can invest in an $1000 investment with a certain return of .055.

The interest rate on government securities of the same life as the investment is .05.

Required: (a) Should the investment be undertaken if the funds have to be borrowed?
   (b) Should the investment be undertaken if the funds are presently held? Assume the alternative is to return the funds to the stockholders.

4. The ABC Company can borrow at .06 and it has a .4 tax rate. Its after-tax borrowing cost has been computed to be .036.

An investment with the following cash flows (without considering financing) is being considered:

0	1	2	
− 1000	80	1080	Before Taxes
	32	32	Taxes
− 1000	48	1048	After Taxes

Required: Should the investment be undertaken based on the information that is given, if the funds are to be borrowed to undertake the investment?

5. (Continue Problem 4–4) Assume the investment could not be financed with 100% debt since it is necessary to have at least .6 stock equity capital.

   Required: Should the investment be undertaken?

6. Assume an investment has uncertain results. In each of two consecutive periods of time (there are two outcomes) there is

   .6 probability of winning $1000
   .4 probability of winning $0

   The cost of the investment is $900. The time value of money is .05 per year. The two outcomes are independent.

   Required: (a) Assume the periods separating the investment and two outcomes are very close together (e.g., one hour apart). Prepare an analysis for determining whether or not the investment should be undertaken.
   (b) Assume the first outcome is determined one year after the investment and the second outcome is determined two years after the first outcome.
   (c) Assume the first outcome is determined five years from now and the second outcome ten years from now.
   (d) Assume the time value of money is .20 and the outcomes occur one and two years from now.

7. The April 15, 1967, issue of *Forbes* in discussing the use of tax-exempt securities by communities to finance (and attract) industry made the following comment (p. 58).

   The company can charge off rent as a business deduction and had the choice of either paying relatively low rent—due to the cheap money—or very high rent over a short period to take advantage of a tax benefit similar to accelerated depreciation.

   Required: Discuss this statement assuming the total amount of rent paid over the period being discussed is fixed.

8. The Jones Oil Company has debt outstanding on which it is paying .06 interest. It can buy municipal securities that are maturing within a year to yield .05 (Assume the securities have been issued by the city of New York.)

The Jones Oil Company can buy and retire its own debt at face value. Ignore other investment possibilities that may be competing for funds within the firm. The corporate income tax rate is .48.

Required: Should the Jones Oil Company buy its bonds or the municipal bonds?

REFERENCES

See also References of Chapters 5 and 6.

Barges, A. *The Effect of Capital Structure on the Cost of Capital*, The Ford Foundation Doctoral Dissertation Series (Prentice-Hall, Englewood Cliffs, N.J., 1963).

Bierman, H., and Smidt, S. *The Capital Budgeting Decision*, 2nd ed. (Macmillan, New York, 1966).

Durand, D. "The Cost of Capital, Corporation Finance, and The Theory of Investment: Comment," *The American Economic Review* (September), 1959.

Gordon, M. J. *"The Investment, Financing and Valuation of the Corporation,"* (Irwin, Homewood, Ill., 1962).

Hirschleifer, J. "On the Theory of Optimal Investment Decisions," *Journal of Political Economy* (August), 1958.

Mao, J. C. T. *Quantitative Analysis of Financial Decisions* (Macmillan, New York, 1969).

Markowitz, H. M. *Portfolio Selection: Efficient Diversification of Investments*, Cowles Foundation Monograph No. 16 (Wiley, New York, 1959).

Lerner, E., and Carleton, W. "The Integration of Capital Budgeting and Stock Valuation," *The American Economic Review* (September), 1964, pp. 683–702.

Modigliani, F. and Miller, M. H. "The Cost of Capital, Corporation Finance, and the Theory of Investment," *The American Economic Review* (June), 1958, pp. 261–297.

———. "The Cost of Capital, Corporation Finance, and the Theory of Investment: Reply," *The American Economic Review* (September), 1959.

———. "Taxes and the Cost of Capital: A Correction," *The American Economic Review* (June), 1963.

Solomon, E. *The Theory of Financial Management* (Columbia University Press, New York, 1963).

Vickers, D. *The Theory of the Firm* (McGraw-Hill, New York, 1968).

CHAPTER 5

The Components of the Cost of Capital

SYMBOLS

P_t price per share of common stock at time t (P_0 is the price at time zero)

D_t dividend at time t

r the discount rate used by stockholders

g growth rate of dividends

V total amount of capital (debt plus stock)

α the ratio of debt to capital

B the amount of debt

S the amount of stock

$i(\alpha)$ the average cost of debt with α debt outstanding

K the average cost of capital; also the marginal return available on investments

$r(\alpha)$ the average cost of stock with α debt

I the total cost of debt

R total cost of stock

m marginal cost of debt

L the amount of leverage. Two measures are

$$L_1 = \frac{B}{V} = \alpha$$

$$L_2 = \frac{B}{S}$$

Y_i the earnings before interest before taxes (EBIT)

t_c the corporate income tax rate

r_{d_i} the return per dollar of common stock investment for d_i amount of debt

b the proportion of the earnings retained

This chapter investigates the nature of two of the components of the cost of capital—the cost of debt and the cost of stock equity. These terms have been used extensively but frequently are not defined in a reasonably exact manner. While on the surface the problem seems trivial, there are many interesting complexities to defining and distinguishing the average cost, the marginal cost, and market yield curves for bonds and stocks. Unfortunately, the literature in this area has occasionally been confused in discussing these cost curves.

The Cost of Common Stock Equity

We can describe the price now of a share of common stock P_0 in terms of the next dividend to be received (assume the dividend is to be received today and we can use D_0 to designate this dividend) plus the price of the common stock one time period in the future P_1 discounted back to the present by dividing by $1 + r$.

$$P_0 = D_0 + \frac{P_1}{1 + r}.$$

This equation states the well-known fact that barring uncertainty the price today is equal to the dividend plus the discounted value of the future price. We can now write P_1 in terms of the next dividend and the price at Time 2.

$$P_1 = D_1 + \frac{P_2}{1 + r}.$$

Substituting $[D_1 + P_2/(1 + r)]$ for P_1 in the first equation we would have

$$P_0 = D_0 + \frac{D_1}{1 + r} + \frac{P_2}{(1 + r)^2}.$$

Continuing this process of substitution we would obtain an infinite series of dividends discounted back to the present.

$$P_0 = D_0 + \frac{D_1}{(1 + r)} + \frac{D_2}{(1 + r)^2} + \cdots$$

$$= \sum_{t=0}^{\infty} D_t (1 + r)^{-t}$$

If we assume that dividends grow at a constant rate g we would obtain

$$P_0 = \sum_{t=0}^{\infty} D_0 (1 + g)^t (1 + r)^{-t}.$$

If g is less than r then this infinite series can be summed to obtain

$$P_0 = \frac{D_0}{r - g}.$$

Solving for r we obtain

$$r = \frac{D_0}{P_0} + g.$$

We can define r to be the cost of common stock equity. While r is defined in terms of future dividends it should be noted that the growth in dividends (g)

that is forecasted cannot be independent of the forecasted future incomes. In practice, a forecast of future dividends is apt, to some extent, to be based on past incomes and past dividends.

Note also that the above derivation of r in terms of (D_0, P_0, g) assumes that transforming the future price per share (or dividends) back to the present can be accomplished by using a constant r each time period and compounding the term 1 plus r for the number of time periods. With an assumption of certainty this procedure would be completely acceptable. Relaxing this assumption, it is not clear that investors do, or should, behave in this manner. Nevertheless, the normal interpretation of the required return of common stockholders is consistent with the interpretation implicit in the above derivation.

The use of dividends in the above relationship is confusing to some. They would prefer to see earnings used. Letting Y be earnings, b the proportion of the earnings retained (the dividends are $1 - b$ times Y), and if reinvested funds earn K, we have:

$$g = bK$$

$$r = \frac{D_0}{P_0} + g = \frac{(1 - b)Y}{P_0} + bK = \frac{Y}{P_0} - b\frac{Y}{P_0} + bK.$$

The term Y/P_0 relates earnings and the price of stock. The second term, $b(Y/P_0)$, adjusts for the retention of earnings and the third term, bK, is an adjustment for growth in earnings resulting from the retention.

The two relationships illustrated above for r by no means exhaust the possibilities. There are a variety of forms that result from further substitutions.

In the remainder of this chapter when we discuss the yield of common stock we will be referring to the rate of interest that equates the future expected dividends to the current market price of the stock.

The Cost of Debt

The definition for cost of debt is analogous to the definition of cost of common stock equity. We defined the cost of equity funds to be the rate of interest that equated all future dividends to the current market price of the stock. We will define the cost of debt to be the rate of interest that equates all future contractual payments of interest and principle to the holders of the debt. Thus if the debt promises to pay $50 a year interest for twenty years and $1000 at maturity, and the bonds are issued at $1000 we would conclude that the cost of the debt was .05. If the bonds were issued at a price of $885 we would assume that the cost of debt was .06, since that is the discount rate that equates the sum of the present value of all future payments to $885.

Again it must be admitted that the definition of cost being used is not exact. If we considered uncertainty explicitly we would recognize that the payment of interest and principal are not certain, that the expected values to be collected are likely to be less than the contractual amounts, and that the investors are not likely to be making their decisions using expected monetary values (there may be an element of risk aversion). Despite these complications we will use the common and simple interpretation of cost of debt that has been described.

Leverage

A firm may be said to be levered when there are securities of ownership outstanding, which have different priorities of payment, and where some of the promised payments for the use of funds are of limited amount (so that if more than the limited amount is earned the holder of a different type of security benefits). Bonds and preferred stock are the securities commonly used to attain leverage for the common stockholders. In this chapter we shall be dealing only with the use of bonds as a form of leverage.

The Measurement of Leverage

We want to measure the amount of leverage since we associate leverage both with the risk and opportunities for profit.[1] Thus the measure of leverage is an important input into our evaluation of the value of common stock and also the value of debt.

One of the more widely used classical definitions of leverage is long-term debt divided by long-term debt plus stockholders' equity. That is, $L_1 = B/V$, where B is the amount of long term debt and V is the sum of long-term debt and common stock. Both B and V are obtained from the accounting reports.

The definitions of B and V can be changed to include short-term debt without doing any harm to the logic of the computation.

A variation of this definition is to define leverage as the ratio of long-term debt (or total debt) to common stock equity (S):

$$L_2 = \frac{B}{S}.$$

[1] For an interesting and reasonably complete discussion of leverage see J. K. S. Ghandi, "On the Measurement of Leverage," *The Journal of Finance* (December, 1966), pp. 715–726.

L_1 and L_2 are tied together by the following relationship:[2]

$$L_1 = \frac{L_2}{1 + L_2}.$$

EXAMPLE: Let

$$S = 1,000,000$$

$$B = 2,000,000$$

$$V = 3,000,000$$

$$L_1 = \frac{B}{V} = \frac{2}{3} = .67 \qquad L_2 = \frac{B}{S} = 2 \qquad L_1 = \frac{L_2}{1 + L_2} = \frac{2}{1 + 2} = \frac{2}{3}$$

The advantage of using L_1 is that its possible values are all between 0 to 1. On the other hand, L_2 can take on values ranging from zero to very large numbers. For many purposes it is somewhat more convenient to deal with the bounded measures of leverage associated with L_1 than the unbounded measures obtained when using L_2.

Instead of using the accounting information as presented it would be possible to adjust the accounting data based on information that would result in more meaningful measures of B, S, and V. A second alternative is to abandon the accounting-based measures completely and to use market values. For example, assume that the market value of the bonds is $1,500,000, and the market value of the stock is $8,500,000. We now have new measures of L_1 and L_2:

$$L_1 = \frac{B}{V} = \frac{1.5}{10} = .15 \qquad L_2 = \frac{B}{S} = \frac{1.5}{8.5} = .18$$

The difference between book values and market values may reflect faulty accounting measures or may reflect the fact that the market has expectations that cannot be recorded by the accountant. In any event, the use of market values will often give greatly different measures of leverage than the use of book values.

The measures to this point have focused on the static measures of book value and market value. Now we will switch to considering the relevance of flow measures. Continuing the example, assume the interest rate on the bonds

---

[2] Since $L_1 = B/V$, we can obtain $B = VL_1$.
Since $L_2 = B/S$, we can obtain $B = SL_2$.
Equating the two B's:

$$VL_1 = SL_2,$$

$$L_1 = \frac{S}{V}L_2 = \frac{V - B}{V}L_2 = L_2 - \frac{B}{V}L_2 = L_2 - L_1L_2,$$

$$L_1 = \frac{L_2}{1 + L_2}.$$

is .05 and the annual interest payment is $100,000. The income of the stockholders and the dividend on the common stock is $150,000 (the income before interest is $250,000). Assume a zero corporate income tax rate. The depreciation expense is $50,000.

The total income flow into the firm is $250,000. Of this amount two-fifths is designated for the bondholders and three-fifths for the stockholders. Based on the assignment of the income one might well say that the leverage is .4.

Rather than focusing on income let us consider the assignment of the $300,000 cash flow of the firm. We might want to consider not only the interest payments but also the repayment of principal of the debt where the debt has a life of twenty years. Assuming a .05 interest rate, dividing the $2,000,000 of debt by the annuity factor for twenty years we obtain the annual equivalent debt payment of $156,000:[3]

$$\frac{2,000,000}{12.82115} = 156,000$$

To Bondholders	$156,000	.52
$300,000		
To Stockholders	$144,000	.48

However we could measure the debt service only for the first year assuming that equal amounts of principal are retired each year. This would mean that in year one $100,000 principal would be repaid as well as $100,000 interest (the interest payments in the future will be less). The measure for year one would now be

$$\frac{200,000}{300,000} = .67.$$

Since this measure is extremely sensitive to the rate of debt repayment, it is a better measure of short run liquidity than it is of leverage.

Assume that the book values and market values coincided, and S equalled $1,000,000 and B equalled $2,000,000. Assume also that the interest payment is $100,000, the income before interest is $150,000, and the cash flow is $450,000 with $200,000 of the debt being retired in the first period:

$$L_1 = \frac{B}{V} = \frac{2}{3}.$$

[3] If the coupon rate (.05) were not equal to the current interest rate (.05) the market value of the debt would likely differ from the book value. In this situation one should use the market value of the debt in the numerator for computing the annual equivalent outlay for debt.

The ratio of interest to income before interest deductions is

$$\frac{100,000}{150,000} = \frac{2}{3}.$$

The cash flow required to service the debt divided by the total cash flow would be

$$\frac{200,000 + 100,000}{450,000} = \frac{2}{3}.$$

With this highly restrictive set of assumptions, each of the measures is identical. Note that both the stock and bonds earned .05 and that the non-fund-utilizing expenses were $300,000 or 3/2 of the funds used for bond retirement.

In a general situation the measures will differ. It would be possible for the cash flow after interest and principal, or the income after interest, to be zero. Using the flow measures, this would result in measures of 100% leverage. In a situation where the projection for these two measures of flows was to be zero, the value of the stock equity would be zero (despite a possible positive book value) and the leverage would be correctly measured.

Each of the above measures has some desirable features. The use of the book value is highly objective and more importantly is the measure most likely to be used by practical men. Thus if the ratio of book debt to book stock equity is .8, the average investor is likely to think of the situation as being highly levered even if the market value of the stock is a high multiple of the book value.

The use of the market value is desirable since it tends to soften the effect of the conservative accounting practices and also reflects the expectations of the market as to the future cash flows of the company. An important drawback is that this measure is not extensively used. Thus decisions based on this ratio could lead to reactions by the markets for its securities, which would not be beneficial to the stockholders.

The flow measures (either income or cash flow) are both extremely useful though they are not widely used as measures of leverage. These flows are used however in computing the coverage of interest payments (the reciprocal of the measures computed in this section). The use of the income measure has the important advantage of not requiring an assumption as to the appropriate rate of interest to be used in computing the present value of debt or stock (using values the interest rate is used either implicitly or explicitly). Measures of market value of debt or stock equity both implicitly assume rates of interest as well as adjustments for risk. The use of the income measure of leverage (the ratio of interest to income before interest) avoids making these assumptions.

It is extremely unlikely that all the measures would be identical for a real situation. For many firms all the measures will be reasonably close, but this closeness should not be assumed. It is desirable that the several leverage measures be computed and be compared. An inspection of the set of ratios will leave the user with a "feel" for the amount of leverage that is being used.

Measuring the Effects of Leverage

What happens to the income of the stockholders when debt is issued? We will make the analysis in terms of the return per dollar of common stock investment. Assume that the size of the firm is kept constant and that debt is substituted for stock when it is issued.

For zero debt and a tax rate of t_c we would have the following return per dollar of common stock investment

$$r_0 = \frac{(1 - t_c)}{V} Y_i.$$

For B_i amount of debt we have

$$r_{d_i} = \frac{(Y_i - iB_i)(1 - t_c)}{V - B_i}.$$

Rewriting this equation so that the linear nature of the relationship becomes apparent:

$$r_{d_i} = -\frac{(1 - t_c)iB_i}{V - B_i} + \frac{(1 - t_c)}{V - B_i} Y_i.$$

Let

$$-\frac{(1 - t_c)iB_i}{V - B_i} = a, \text{ the vertical axis, intercept}$$

$$\frac{(1 - t_c)}{V - B_i} = b, \text{ the slope.}$$

We then have

$$r_{d_i} = a + bY_i.$$

EXAMPLE

$$V = 1,000,000$$

$$B_i = 900,000 \qquad S = V - B_i = 100,000$$

$$i = .06,$$

$$t_c = .4 \qquad (1 - t_c) = .6,$$

$$a = -\frac{(1 - t_c)iB_i}{V - B_i} = -\frac{.6 \times .06 \times 900,000}{100,000} = -.324,$$

$$b = \frac{(1 - t_c)}{V - B_i} = \frac{.6}{100,000}.$$

We can now compute the return per dollar of common stock investment for different levels of Y (i.e., EBIT).

Y_i (EBIT)	bY_i	a	$r_{d_i} = a + bY_i$
− 100,000	− .6	−.324	− .924
0	0	−.324	− .324
100,000	.6	−.324	.276
200,000	1.2	−.324	.876
800,000	4.8	−.324	4.476

Instead of .90 debt, assume we have .50 debt:

$$a = -\frac{.6 \times .06 \times 500,000}{500,000} = -.0036 \qquad b = \frac{.6}{500,000}$$

Y_i (EBIT)	bY_i	a	$r_{d_i} = a + bY_i$
− 100,000	− .12	−.0036	−.1236
0	0	−.0036	−.0036
100,000	.12	−.0036	.1164
200,000	.24	−.0036	.2364
800,000	.96	−.0036	.9564

The calculation of r_{d_i} can also be done in a conventional manner. For example, for $B = \$900,000$, we would have

Y_i (EBIT)	100,000	0	100,000	200,000	800,000
Interest	54,000	54,000	54,000	54,000	54,000
Taxable income	− 154,000	− 54,000	46,000	146,000	746,000
Tax (or tax saving)	− 61,600	− 21,600	18,400	58,400	298,400
Income	− 92,400	− 32,400	27,600	87,600	447,600
Return per $1 of common stock	− .924	− .324	.276	.876	4.476

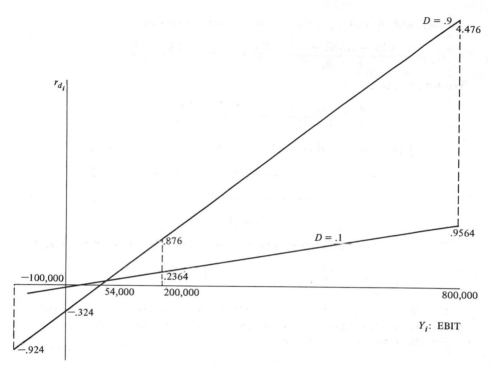

FIGURE 5–1

Figure 5–1 shows the advantage of debt if operations are highly profitable (EBIT is large) and the disadvantage of debt if operations are not profitable (EBIT is negative or close to negative). Figure 5–1 and the calculations on which it is based assume that tax deductions for interest can always be used to reduce taxes. If taxes are zero because of a long period of loss operations, then this assumption is not valid. We could assume that the equation for r_d holds only for $Y_i \geq iB$ and that for values of $Y_i < iB$ we should use

$$r_{d_i} = \frac{Y_i - iB_i}{V - B_i}.$$

The Indifference Point

In Fig. 5–1 the lines for D equal to $900,000 and D equal to $100,000 intersect at Y_i equal to $60,000. We will show that for any amount of debt the line representing the return will intersect all other debt lines at the same point. This point will be

$$Y_i = iV,$$
$$r_b = i(1 - t_c)$$

Proof: Let B_1 and B_2 be two different amounts of debt.

$$r_{d_1} = -\frac{(Y_i - iB_1)(1 - t_c)}{V - B_1} \quad \text{and} \quad r_{d_2} = \frac{(Y_i - iB_2)(1 - t_c)}{V - B_2}.$$

We want r_{d_1} to equal r_{d_2}.

$$\frac{(Y_i - iB_1)(1 - t_c)}{V - B_1} = \frac{(Y_i - iB_2)(1 - t_c)}{V - B_2},$$

$$Y_i(V - B_2) - iB_1(V - B_2) = Y_i(V - B_1) - iB_2(V - B_1),$$

$$Y_i(V - B_2 - V + B_1) = i[B_1(V - B_2) - B_2(V - B_1)],$$

$$Y_i(B_1 - B_2) = iV(B_1 - B_2),$$

$$Y_i = iV.$$

To solve for the indifference value of r (we know $Y = iV$ when $r_{d_1} = r_{d_2}$):

$$r_b = \frac{(Y - iB)(1 - t_c)}{V - B} = \frac{(iV - iB)(1 - t_c)}{V - B} = i(1 - t_c).$$

For any amount of debt the line representing the return per dollar of common stock investment will pass through the point $[iV, i(1 - t_c)]$.

For the example, this point is

$$Y_i = \$60{,}000,$$

$$r = .036.$$

The debt lines will all have different slopes and intercepts. *If we know* that the earnings before interest and before taxes are to be \$60,000, and if there were other investment opportunities of identical characteristics for the stockholders, we would be indifferent to the amount of debt.

EXAMPLE:

	DEBT: 0	200,000	900,000
Y_i: EBIT	60,000	60,000	60,000
Interest	0	12,000	54,000
Taxable income	60,000	48,000	6,000
Tax	24,000	19,200	2,400
Income	36,000	28,800	3,600
Return per dollar of common stock	.036	.036	.036

If the coming period's EBIT was known to be $60,000 and if other possible investments available to stockholders are not as good as the investment in this firm, then the optimum leverage would be 0 since the income is highest with zero leverage (i.e., there is a larger common stock investment earning a "good" return). If we return to the assumption that there are identical investments available the stockholder would be indifferent among the different capital structures.

We can also compute the value of Y_i (EBIT) for which r is equal to zero:

$$r_d = \frac{(Y_i - iB)(1 - t_c)}{V - B}.$$

Let r_d equal zero:

$$\frac{(Y_i - iB)(1 - t_c)}{V - B} = 0,$$

$$Y_i - iB = 0,$$

$$Y_i = iB.$$

Thus the intercept on the horizontal axis when $B = \$900,000$ is $54,000.

Let us assume that EBIT has a mean of $200,000, a standard deviation of $100,000, and is normally distributed. With zero debt there is .023 probability of loss.[4]

If we add $900,000 debt that has $54,000 annual interest payments, the probability of a loss is .072.[5] This is three times as large as the probability of a loss with zero debt. Remember these probabilities are for the operating results of one year.

A combination of the normal income-activity break-even chart (operating income) and the financial leverage chart are of interest. This combination of the two types of leverage enables us to evaluate how the riskiness of the operating characteristics of the firm combined with the financial leverage will affect the returns to stockholders (see Fig. 5–2).

When the activity level is $0Q$ the income (EBIT) will be $0B$. With debt equal to .8 of the total capital, $0B$ of income will lead to a return per dollar of common stock investment of $0C$. We could continue the analysis on to the third quadrant and convert the return per dollar of investment into earnings per share, and into the fourth quadrant for conversion into utility (see Fig. 5–3).

In this section we considered the effect of leverage on the return to the common stock investors if there are different possible values of earnings

[4] $d = \dfrac{200,000}{100,000} = 2: \qquad F(2) = .023.$

[5] $d = \dfrac{146,000}{100,000} = 1.46: \qquad F(1.46) = .072.$

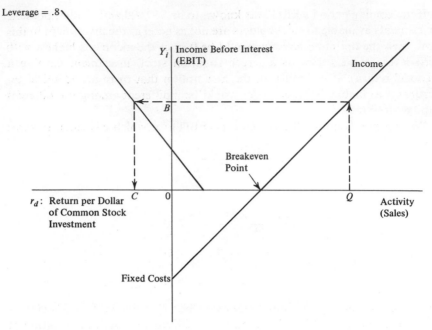

FIGURE 5–2

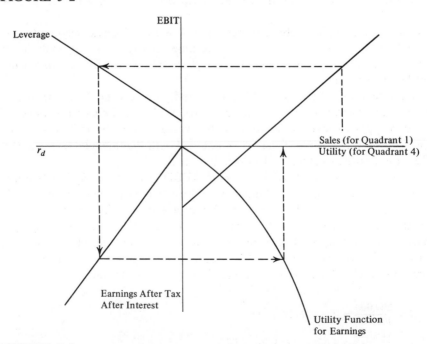

FIGURE 5–3

before interest before taxes. We did not consider the effect of more debt on the cost of common stock or on the cost of debt (or equivalently on the value of the firm). We shall now consider systematically the effect of adding debt on the risk to the present debt-holders and the common stockholders.

Leverage and the Cost of Debt

Assume that the amount of capital V is constant and is equal to the amount of debt B plus the amount of stock S. It is reasonable to expect that if we increase α, the ratio of debt (B) to total capital (V), the required return or the expected cost of debt increases. We will define $i(\alpha)$ to be the expected average cost of debt.

Note that the average market yield as measured using contractual interest payments, maturity amount, and market price is likely to be higher than the value of $i(\alpha)$. The average market yield is a modal value (the most likely value), but it is not the mathematic expectation of the return. The contractual return might not be realized by the investors, thus the expected return for any security will differ from the contractual return of that security if there is any uncertainty. If there is some probability of not receiving the interest or being paid the principal the expected yield from the point of view of the investor is likely to be less than the market yield. The modifier "average" is used to describe the market yield because the required returns of each of the several issues of debt securities are being weighted by the size of the issues to obtain a weighted average return.

The Common Stock Yield Curve

The essential question being considered in this section is the shape of the common stock yield curve. That is, what happens to the expected (required) yield curve for common stock as we increase the ratio of debt to common stock of a firm. Figure 5–4 shows three basic alternatives.[6]

The common stock yield curve must increase monotonically to the right. It cannot logically have a negative slope, but it has been incorrectly argued that beyond some large amount of leverage the required yield may fall.

The risk of leverage can be reduced by a person buying both stocks and bonds. While this strategy reduces the financial risk (i.e., the risk to an investor arising from the type of securities outstanding), it does not reduce the risk arising from the basic economic activity of the firm. An investor holding

[6] F. Modigliani and M. Miller, "The Cost of Capital, Corporation Finance, and the Theory of Investment," *The American Economic Review* (June, 1958), p. 275.

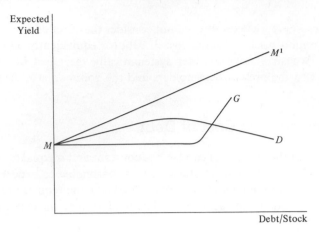

FIGURE 5-4

stock yielding .09 in a corporation with .5 debt can improve his position by shifting to a stock yielding .10 in an otherwise comparable corporation with .2 debt. He has a higher yield and less risk.[7] Unless one takes the position that the market prices of securities are set by individuals willing to give up expected yield in order to have more risk, one must reject curve MD, and label it as not being feasible in a world of rational decision makers.

We can use a quote from Modigliani and Miller to reinforce our position:[8]

Economic theory and market experience both suggest that the yields demanded by lenders tend to increase with the debt-equity rates of the borrowing firm (or individual).

We extend this observation to the situation where the "lending" is done by stockholders and where the stock certificates are received instead of debt securities.

The Cost of Capital

So far we have claimed that both the expected cost of debt and the expected cost of equity should increase with leverage. There remains a more general problem of how the expected cost of common stock is related to the expected cost of debt and the amount of debt outstanding, and how these changes affect the average cost of capital.

Modigliani and Miller have argued that if the cost of debt increases with leverage, the required yield of common stock will increase as the debt/capital

[7] If the individual wants more debt and the same risk he can make some homemade leverage, increasing his effective debt-stock ratio to .5 and increasing his yield even higher than .10.

[8] Modigliani and Miller, *op. cit.*, p. 273.

ratio increases, but at a decreasing rather than a constant rate.[9] They conclude that K (the average cost of capital) is constant as the amount of debt changes (there is a highly restrictive set of assumptions including zero taxes).

In a 1963 article, Ezra Solomon correctly objected to the M–M proposition that K is a constant.[10] However, he defined a constant interest rate as a necessary condition for K to be constant. The cost of stock (r) can increase with leverage even though the cost of debt (i) increases. In fact r may increase in many different ways and we can still satisfy the basic relationship resulting in a constant K.

We will define the cost of stock in terms of the expected yield required by the stockholders for different amounts of debt (since the size of the firm is being held constant α, the proportion of debt is changing). As we argued earlier, it is reasonable to expect that as α increases the expected cost of stock (the required return) will also increase.

The function $r(\alpha)$ for the cost of stock equity should be determined empirically, but we shall assume that K is constant and equal to a weighted average of the cost of stock and debt:

$$K = \alpha i(\alpha) + (1 - \alpha)r(\alpha).$$

Solving for the cost of stock:

$$r(\alpha) = \frac{K - \alpha i(\alpha)}{1 - \alpha}.$$

Let K, the average cost of capital, be .10.

We could assume many functional relationships for the average cost of debt. Let us assume for simplicity that i increases linearly and that

$$i(\alpha) = .03 + .07\alpha$$

We assume with $\alpha = 1$ that the bondholders would expect the same return that stockholders would want with $\alpha = 0$. This is not an unreasonable assumption since with $\alpha = 1$ the bondholders would essentially be equivalent to stockholders (all the capital is coming from debt).[11]

Substituting for $i(\alpha)$ and K we obtain the following relationship for $r(\alpha)$:

$$r(\alpha) = \frac{.10 - \alpha(.03 + .07\alpha)}{1 - \alpha}.$$

The values of r for different values of α are given in Table 5–1.

[9] Ibid., p. 274.
[10] Ezra Solomon, "Leverage and the Cost of Capital," The Journal of Finance (May, 1963), p. 276.
[11] It may be somewhat difficult to imagine a company with no stock, thus we can imagine the amount of debt approaching V rather than being equal to V.

TABLE 5-1   Cost of Stock Equity with Different Capital Structures

α	r
0	.100
.2	.114
.4	.128
.5	.135
.6	.142
.8	.156
Near 1.0	Large

EXAMPLE OF COMPUTATIONS: Let

$$r = .03 + .07\alpha$$

$$K = .10$$

We have found that

$$r = \frac{.10 - \alpha(.03 + .07\alpha)}{1 - \alpha}.$$

If $\alpha = .2$ then $i = .044$, and

$$r = \frac{.10 - .2(.03 + .014)}{.8} = \frac{.10 - .0088}{.8} = \frac{.0912}{.8} = .114.$$

The cost of capital is

$$K = \alpha i(\alpha) + (1 - \alpha)r(\alpha)$$

$$= .2 \times .044 + .8 \times .114$$

$$= .0088 + .0912 = .10.$$

If $\alpha = .5$, then $i = .065$ and $r = .135$. The cost of capital is again .10.

$$K = .5 \times .065 + .5 \times .135 = .10.$$

Note that as i (the cost of debt) increases, r (the cost of stock) also increases, and K is constant.

The Marginal Costs of Debt and Stock

The average rate of interest will rise as leverage is increased. But is it likely that the average cost of debt will be above the cost of capital for positions of extreme leverage?[12] The average cost of debt could only be above the cost

---

[12] See Solomon, *loc. cit.*, p. 276 for a somewhat different argument than that presented here.

of capital if the required (desired) yield on common stock were below both the cost of capital and the cost of debt. This is not consistent with logic or actual experience in the real world. However the observed interest rate on debt could be above the desired return on common stock because the observed interest rate is not the real expected return on debt because of the possibility of default or price level changes.

In addition to the average cost curves we need marginal cost curves to help analyse the cost of substituting more debt for stock. We will again assume that

$$i = .03 + .07\alpha$$

$$= .03 + .07\frac{B}{V}.$$

If we multiply the average cost by the amount of debt B, we have the total cost of debt, I:

$$I = .03B + .07\frac{B^2}{V}.$$

The marginal cost of debt is[13]

$$.03 + .14\frac{B}{V}.$$

Since $I = iB$ the marginal cost of debt may also be defined as

$$i + B\frac{di}{dB}.$$

For the example

$$\frac{di}{dB} = \frac{.07}{V}$$

the marginal cost is again

$$.03 + .14\frac{B}{V}.$$

When $B/V = 1$, the marginal cost is .17 and the average cost is .10.[14] The marginal cost of the stock is[15]

$$-.03 - .14\frac{B}{V}.$$

[13] If $i(\alpha)$ is the average cost, then $Bi(\alpha)$ is the total cost of debt and the marginal cost is $dI/dB = .03 + .14B/V$. We are assuming that the size of the firm is constant, thus debt is being substituted for stock.

[14] The last issue of debt must be subordinate to previous issues in order for the above conclusions to hold.

[15]
$$r = \frac{.10 - B/V(.03 + .07B/V)}{1 - B/V} = \frac{.10V - .03B - .07B^2/V}{V - B}.$$

Multiplying by the amount of stock $(V - B)$ we obtain the total cost R: $R = .10V - .03B - .07B^2/V$.

The marginal cost is $dR/dB = -.03 - .14B/V$.

The marginal cost of adding debt is $.03 + .14B/V$, the marginal cost of decreasing the amount of stock outstanding is $-.03 - .14B/V$, and the sum is zero. Since we are assuming that the average cost of capital is constant, the net change to the total cost of obtaining capital should be zero.

The negative marginal cost of stock does not mean that stock will cost less as we increase debt, but that there will be less stock outstanding. Table 5–1 shows that the average cost of stock is increasing as α increases.

Instead of making the analysis in terms of changing the amount of debt, we can increase the amount of stock. We obtain

$$.03S + .14 \frac{V - S}{V}$$

as the marginal cost of issuing more stock, and

$$-.03S - .14 \frac{V - S}{S}$$

as the marginal cost of substituting the stock for debt.[16]

The marginal cost of issuing more stock is positive despite the fact that the average cost will decrease as more stock is issued to replace debt. The marginal cost of retiring the debt is negative reflecting less total debt outstanding as well as lower average interest costs with the stronger capital structure.

Conclusions

Several journal articles have described the relationships between cost of debt, stock, and the average cost of capital. Unfortunately, some confusion has entered the analysis. We have attempted to show that:

1. We should expect the required expected return on common stock to increase as debt is substituted for stock.[17]

[16] The total cost of the stock is: $R = .10V - .03B - .07B^2/V$.
Substituting $(V - S)$ for B:
$$R = .10V - .03(V - S) - .07 \frac{(V - S)^2}{V}.$$
Taking the first derivative
$$\frac{dR}{dS} = -.03(-1) - .14 \left(\frac{V - S}{V} \right) (-1)$$
$$= .03 + .14 \frac{V - S}{V}.$$
The total cost of the debt is $I = .03B + .07B^2/V$.
Substituting $(V - S)$ for D:
$$I = .03(V - S) + .07 \frac{(V - S)^2}{S}$$
Taking the first derivative:
$$\frac{dI}{dS} = -.03 - .14 \frac{V - S}{S}.$$

[17] Douglas Vickers, in "Elasticity of Capital Supply, Monopsonistic Discrimination, and Optimum Capital Structure," *The Journal of Finance* (March, 1967), pp. 1–9, makes

2. We should expect the required expected return on debt to increase as debt is substituted for stock.
3. Neither of the above conditions is inconsistent with a constant cost of capital as debt is substituted for stock.

Appendix

Necessary Conditions for a Decline in the Average Cost of Stock Equity with an Increase in the Debt Capital Ratio

Let α equal B/V where B is the total debt and V the total capital of the firm. We will hold V constant as we vary the amount of debt.

In addition, i is the average cost of debt, r is the average cost of stock, S is the amount of stock and $S = V - B$, and K is the average cost of capital and is constant. K is equal to:

$$K = \alpha i + (1 - \alpha)r$$
$$= \frac{B}{V} i + \left(1 - \frac{B}{V}\right)r.$$

Multiplying both sides by V, $VK = Bi + (V - B)r$. Taking the derivative of the total cost VK with respect to B:

$$\frac{d(VK)}{dB} = i + B\frac{di}{dB} + V\frac{dr}{dB} - r - B\frac{dr}{dB}.$$

We know that

$$\frac{d(VK)}{dB} = 0$$

since V and K are both constant. Also

$$\frac{dr}{dB} = 0$$

since we want to find the point where r turns from being upward sloping to downward sloping.

Therefore:

$$i + B\frac{di}{dB} - r = 0$$

$$r = i + B\frac{di}{dB}$$

---

the point that the cost of equity will decrease when the marginal cost of borrowing has risen to equal that rate. He states that such an occurrence is empirically improbable. The same point is made by A. A. Robichek and S. C. Myers, *Optimal Financing Decisions*, Prentice-Hall, Englewood Cliffs, 1965, Chapter 3. Also see the appendix to this chapter.

Let $I = iB$ where I is the total interest cost. $dI/dB = i + B(di/dB) = m$ where m is the marginal cost of the debt. Combining the two equations for r and m:

$$r = i + B\frac{di}{dB} = m.$$

In order for the average cost of stock to be at a maximum it is necessary for the marginal cost of debt to be equal to the average cost of stock. Also, the marginal cost of additional stock has to be less than the average cost to the right of point t since the average cost is decreasing. This implies that debt-holders could obtain a higher expected marginal return than stockholders in a situation, where by definition of the term debt and barring price level changes, the debtholders had less risk than the stockholders. We would argue that the average cost of stock equity is monotonically increasing as the debt/capital ratio increases (see Fig. 5–5).

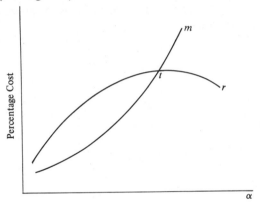

FIGURE 5–5

Relationship of Marginal Cost of Debt and Average Cost of Stock

Again assuming that V and K are constant we have

$$\frac{d(VK)}{d(B)} = i + B\frac{di}{dB} + V\frac{dr}{dB} - r - B\frac{dr}{dB}.$$

$$\frac{d(VK)}{dB} = 0$$

We know that since V and K are both constant. Also

$$i + B\frac{di}{dB} = m \text{ the marginal cost of debt,}$$

and by substitution we obtain

$$m + V\frac{dr}{dB} - r - B\frac{dr}{dB} = 0.$$

Solving for m,

$$m = r + (B - V)\frac{dr}{dB}.$$

If we accept the previous proof that r does not decline with an increase in B, dr/dB will be positive and since V is greater than B, the term $(B - V)\,dr/dB$ will be negative. Therefore $m < r$, that is, the marginal cost of debt will be less than the average cost of stock.

PROBLEMS

1. Assume a company is currently paying dividends of $1 per share. The stockholders expect a return of .12 (they apply this discount factor to future cash flows).

   (a) If an investor expects the dividends to grow at a rate of .08 per year per share, how much would the investor pay for a share of the stock?
   (b) If an investor was willing to pay $100 for a share of the stock, what dividend growth rate would this imply?

2. Mr. Smith has a time value of money of .06. He has just bought for $101 a stock that is paying a $1 per share dividend. At what price does Mr. Smith expect the stock to be selling one period from now?

3. A company is currently paying a dividend of $1 and the stock is selling for $100. Investors think the dividend growth will be at a rate of .06 per year. What is the implied time value of money of the investors?

4. Assume a twenty year bond with a coupon rate of .05 is sold at a price of $855.30. What is the cost of the debt (the yield of a $1,000 bond)?

5. Assume that the average cost of capital is a constant (.15) as the amount of debt is increased, and that the interest rate i is a function of the per cent of debt α.

$$i(\alpha) = .05 + .10\alpha.$$

Assume that $r(\alpha)$ is the cost of common stock equity.

   Required: (a) Give the cost of debt and common stock equity for the four values of α.

$$\alpha = 0, .25, .75, 1.0$$

   (b) Compute the weighted average cost of capital.

6. Continue Problem 5. What is the marginal cost of debt when α is equal to .25?

7. The ABC Company has the following balance sheet as of December 31, 1968.

Current Assets	20,000	Current liabilities	10,000
Long-lived assets	80,000	Long term liabilities	40,000
		Stockholders' equity	50,000
	100,000		100,000

The projected income statement for the year 1969 is:

Revenues	15,000
Expenses	10,000
Income before interest	5,000
Interest expense	2,000
Income after interest	3,000

The expenses included $4000 of depreciation.

At December 31, 1968 the common stock was selling for $90 per share (there were 1000 shares outstanding). The bonds with a twenty-year maturity were selling for $885 per bond (there were forty bonds outstanding). The time value of money for the firm is .06.

Required: Compute four meaningful measures of leverage (in your judgment). Attempt to maximize the information presented.

REFERENCES

See also References of Chapters 4 and 6.

Ghandi, J. K. S. "On the Measurement of Leverage," *The Journal of Finance* (December), 1966.

Miller, M. H., and Modigliani, F. "Some Estimates of the Cost of Capital to the Electric Utility Industry, 1954–57," *The American Economic Review* (June), 1966.

Robichek, A. A., and Myers, S. C., *Optimal Financing Decisions* (Prentice-Hall, Englewood Cliffs, N.J., 1965).

Schwartz, Eli. "Theory of the Capital Structure of the Firm," *The Journal of Finance* (March), 1959.

Solomon, E. "Leverage and the Cost of Capital," *The Journal of Finance* (May), 1963.

————. *The Theory of Financial Management* (Columbia University Press, New York, 1963).

Vickers, D. "Elasticity of Capital Supply, Monopsonistic Discrimination, and Optimum Capital Structure," *The Journal of Finance* (March), 1967.

CHAPTER 6

Risk and the Addition of Debt to the Capital Structure[1]

SYMBOLS

V debt plus stock

S the value of the outstanding stock

X the earnings of the firm with mean $E(X)$ and var (X)

Y the earnings of the stockholders with mean $E(Y)$ and var (Y)

Y_n the earnings after the addition of capital with mean $E(Y_n)$ and var (Y_n)

B the amount of debt

α ratio of debt to debt plus stock

$i(\alpha)$ the average cost of debt with α debt

V_0 the initial size of firm (debt plus stock)

r_d the return (earnings) per dollar of common stock investment with mean $E(r_d)$ and var (r_d)

This chapter investigates how the addition of debt to the capital structure of a corporation affects the risk of the stockholders. In the first instance we will hold the size of the firm constant and substitute debt for common stock.[2] In the second situation we will allow the size of the firm to change and will accomplish the increase in size by issuing debt.

For both situations we will first observe the effect of debt on the earnings per dollar of common stock investment. The analysis could also be made using the number of shares of common stock. Since the number of shares of common stock may be changed quite arbitrarily (as, e.g., by stock dividends), we want to make the measure invariant to the number of shares outstanding. We will do this by using the value of the common stock and the value of the debt. We are then computing the variance of the return on common stock investment when we compute the variance of the earnings per dollar of common stock investment.

---

[1] This chapter is based on an article by the author, which appeared in the December, 1968, issue of *The Journal of Financial and Quantitative Analysis*.

[2] See W. Beranek, *Analysis for Financial Decisions*, Homewood, Irwin, 1963, pp. 243–248, for a similar approach. For a different approach see G. Donaldson, *Corporate Debt Capacity*, Boston: Harvard Graduate School of Business, 1961.

After considering how debt affects earnings per dollar of stockholders' investment, we will investigate the effect of debt on the total earnings of the stockholders, and on the probability of a deficit.

Substitution of Debt for Stock

First assume that the cost (interest) of the debt is exactly equal to the current expected earnings per dollar of investment of the common stock. Let V be the total of debt plus stock, S be the value of the common stock outstanding, and X be the earnings of the firm in any future time period. X is a random variable with mean $E(X)$ and variance var (X). The interest cost per dollar of debt is equal to the average return per dollar of investment $E(X)/V$. The future earnings are unknown, but the interest rate is being set equal to the expectation of the earnings divided by the dollars of total investment. With this assumption the expected earnings per dollar of common stock will not be affected by the issuance of the debt (tax considerations are being ignored)[3]

EXAMPLE: Assume that $E(X) = \$80,000$ for a firm of size $\$1,000,000$. The firm can issue $\$400,000$ of debt (to replace $\$400,000$ of stock) at a cost of $\$32,000$ interest per year.

The earnings per dollar of common stock before the issuance of debt is .08 and after the issuance of debt .08.

$$E(r_d) = \frac{E(X) - Bi(\alpha)}{V - B} = \frac{80,000 - 32,000}{600,000} = .08.$$

While the expected earnings are not affected by the issuance of the debt, the actual earnings per dollar of common stock may be affected (they will be affected unless the actual earnings are equal to the mean earnings). For example, assume that the expected earnings per $\$100$ of investment are $\$8$, and that $\$8$ is being paid on $\$100$ of debt that has been substituted for common stock. If the actual earnings are $\$6$ per $\$100$ of investment the stockholders are going to be hurt by the fixed obligation to pay the bondholders $\$8$. On the other hand, if the actual earnings are $\$10$ per $\$100$ of investment the stockholders are going to benefit by the fact that the bondholders will receive a fixed $\$8$ return.

We want to determine how the substitution of debt for common stock increases the variance of the return per dollar of investment of the common stockholders. Let var (r_d) be the variance of stockholder earnings per dollar of common stock investment. With no debt var (r_d) is equal to var (X/S) or $1/S^2$ var (X). Since S is equal to V the total investment, we could write

[3] See Appendix 1 to this chapter for a proof.

var $(r_d) = 1/V^2$ var (X). With B dollars of debt paying $BE(X)/V$ interest, the variance of earnings per dollar of common stock investment is[4]

$$\text{var } (r_d) = \frac{1}{(V - B)^2} \text{ var } (X) = \frac{1}{S^2} \text{ var } (X).$$

While the expectation of the before-interest earnings of the firm is not changed by the issuance of debt, the variance of the earnings per dollar of common stock investment is greatly affected.[5] However, the variance of the earnings per dollar of common stock investment is invariant to the interest rate if we assume that the incurrance of interest cost is a certainty even though the actual interest payment may be uncertain.

EXAMPLE: Assume that var (X) is equal to \$100,000,000 and that common stockholders have invested \$10,000 and there is zero debt. We then have

$$\text{var } (r_d) = \text{var } \left(\frac{X}{S}\right) = \frac{1}{S^2} \text{ var } (X) = \frac{10^8}{10^4 \times 10^4} = 1.$$

If we issue \$6000 of bonds and retire \$6000 of stock, we now have

$$\text{var } (r_d) = \frac{1}{(4000)^2} \times 100,000,000$$

$$= \frac{10^8}{(4 \times 10^3)(4 \times 10^3)} = \frac{10^2}{16} = 6.25.$$

If we issue \$9000 of bonds and retire \$9000 of stock we now have

$$\text{var } (r_d) = \frac{100,000,000}{1000 \times 1000} = \frac{10^8}{10^3 \times 10^3} = 100.$$

The variance of the earnings per dollar of common stock investment is very sensitive to the substitution of debt for common stock, especially if the firm has a relatively large amount of debt, say over .5 debt.

The ratio of the variance of earnings per dollar of common stock with debt compared to the variance with no debt is equal to $V^2/(V - B)^2$ or $[V/(V - B)]^2$. Dividing the numerator and denominator by V we obtain $[1/(1 - B/V)]^2$. Thus the ratio of the variances of earnings per dollar of common stock (with and without debt) depends only on the size of B compared to V. Table 6–1 shows the increase in this ratio as debt is substituted for stock. The equality of the fourth and sixth columns occurs since var (X) equals V^2.

---

[4] See Appendix 1 to this chapter.
[5] The magnitude of the change will depend on the value of var (X). Different investors will have different estimates of var (X), thus will interpret the issuance of debt differently.

TABLE 6-1.   Impact of Debt on the Variance in Earnings on Common Stock

B	V − B	DEBT/ COMMON STOCK, i.e., B/V	VARIANCE OF EARNINGS PER DOLLAR OF COMMON STOCK WITH DEBT $\left(\dfrac{1}{V-B}\right)^2 \text{var}(X) \left(\dfrac{1}{1-B/V}\right)^2 =$		RATIO OF VARIANCE OF EARNINGS PER DOLLAR OF COMMON STOCK WITH DEBT COMPARED TO THE VARIANCE OR EARNINGS WITH NO DEBT
0	10,000	.00	1	$\left(\dfrac{1}{1}\right)^2$	1
2,500	7,500	.25	1.8	$\left(\dfrac{1}{.75}\right)^2$	1.8
5,000	5,000	.50	4	$\left(\dfrac{1}{.50}\right)^2$	4
7,500	2,500	.75	16	$\left(\dfrac{1}{.25}\right)^2$	16
9,000	1,000	.90	100	$\left(\dfrac{1}{.10}\right)^2$	100
9,900	100	.99	10,000	$\left(\dfrac{1}{.01}\right)^2$	10,000
10,000	0	1.00	Undefined	$\left(\dfrac{1}{0}\right)^2$	Undefined

The increase in the variance of earnings per dollar of common stock is very dramatic as B/V passes the .5 point.

If the debt is held proportionately by the present stockholders, the increase in the variance of the earnings per dollar of common stock is not disturbing since they will be receiving the interest from the debt. Var (X), the variance of the total earnings, is not affected by the capital structure.

We will now assume that the rate of interest on the debt is not necessarily equal to the expected earnings divided by the common stock investment. Let the interest rate now be $i(\alpha)$, where α is the ratio of debt to total assets. The expected earnings per dollar of common stock is

$$E(r_d) = \frac{E(X) - Bi(\alpha)}{V - B}.$$

The expected earnings of the common stock may be affected by the issuance of the debt.

Since the interest cost is a constant sum the value of the variance of earnings per dollar of common stock investment is again

$$\text{var}(r_d) = \text{var}\left(\frac{X - Bi(\alpha)}{V - B}\right) = \frac{1}{(V - B)^2}\text{var}(X).$$

EXAMPLE THE ADDITION OF DEBT: Assume a firm has $10,000,000 of stock equity with no debt. The forecast of earnings and the expected earnings of the next period as follows:

EARNINGS	PROBABILITY	Y/S EARNINGS/STOCK EQUITY	$E(Y/S)$
500,000	.25	.05	.0125
1,000,000	.50	.10	.0500
2,000,000	.25	.20	.0500
		$E(r_d) = E(Y/S) = $	.1125

The variance of the earnings per dollar of investment is:

Y/S	E(Y/S)	$(Y/S - E(Y/S))^2$	$P(Y/S)$	$E(Y/S - E(Y/S))^2$
.05	.1125	$(.0625)^2 = .0039065$	.25	.000977
.10	.1125	$(.0125)^2 = .00015625$	.50	.000078
.20	.1125	$(.0875)^2 = .00765625$	.25	.001914
			$\text{var}(r_d) = \text{var}(Y/S) = $	.002969

Let us now substitute $9,000,000 of debt for $9,000,000 of the stock equity. Assuming the debt costs .07 there is $630,000 of fixed interest charges. There is $1,000,000 of stock equity. *After interest earnings* are:

EARNINGS	Y/S	PROBABILITY	$E(Y/S)$
− 130,000	−.13	.25	−.0325
370,000	.37	.50	.1850
1,370,000	1.37	.25	.3425
		$E(r_d) = E(Y/S) = $	.4950

The expected return with debt increases since the cost of the debt is less than the return earned by the investment.

The variance is now:

Y/S	$E(Y/S)$	$(Y/S - E(Y/S))^2$	PROBABILITY	$E(Y/S - E(Y/S))^2$
−.13	.4950	$(.6250)^2 = .39063$	.25	.0977
.37	.4950	$(.1250)^2 = .01526$	.50	.0078
1.37	.4950	$(.8750)^2 = .76563$	.25	.1914
			var (r_d) = var (Y/S) =	.2969

The variance of the stockholders earnings (Y/S) with the debt is 100 times greater than it was without the debt.

Changing the Size of the Firm

Instead of substituting debt for common stock we will now add debt to the common stock investment and increase the size of the firm. If the additional debt earns interest at a rate equal to the return currently being earned on the common stock investment the addition of the debt will not affect the expected return of the common stock. However, the variance of earnings per dollar of common stock investment is affected by the addition of the debt. Assuming that new capital is added in the form of debt and the debt earns the same return as is currently being earned, the variance of the new return will be:[6]

$$\text{var}(r_d) = \frac{1}{S^2}\left(\frac{S+B}{S}\right)^2 \text{var}(X).$$

Without the addition of debt we would have the following return:

$$\text{var}\left(\frac{Y}{S}\right) = \frac{1}{S^2}\text{var}(X).$$

The ratio of the variance of the earnings per dollar of common stock with debt to the variance without the additional debt is

$$\text{Ratio} = \left(\frac{S+B}{S}\right)^2 = \left(\frac{1+B/S}{1}\right)^2 = (1+B/S)^2.$$

Table 6–2 shows the values of the ratio for different amounts of debt being added to the present common stock.

[6] See Appendix 2 at the end of this chapter. We are assuming that the new earnings will be perfectly correlated with the old earnings. When we substituted debt for common stock the variance of the earnings was var (X). Now that we are adding debt the variance of the earnings is var $(X + BX/V_0)$, where V_0 is the initial size of the firm.

TABLE 6–2.   **Changing the Size of the Firm by Adding Debt**

B	S	B/S	$(1 + B/S)^2$	RATIO OF VARIANCES OF EARN-INGS WITH DEBT COMPARED TO NO DEBT
0	10,000	0	$(1)^2$	1
2,500	10,000	.25	$(1.25)^2$	1.56
5,000	10,000	.50	$(1.50)^2$	2.25
7,500	10,000	.75	$(1.75)^2$	3.06
9,000	10,000	.90	$(1.90)^2$	3.61
9,900	10,000	.99	$(1.99)^2$	3.96
10,000	10,000	1.00	$(2)^2$	4.00
50,000	10,000	5.00	$(6)^2$	36.00
100,000	10,000	10.00	$(11)^2$	121.00

In Table 6–1 we used the relationship $1/(1 - B/V)$ to determine the ratio of the variance of earnings with debt compared to the variance with no debt. Substituting $B + S$ for V:

$$\frac{1}{1 - B/V} = \frac{1}{1 - B/(S + B)} = \frac{S + B}{S + B - B} = 1 + \frac{B}{S}.$$

Table 6–2 is based on $(1 + B/S)$. Since V is a constant in Table 6–1 the expression $1/(1 - B/V)$ is easier to use in that table. In like manner S is a constant for the computations of Table 6–2, thus $1 + B/S$ is used in that table.

The Variance of Total Common Stock Earnings

The total earnings of the common stockholders are Y and the variance with B dollars of debt paying $E(X)/V$ interest is

$$\text{var}(Y) = \text{var}\left(X - \frac{BE(X)}{V}\right) = \text{var}(X).$$

The variance of the *total* earnings of the common stockholders is unchanged by the issuance of debt to be used to retire common stock. Before concluding erroneously that the risk is unchanged we should note the effect of the debt on the expected total earnings of the common stockholders.

$$E(Y) = E\left(X - \frac{BE(X)}{V}\right).$$

Let $i = E(X)/V$,

$$E(Y) = E(X - Bi) = E(X) - Bi.$$

The expected total income is decreased as the amount of debt increases. We could say that the expected value of the common stock earnings is being moved closer to the break-even value of earnings. The probability of a deficit is being increased since the variance is unchanged by the substitution of the debt for common stock and the mean of common stock earnings is being moved to the left.

We can gain an idea of the magnitude of the probability of the deficit using Chebyshev's inequality:[7]

$$P\{|X - u| > t\} < \frac{\sigma^2}{t^2} = \frac{\sigma^2}{Z^2\sigma^2} = \frac{1}{Z^2},$$

where t is equal to the expected earnings u, and Z is the number of standard deviations, the expected earnings u is from zero.

EXAMPLE: Assume a firm with $10,000,000 assets financed with stock is considering the substitution of $6,000,000 of debt for common stock. The debt will have an interest cost of .10. The company is currently expected to earn $1,000,000 with a standard deviation of $250,000.

Using Chebyshev's inequality:

$$P\{|X - u| > t\} < \frac{\sigma^2}{t^2},$$

$$P\{|X - 1,000,000| > 1,000,000\} < \frac{(250,000)^2}{(1,000,000)^2} = \frac{1}{16}.$$

The probability that the actual income is $1,000,000 greater (or less than) the mean value is less than 1/16. The probability that the actual income is $1,000,000 smaller than the mean income is less than 1/32 (i.e., $\frac{1}{2}$ of 1/16).

If $6,000,000 of debt pays $600,000 of interest (10%) the expected income of the common stockholders is $400,000. We now have

$$P\{|X - 400,000| > 400,000\} < \left(\frac{250,000}{400,000}\right)^2 = \left(\frac{5}{8}\right)^2 = \frac{25}{64}.$$

The probability of a deficit is less than 25/128.

With $9,000,000 of debt the probability of a deficit is

$$P(\text{deficit}) < \frac{1}{2}\left(\frac{250,000}{100,000}\right)^2 = \frac{1}{2}(2.5)^2 = \frac{1}{2} \times 6.25 = 3.125.$$

This computation tells us less than we would like to know since we already know that the probability of a deficit is less than 1.

If we assume that the earnings of the firm are normally distributed, we can

---

[7] The advantage of using Chebyshev's inequality is that no assumption has to be made about the probability distribution of earnings.

estimate the probability of deficits for different amounts of debt substituted for stock.

PERCENTAGE OF DEBT	t: EXPECTED EARNINGS OF STOCKHOLDERS	$Z = \frac{t}{\sigma}$	P (DEFICIT)	P (NO DEFICIT)
0	1,000,000	4	.00003167	.99996833
.25	750,000	3	.001350	.998650
.5	500,000	2	.02275	.97725
.6	400,000	1.60	.05480	.94520
.9	100,000	.40	.3446	.6554

We have obtained the probability of a deficit in a specific year. The probability of encountering a deficit in one or more years during the n years of life of the debt would be

$$P(\text{deficit in one or more years}) = 1 - [P(\text{no deficit})]^n.$$

With .9 debt and a life of 32 years we would have

$$P(\text{deficit in one or more years}) = 1 - (.6554)^{32} = .999998657.$$

With .5 debt we would have

$$P(\text{deficit in one or more years}) = 1 - (.97725)^{32} = .52117.$$

With .9 debt the probability of a deficit in one or more years is essentially 1. With .5 debt the probability of a deficit in one or more years goes down to .52117.

These computations assume that the operating results in each year are independent of each other. While this assumption may not be entirely valid, the probabilities that we obtain are of interest. They help us to understand what is happening when we increase the amount of debt outstanding (i.e., increasing the percentage of debt in the capital structure).

Conclusions

In this chapter we are considering the consequences of adding more debt or substituting debt for common stock. Inspection of Tables 6–1 and 6–2 shows that debt will cause the variance of earnings per dollar of stock investment to increase dramatically if debt, as a percentage of the total capital, increases. A larger amount of variance in the earnings may be assumed generally as having increased the amount of risk associated with the earnings of the common stockholders.

Investigating the variance of the total earnings of the common stockholders we find that the variance of these earnings is not affected by the issuance of debt, but that the probability of a deficit is dramatically increased as the percentage of debt becomes large.

The present tax structure offers a large incentive for the issuance of debt. However, assuming the debt is being issued to parties other than common stockholders, this chapter shows that the issuance of debt is accompanied by increasing risk to the common stockholders.

Appendix 1

Substitution for Debt of Stock

We will hold the size of the firm constant and substitute debt for common stock.

Let X be earnings of the firm (when there is no debt, X is the earnings of the stockholders). X is a random variable with mean $E(X)$.

S be the dollars of common stock investment.

r_d be the earnings per dollar of common stock investment and equal to X/S.

B be the dollars of debt issued to replace B dollars of stock. The debt is issued so that the interest on the bonds is equal to $E(X)/S$, the average return on the stock. The total interest is $B(E(X)/V)$.

V be the total investment (stock plus debt)

$V - B$ be dollars of common stock outstanding after the issue of B dollars of debt

$X - \dfrac{BE(X)}{V}$ be total earnings of stockholders after the issue of the debt

$\dfrac{1}{V-B}\left(X - \dfrac{BE(X)}{V}\right)$ be earnings per dollar of common stock after the issue of the debt

Without debt the expected earnings per dollar of common stock are

$$E(r_d) = E\left(\frac{X}{V}\right) = \frac{E(X)}{V}.$$

With debt we have

$$E(r_d) = E\left[\frac{1}{V-B}\left(X - \frac{BE(X)}{V}\right)\right] = \left(\frac{1}{V-B}\right)E\left(\frac{VX - BE(X)}{V}\right)$$

$$= \frac{1}{V-B} \times \frac{1}{V} \times (VE(X) - BE(X))$$

$$= \frac{1}{V-B} \times \frac{1}{V} \times E(X)[V - B] = \frac{E(X)}{V}.$$

Thus the expected earnings per dollar of common stock are not affected by the issuance of the debt (assuming the interest cost is certain to occur).

With no debt the variance of the earnings per dollar of investment is

$$\text{var}(r_d) = \text{var}\left(\frac{X}{V}\right) = \frac{1}{V^2}\text{var}(X).$$

With debt the variance of the earnings per dollar of investment is[8]

$$\text{var}(r_d) = \text{var}\left[\frac{1}{V-B}\left(X - \frac{BE(X)}{V}\right)\right]$$

$$= \frac{1}{(V-B)^2}\text{var}(X).$$

Although the expectation of the earnings of the firm is not changed by the issuance of debt, the variance of the earnings per dollar of common stock investment is affected.

Appendix 2

The Addition of Debt to Accomplish Growth

BX/V_0 is the additional earnings assumed to result from B dollars of debt being added to S dollars of stock where the initial size of the firm is V_0 and where $S = V_0$.

$BE(X)/V_0$ is the amount of the fixed commitment to pay interest.

The new earnings per dollar of common stock investment are equal to

$$r_d = \frac{1}{S}\left(X + \frac{BX}{V_0} - \frac{BE(X)}{V_0}\right),$$ where S is the unchanging common stock investment.

[8] We are assuming that the interest cost is certain even though the payments may be uncertain.

The variance of r_d is

$$\text{var}(r_d) = \text{var}\left[\frac{1}{S}\left(X + \frac{BX}{V_0} - \frac{BE(X)}{V_0}\right)\right]$$

$$= \frac{1}{S^2}\text{var}\left(\frac{V_0X + BX - BE(X)}{V_0}\right) = \frac{1}{S^2V_0^2}\text{var}(V_0 + B)X$$

$$= \left(\frac{V_0 + B}{V_0S}\right)^2\text{var}(X).$$

Since $V_0 = S$ we have

$$\text{var}(r_d) = \left(\frac{S + B}{S^2}\right)^2\text{var}(X) = \frac{1}{S^2}\left(\frac{S + B}{S}\right)^2\text{var}(X)$$

$$= \left(\frac{S + B}{S}\right)^2\frac{1}{S^2}\text{var}(X).$$

We know that $\text{var}(Y/S) = 1/S^2 \text{var}(X)$ if B equals zero, therefore

$$\text{var}(r_d) = \left(\frac{S + B}{S}\right)^2\text{var}\left(\frac{Y}{S}\right).$$

The ratio of $\text{var}(r_d)$ to $\text{var}(Y/S)$ is

$$\frac{\text{var}(r_d)}{\text{var}(Y/S)} = \left(\frac{S + B}{S}\right)^2.$$

PROBLEMS

1. Assume the ABC Company expects to earn .10 per year on a newly acquired asset that costs $10,000,000. The asset is currently being financed by common stock but the firm is considering issuing $6,000,000 of debt paying .10. The variance of the earnings estimate is 3×10^{12} with 100% common stock financing.

Required: (a) With zero debt the variance of the common stockholders' annual earnings would be 3×10^{12}. What is the variance of stockholders' earnings with $6,000,000 of debt replacing 6,000,000 of stock?

(b) In both cases described in (a) what would be variance per dollar of common stock investment?

(c) What is the expected earnings per dollar of common stock investment with and without the debt?

(d) If the $6,000,000 of debt were issued at a cost of .08 what would be the expected earnings of the common stockholders' per dollar of investment?

2. Continue Problem 1. Prepare a table showing the variance of earnings per dollar of common stock investment with the following amounts of debt: 0, 2,000,000; 4,000,000; 6,000,000; 8,000,000; 9,000,000; 9,900,000; 10,000,000.

3. Continue Problem 1. Assume the initial asset was acquired entirely with common stock. The ABC Company is now considering issuing debt paying .10 to acquire a second asset. The new asset can be of any size from $0 to $90,000,000, is expected to earn .10 per year. The new earnings will be perfectly correlated with the earnings of the original $10,000,000 investment.

Required: (a) Prepare a table showing the ratio of the variance of the new earnings per dollar of common stock investment (the present $10,000,000) compared to no debt for the different amounts of debt: $0; $5,000,000; $10,000,000; $50,000,000; $90,000,000.

(b) What would be the variance of the earnings per dollar of common stockholder investment if $90,000,000 of debt is issued.

4. Continue Problems 1 and 3.

(a) Compute the variance of the total earnings of the stockholders for the following three situations:
(1) the investment is financed entirely with stock (the size of the total investment is $10,000,000).
(2) $6,000,000 is used to retire $4,000,000 of stock (the size of the total investment is $10,000,000).
(3) $90,000,000 of debt costing .10 is added to the $10,000,000 of common stock.

(b) Compute the expected earnings of the common stockholders in the three situations.

(c) Assume the probability distribution of earnings is normal. Compute the probability of a loss to the stockholders in any one year for the three situations.

(d) If the $90,000,000 debt has a three-year life what is the probability that there will be no year in which there is a loss to the common stockholders?

5. PUBLIC UTILITIES AND FINANCIAL DECISIONS[9]

So enormous are the capital requirements of the electric utilities that skilful money management is at least as important in lifting earnings per common share as the ability to generate power economically. That is especially true in the current high-priced money market where electric utilities must pay 5%–5½%, not only for expansion money but also to refund old 3% debt floated during the 1930's and early 1940's. For the standard industry practice is never to retire old debt but rather to refund it.

Of course, utility capital costs are not rising nearly so precipitately as the percentage figures above might suggest. New issues have only a slight impact upon a company's over-all debt cost, so that the average figure for Middle South, for example, is now about 4%. Moreover, an alert management can often use the higher cost of money to persuade the regulatory authorities to allow a higher rate of return, as new production economies build operating income. But since money costs seem destined to remain well above the levels of the prewar and early post war years, clearly it behooves a management to keep the interest burden as low as possible.

One way that has been demonstrated by several of the electric utility holding companies is to issue debt without call protection—that is, without an agreement to forego refunding for a specified number of years. Because it cuts down on their portfolio turnover, large financial institutions are currently willing to pay perhaps a fifth of one percentage point for such protection.

The electric utility holding companies are prohibited by Securities & Exchange Commission regulation from offering such call protection. "But I wouldn't sell with call protection anyway," comments AEP's Don Cook. If interest rates go down, he reasons, the company refunds the bonds at once. If they go up, the company sits tight with what has become low-cost debt. "In the last credit cycle," adds Middle South's Winfield, "I was able to refund a 5–5⅝% issue at 4⅜% in less than five years. Call protection would have prevented this."

HOW MUCH DEBT?

One classic way to lift per-share earnings is to increase leverage, and there are few hotter arguments in the industry than that over how much debt is desirable or permissible or even safe in an electric utility's capital structure.

At one extreme is Cook of American Electric Power, who maintains flatly that a 65% debt ratio is perfectly sensible, even if the relatively thin equity cushion causes a company's bonds to be rated somewhat lower. "In my opinion," he says, "a triple-A bond, instead of being a hallmark of excellence, is a badge of poor financial management."

As competent an operating man as President William B. McGuire of Duke Power maintains the exact oppposite, feeling that it would leave companies too vulnerable to economic depression. "We've had a wonderful long period of prosperity," he says. "I suspect young fellows your age don't believe that we can ever have hard times again. Well, I hope that's right, but I don't know who's going to guarantee it."

Between these two, but sidling perceptibly in Cook's direction, are most of the rest of the industry: They give the appearance of wanting to hang their clothes on a hickory limb but not go near the water. "Our policy," says Southern California Edison's Horton, "is gradually to move our debt ratio up—consistent with keeping our double-A rating."

To those unschooled in the often venerable traditions of the industry the arguments for more leverage seem strong. Although debt ratios have edged up gradually, with 55% debt becoming respectable lately, the ratio in real terms is still not as high as it was back in the 1930's. It has been the lesson of that decade, when assets of electric utility holding companies were found to have been overstated, and when, of course, the United States suffered its more severe economic decline, that has governed thinking about capitalization in the industry. But today, in view of the growth that the industry has continually enjoyed, and for which it is even now busily preparing, it would seem strange to let the industry's capital structure be controlled by the least likely of eventualities.

A simpler means of lifting per-share net would be to retain more than the one-third of earnings now commonly kept. For a dollar retained adds immediately to equity; and that extra dollar of equity, in a capital structure that is 55% debt, 20% preferred and 25% common, could then be matched by three extra dollars of senior money. Yet the tradition that an electric utility must raise dividend payout as it raises per-share earnings is so strong as to have kept per-share results from improving as rapidly as they might.

IMAGE OF GROWTH

Tri-Continental's Frederick Page contends that the best way for an electric company to lift per-share earnings is to be able to sell equity, when new equity money is necessary, at a price well above book value. Fortunately all major electric utility common stocks, including those of the 55 companies listed on page 37, sell well above book value, and often at two and three times book, even in today's dull utility market. Even a company with as many troubles and as poor a recent earnings record as Consolidated Edison was recently quoted at $35.75 as compared with a book value of $28.86.

To show the influence of this factor upon per-share earnings growth, take the admittedly over-simplified case of a hypothetical company with $100 million of total capital on which it is permitted a return of 6%. Half of that total capital is 4% debt, the other half 1 million shares of common. The table below demonstrates what happens if the company doubles its investment (as the electric utility industry commonly does every decade) by selling half new debt and half common shares at twice their book value. This example, it should be noted, assumes a minimum of debt leverage, no preferred stock and no build-up of common equity through retained earnings.

The electric utility companies that sell at the greatest premium above book are, naturally enough, those that show the best per-share earnings growth, and thereby come to be regarded by investors as growth companies. A company comes to be regarded as a growth company first by acting like one, and then by presenting the image of one.

This is the dual achievement of American Electric Power, which by continuous effort toward lower costs and prices, along with equally continuous drumbeating, earned the growth label even though much of its service area was in the heart of depressed Appalachia. This is also the tragedy of Consolidated Edison, whose operating shortcomings piled up and gave it such a bad public reputation as to threaten its chances of getting approval for its much-needed 2-million-kw Cornwall pumped-storage plant.

	PRESENT	NEW CAPITAL	RESULT
Invested capital	$100 million	$100 million	$200 million
Debt	$50 million	$50 million	$100 million
Common	$50 million	$50 million	$100 million
Number of shares	$1 million	$.5 million	$1.5 million
Return, 6%	$6 million		$12 million
Prior charges	$2 million		$4 million
Balance for common	$4 million		$8 million
Per share	$4		$5.33 (+33%)

It was an attempt to break out of this vicious circle that led to the recent appointment of Interior Undersecretary Charles F. Luce, a man from the public power side of the fence, as Con Edison's new chairman and chief executive. The problems he faces are vast. His appointment also underscores something the investor should never forget: Even in this sure-growth industry you need good management not mere seat-warmers. But given the right kind of management, it's tough to see how the electric utilities can lose.

Required: Discuss the pros and cons of more debt for public utilities.

REFERENCES

See also References for Chapters 4 and 5
Beranek, W. *Analysis for Financial Decisions* (Irwin, Homewood, Ill., 1963).

Cohen, K. J., and Hammer, F. S. "Critical Comments on 'Measuring Risk on Consumer Installment Credit' by Paul F. Smith," *Management Science* (May), 1966.

————. *Analytical Methods in Banking* (Irwin, Homewood, Ill., 1966). See the Appendix to Chapter 6.

Donaldson, G. *Corporate Debt Capacity* (Harvard Graduate School of Business, Boston, 1961).

Fisher, L. "Determinants of Risk Premiums on Corporate Bonds," *Journal of Political Economy* (June), 1959.

CHAPTER 7

Capital Structure and the Cost of Capital

SYMBOLS

$E(X)$ the expectation of a constant annual payment to the investors (X, the annual payment is a random variable)

K the average cost of capital

t_c the corporate tax rate

B the amount of debt

i the cost of debt and the time value of money for the firm

V_0 the value of a firm with zero debt

V the value of a firm with debt

Let us define the value of a firm as being equal to the present value of all the cash distributed to all capital contributors. Initially we will assume that there is no debt outstanding, no taxes, and the firm is not growing. The value of a firm, is defined to be

$$V_0 = \frac{X}{K},$$

where X is a constant known annual payment to the investors (they are all stockholders) and K is the discount rate being applied to the future cash flows by the investors. We will define K to be the firm's average cost of capital (with zero debt it is also the cost of common equity funds).

If we can reduce K by manipulating the capital structure then V_0 would be increased since the total annual payment X to investors would not be affected by the capital structure decision in the absence of taxes, and K is reduced.

If we recognize that X is a random variable and if there is no adjustment for risk (in addition to that incorporated into K), the value of the firm is:

$$V_0 = \frac{E(X)}{K}$$

EXAMPLE: Assume $E(X)$ is \$1,000,000 and K (with no debt) is .10. The value of the firm is

$$V_0 = \frac{1,000,000}{.10} = 10,000,000.$$

If K can be decreased to .05 by adding debt, we would then have

$$V = \frac{1,000,000}{.05} = 20,000,000.$$

Since the famous Miller and Modigliani article on capital structure and the cost of capital in 1958, a continuing controversy has raged about the sensitivity of the cost of capital of a firm to changes in its capital structure.[1] The controversy is of importance to financial officers since the effect of capital structure on the cost of capital affects the debt versus common stock decision and the determination of the cost of capital affects the cut-off rate that is conventionally used to determine which independent investments are acceptable. In addition, with income taxes, the capital structure affects the cash flows available for investors.

The broad assumptions made by the several parties to the discussions are worthy of review. The capital structure debate implicitly assumes that:

1. There is a definable something which we can label "cost of capital."
2. It is possible to compute the cost of capital with reasonable exactness and meaningfulness.
3. The cost of stock equity capital is the factor used (either explicitly or implicitly) by an investor in common stock in making his investment decisions.
4. Different risk classes of firms have different costs of capital.
5. We can take the cost of capital and use it in making investment decisions. Using the present value method of making investment decisions it is the rate of discount to be used in choosing the best of a set of mutually exclusive investments, and it is the cut-off rate for accepting or rejecting independent investments.[2]

These assumptions are convenient since they enable us to implement the very logical present value procedure which works in excellent fashion so long as we do not ration capital or allow uncertainty.[3]

---

[1] See Franco Modigliani and Merton H. Miller. "The Cost of Capital, Corporation Finance, and the Theory of Investment," *The American Economic Review* (June, 1958), pp. 261–297; "The Cost of Capital, Corporation Finance, and the Theory of Investment: Reply," *The American Economic Review* (September, 1959), pp. 655–669; and "Taxes and the Cost of Capital: A Correction," *The American Economic Review* (June, 1963), pp. 433–443. Also David Durand, "The Cost of Capital, Corporation Finance, and The Theory of Investment: Comment," *The American Economic Review* (September, 1959), pp. 640–654; and Alexander Barges, *The Effect of Capital Structure on the Cost of Capital,* The Ford Foundation Doctoral Dissertation Series (Prentice-Hall, Englewood Cliffs, N.J., 1963). The first Modigliani and Miller article is a classic article on the cost of capital.

[2] Compare with Modigliani and Miller, *op. cit.,* (1958), p. 288.

[3] See Jack Hirschleifer. "On the Theory of Optimal Investment Decisions," *Journal of Political Economy* (August, 1958), pp. 329–352, or Harry M. Markowitz. *Portfolio*

Although Assumption 1 may be satisfied, there is no reason for assuming that the other four assumptions hold under conditions of uncertainty. No one has shown in a logical manner that the cost of capital can be computed in such a manner as to be used in evaluating investments, if the factor of uncertainty is taken into consideration. For example, Modigliani and Miller state that "nothing in our analysis (or anyone else's, for that matter) has yet established that it is indeed legitimate to 'discount' an uncertain stream."[4] Thus in this chapter we will attempt to determine the effect of leverage on the cost of capital and on the value of the firm but will not be interested in determining the exact cost of capital to be used in investment evaluation. In Chapter 4 we argued that the use of cost of capital to evaluate investments is not correct.

Optimal Capital Structure: No Corporate Taxation

With a zero corporate tax rate, no benefits from limited liability associated with being corporated, and if everyone borrowed funds at the same interest rate, a firm's value should not change because of a modification in its capital structure. This conclusion can be illustrated assuming an individual can borrow at the same interest rate as the corporation and is willing to attain a desired amount of debt and equity by using a diversified portfolio, or by the investor borrowing directly. In a sense we assume the investor consolidates his own financial position with the affairs of the corporations in which he owns stock.

EXAMPLE: Assume a person has $4000 to invest. He wants $1 of debt for each $1 of stock equity. The stocks of two firms are available for acquisition. The characteristics of the two firms are as follows (assume values are being measured):

	A	B
Assets	10,000	10,000
Debt	0	8,000
Common stock	10,000	2,000

To satisfy the requirements described above, the investor will buy $1000 (or .5) of B and $3000 (or .3) of A.

Selection: *Efficient Diversification of Investments*, Cowles Foundation Monograph No. 16 (Wiley, New York, 1959).
    [4] Modigliani and Miller, *op. cit.*, (1963), p. 442 (fn).

The financial position of the investor, including a *pro-rata* share of the two firms, is:

	INDIVIDUAL	A	B	TOTAL "CONSOLIDATED" POSITION
Assets		3000	5000	8000
Investment	4000			
Debt			4000	4000
Common Stock	4000	3000	1000	4000

Instead of buying a mixture of A and B, the investor could have borrowed $4000 and invested all $8000 in A. His financial position would be identical to that indicated in the total "consolidated" position column.

Assume A and B both earn $2000 and that debt costs .05. When the investor owns both A and B we have the following income statements.

	A	B	
Income	2000	2000	
Interest		400	
	2000	1600	
Percentage of ownership	× .3	× .5	
	600 +	800 = 1400	Income of Investor

If the investor bought .8 of A and borrowed $4000 at a cost of .05 he would have:

Earnings of A	2000
Percentage of Ownership	.8
	1600
Interest	− 200
	1400 Income of investor

In both cases the investor's income is $1400. There is no reason to think the investor would pay a premium for B's common stock compared to A's stock. Instead of the investor borrowing on his own credit, arbitrage can be accomplished by purchasing combinations of firms to obtain the desired financial mix (as well as the desired asset mix).

Optimal Capital Structure: Corporate Income Taxes

In the last example we showed that without income taxes the value of a firm could be independent of its capital structure. With corporate income taxes the value of a firm is greatly affected by the fact that interest is deductible for tax purposes and dividends are not.

EXAMPLE: A firm is considering a $2000 investment earning $100. Debt is available at a cost of .05 per year. There is a .4 marginal tax rate. With different financing arrangements, the results would be as follows:

	100% STOCK	50% STOCK 50% DEBT	100% DEBT
Earnings before tax	100	100	100
less: interest	—	50	100
Taxable income	100	50	0
Income tax	40	20	0
Income after tax	60	30	0
plus: interest	—	50	100
Total contribution to capital	60	80	100

There is a larger after-tax distribution with 100% debt than with any other financial arrangement. If the stockholders buy the debt there is no additional risk to the stockholders compared with raising the required capital using common stock. Since the total payoff to the capital contributors can be increased by using more debt, the value of the firm can also be increased. In reaching this conclusion there is an implicit assumption that the capital structures will not be changed in the immediate future.

The question as to whether or not the overall cost of capital of a firm is changed by decisions affecting its capital structure is answered with a yes. If it were not for the income tax laws the answer would not be definite. The present tax laws allowing interest on debt but not dividends on stock to be deducted in computing taxable income results in a clear bias in favor of issuing debt. The reason for this bias is most easily seen where the debt is issued to the common stockholders. In this situation there is no increased risk to the stockholders since they own the debt, but the form of the distribution of earnings is changed.

With all the capital in the form of stock, the cash distributions to the owners would not result in a tax deduction. With all the capital in the form of debt, an amount equal to the tax rate times the cash distribution would be a tax saving. In order to avoid being identified as a "thin corporation" the firm would want less than 100% debt and to avoid arousing the Internal Revenue Service it would not want to issue all its debt to the stockholders. But assuming the firm did not go too far, it is clear that in the presence of the current income tax laws one can change the value of a corporation's earning stream by changing its capital structure. The clearest illustration of benefit arises when we merely change the form of the distribution (a dividend changed to interest) but where the payments are made to the same capital contributors. Where the payment is made to a third party who is not presently a stockholder, the analysis becomes more complex since the risk changes.

A corporation that has debt outstanding, or is issuing debt, is better off with interest being deductible than not deductible, for tax purposes. For example, assume that interest is deductible and that debt is outstanding with an interest rate of .05 and the marginal tax rate is .4 (the after-tax interest rate is .03). We will further assume that the time value of money of both stockholders and bondholders is .05. In this situation the deductibility of interest for tax purposes enables the firm to undertake investments for the benefit of the stockholders with yields of less than .05 (but with after-tax yields of at least .03). Without the deductibility of interest, investments yielding less than .05 would be rejected.[5] The investments are desirable with yields between .03 and .05 because of a combination of tax deductibility of interest and trading on the equity.

With investment yielding over .05, financed by the .05 debt, the stockholders again benefit but with investments yielding over .05, we have a situation of pure trading on the equity and acceptability of the investment is not the result of the tax deductibility of interest (though the fact that interest is deductible may make the investment more desirable).

EXAMPLE: Assume $1000 of debt paying $50 of interest is issued. The amount available for stockholders is illustrated assuming different after-tax earnings.

		SITUATION:				
		1		2		3
After-tax returns		$30		$50		$80
Interest:	$50		$50		$50	
Less:						
tax saving	20	30	20	30	20	30
Net gain to stockholders		$0		$20		$50
Total amount distributed						
to capital contributors		$50		$70		$100

---

[5] Insurance (risk-reducing) type investments are not being considered here.

There is no gain to stockholders when the investment returns just the after-tax yield of the bond. In the second situation there is a net gain to the stockholders of $20 that would not exist if the interest were not deductible for tax purposes. In the third situation the stockholders are $50 better off; $30 is a result of trading on the equity and $20 is a result of the tax saving.

If the investment had been financed by common stock funds the amounts available for distribution in the three situations would be $30, $50, and $80 instead of the $50, $70, and $100 distributed to the capital contributors when the $1000 of debt is used.

The Change in the Value of the Firm

The model that follows makes very special assumptions, and other assumptions would lead to modified results. We assume it is correct to use the cost of debt as the discount factor for time, and that all the cash flows resulting from the operations of the firm should be discounted at the same rate of interest in computing the value of the firm.

Previously we concluded that:

$$V_0 = \frac{X}{K}$$

or more generally

$$V_0 = \frac{E(X)}{K}.$$

Now we will discount for time using i rather than the cost of capital K (risk still must be taken into consideration). With a tax rate of t_c we have:

$$V_0 = \frac{X(1 - t_c)}{i} \quad \text{or} \quad E(V_0) = \frac{(1 - t_c)E(X)}{i}.$$

If we add an amount of debt B that pays i interest we have

$$V = \frac{(X - iB)(1 - t_c) + iB}{i} = \frac{X(1 - t_c) - iB(1 - t_c) + iB}{i}$$

$$= \frac{X(1 - t_c)}{i} + \frac{iBt}{i} = \frac{X(1 - t_c)}{i} + Bt.$$

With X uncertain we can take the expectation of V;

$$E(V) = \frac{(1 - t_c)E(X)}{i} + Bt.$$

The first term is the expected value of V_0, the value with zero debt, and the second term is the value change resulting from issuing B of debt. Since X is uncertain it would be reasonable to also have a "risk adjustment" term subtracted to compute the value of the firm after the debt addition.

With a different assumption about how risk and time value should be taken into consideration we can obtain different measures of the effect of adding debt. However, the above is illustrative of the general approach.

It is interesting that with zero debt the amount available for capital contributors is $X(1 - t_c)$ each year and with debt it is increased to $X(1 - t_c) + iBt_c$. This amount is independent of risk attitudes and discount rates.

Tax Considerations and Costs of Different Capital Sources

Assume for illustrative purposes that holders of bonds, preferred stock, and common stock of the ABC Company all required a return of .05 and there is a .4 tax rate. There are $1000 of each security outstanding (the return to each type of security is $50).

In order to have $50 to distribute to each type of security the company will have to earn $216.67 before tax.

TABLE 7–1

	BEFORE INTEREST, BEFORE-TAX EARNINGS	(1-TAX RATE)	NECESSARY AFTER-TAX EARNINGS
Bonds	50		50
Preferred stock	83.33	.6	50
Common stock	83.33	.6	50
	216.67		150

Since the bond interest is deductible for tax purposes we only need $50 of before-tax earnings to satisfy the interest payment to the bondholders.

If we take the ratio of the necessary after-tax earnings to the capital contributed, we find the cost of each type of security is .05 (we could also say that the return to each type of investor is .05).

But let us consider more exactly the after-tax cost of debt. The $50 of interest results in a tax saving of $20, thus the net cost of the debt is $30 or .03 (30/1000 = .03). We can extend Table 7–1 to show the after-tax cost of each security.

TABLE 7–2

	NECESSARY AFTER-TAX EARNINGS[a]	TAX SAVING[b]	NET COST TO CORPORATION
Bonds	50	20	30 or .03
Preferred stock	50	0	50 or .05
Common stock	50	0	50 or .05

[a] From Table 7–1.
[b] Equal to the tax rate times the tax deductible interest.

We have three sets of costs. These are set forth in Table 7–3.

TABLE 7–3. Costs of Each Type of Capital

	NECESSARY EARNINGS BEFORE TAX[a]	AFTER-TAX DISTRIBUTION AS A FRACTION OF CAPITAL[a]	AFTER-TAX COST[b]
Bonds	.05	.05	.03
Preferred stock	.083	.05	.05
Common stock	.083	.05	.05

[a] From Table 7–1.
[b] From Table 7–2. Each number in this column is .6 of the same line of Column 1 of this table.

Instead of assuming that the returns of each type of security are equal we will assume the returns are .05 for debt, .06 for preferred stock, and .10 for common stock. The magnitude of these costs are consistent with our experience. Table 7–4 shows the costs of the alternative sources:

TABLE 7–4. Costs of Each Type of Capital

	BEFORE-TAX NECESSARY EARNINGS	AFTER-TAX DISTRIBUTION	AFTER-TAX COST
Bonds	.050	.05	.03
Preferred stock	.100	.06	.06
Common stock	.167	.10	.10

In the current example the common stockholders require twice as large a return as the bondholders but the before-tax cost is more than three times as large. The difference in cost between preferred stock and bonds is also interesting. The preferred stock is twice as expensive as the bonds despite the fact that the return to the preferred stockholders is only .06 compared to .05 for bondholders.

The differences in the cost would be less dramatic if a tax rate less than .4 were used. A higher tax rate would make the cost differences more dramatic.

Conclusions

The use of debt in the capital structure of a corporation does enable the firm to reduce its cost of raising capital since the interest payments are deductible for tax purposes. The desirability of debt compared to common stock is dramatized when the debt is purchased by the common stockholders since in this situation there is no increase in the risk to the investors. One could be led to the conclusion that a firm should issue as much debt as possible, with the stockholders purchasing the debt if they fear an excessive increase in risk arising from the highly levered capital structure. However, the Internal Revenue Service will limit the amount of this type of debt that a corporation may issue and too much debt may result in the distribution being relabeled as dividends. Also the points made in Chapter 6 should not be forgotten. The addition of debt, even where the debt is a relatively cheap source of capital because of the tax structure, does add risk. If there is no taxable income, the full cost of the interest falls on the corporation and ultimately on the stockholders. Thus we can conclude that the present tax structure offers strong incentives to issue debt, but that there are forces (the risk of bankruptcy and the conventions of the investment banking community) that restrain the corporation considering the issuance of unusually large amounts of debt compared to common stock.

We conclude that the cost to a firm of obtaining capital is a function of its capital structure. Thus with real world institutions the "cost of capital" is a variable dependent on decisions of corporate managers. In Chapter 4 we suggested that the rate of discount to be used in evaluating investments should measure the time value of money and not include risk adjustments. If we assume that the firm has optimized its capital structure, and if we omit situations where the firm is not willing to enter the capital market, its time value of money is determined by the money market. Its time-value factor may not be equal to the weighted average cost of capital, which by definition includes an adjustment for risk. The cost of capital expresses in one measure the return required on the average by the investors. It does not express investor preferences for a unique investment opportunity with different risk characteristics than the average risk characteristics of the firm.

PROBLEMS

1. Assume a firm is expected to earn $10,000,000 per year over and above the capital outlays (or expenses) necessary to maintain this stream of earnings. Interpret the $10,000,000 to be a perpetuity.

   Required: (a) Determine the value of the firm assuming a value of money of .10

   (b) Determine the value of the firm assuming a value of money of .04.

2. Assume the market value of the common stock of a firm to be $100,000,000 Stockholders can expect future dividends to be a constant $12,500,000.
   Required: What is the implied cost of common stock equity capital?

3. Mr. Jones has $10,000 to invest and he has zero debt. He can invest in either of two firms. These firms are identical except for capital structure.

	FIRM X	FIRM Y
Assets	100,000	100,000
Debt (.05)	0	60,000
Common stock	100,000	40,000

Assume the above statements correctly state the value of assets and debt. Each firm has 100,000 shares of common stock outstanding. Because of the leverage, Y's stock is selling for $.50 per share while X's stock is selling for $1 per share. Both firms are earning .10 on capital, and the income statements of the two firms are:

	X	Y
Income before interest	10,000	10,000
Interest		3,000
Income to stockholders	10,000	7,000
Income per share	$.10	$.07

X is selling at 10 times earnings.
Y is selling at 7.14 times earnings.

Assume that Mr. Jones is willing to have debt in his portfolio but would like to limit it to $1.20 of debt to $1 of owner's equity on a consolidated basis. Mr. Jones can borrow money at a cost of .05.

Required: How should Mr. Jones invest his funds? Assume that the investments are limited to X and Y and we are ignoring risk considerations (we want to maximize the earnings of Mr. Jones).

4. Mr. Smith does not want to add any debt to his personal account. He has $10,000 to invest. There are three firms, which are identical except for capital structure. He is willing to invest in one or more of these firms and only places two constraints on the investment:

   (a) on a consolidated basis the total debt is equal to 50% of the total stock equity.
   (b) the total earnings of his $10,000 investment are maximized.

The financial information of the three companies follows:

	X	Y	Z
Assets	100,000	100,000	100,000
Debt	0	40,000	60,000
Stock equity	100,000	60,000	40,000
Income (before interest)	10,000	10,000	10,000
Interest	0	2,800	4,200
Income of stockholders	10,000	7,200	5,800
Income per share	$1	$.72	$.58
Number of shares	10,000	10,000	10,000
Market value (per share)	$10	$6	$4.64
Ratio of market price to earnings	10	8.33	8.

Required: How should Mr. Smith invest?

5. Continue Problem 4. Assume a .4 marginal tax rate for corporations; also assume that dividends and interest are taxed the same when received by individuals.

   Required: (a) Compute the amount available for distribution to the various capital contributors after taxes.
   (b) If a firm could be financed with 100% debt paying .10 interest, how much could be distributed?

6. The ABC Company can issue $100,000 of the *one* of the following securities at the below costs:

Bonds	.06
Preferred stock	.08
Common stock	.10 (this is the cash dividend)

The current corporate tax rate is .40.

Required: (a) Assuming $100,000 of new capital is obtained, how much would have to be earned before taxes to meet the interest or dividend payments of each type of capital source? What is the before-tax cost as a per cent of the dollars obtained?

      (b) What is the net cost to the corporation of each type of security on an after-tax basis?

      (c) Assume the revenues net of all expenses other than taxes and interest are $16,667. Prepare a table showing the net available to the corporation after the payment to the capital contributors.

      (d) Assume the revenues net of all expenses other than taxes and interest are $20,000. Prepare a table showing the net available to the corporation after the payment to the capital contributors.

7. The Federal Communications Commission's investigation of the Bell System in 1966 led to a discussion of the company's capital structure. Some witnesses said that a debt ratio of 35% (65% stock) was too low. They suggested a debt ratio of 45 or 50% since it would be cheaper to pay interest than to pay dividends to stockholders. The company felt that the greater the debt, the greater the risk to the common stockholders, and the higher the cost of attracting common stock funds.

Required: Comment on the two positions.

8. The Smith Oil Company has $1,500,000 of taxable income. It has the opportunity of purchasing $20,000,000 of common stock in the XYZ Oil Company. This stock is currently paying a dividend of $1,200,000 per year on the common stock described and may be expected to pay this dividend in the future. The Smith Oil Company can obtain debt capital at a cost of .07 to finance the stock purchase. The corporate income tax rate may be assumed to be .48.

Required: Should the Smith Oil Company purchase the common stock? Ignore other investment possibilities that may be competing for funds.

9.   DELAYED INVESTMENTS

In a *Journal of Finance* article Cheng and Shelton consider the situation where a firm is considering more than one investment opportunity.[6] They conclude that the cost of capital, though it is the proper hurdle rate for evaluating one project, does not provide the correct cut-off point when more than one project (involving different marginal rates of return) is under consideration. They specifically object to the fact that earnings

[6] P. L. Cheng and J. P. Shelton, "A Contribution to the Theory of Capital Budgeting—The Multi-Investment Case," *The Journal of Finance* (December, 1963), pp. 622–636.

per share will not necessarily be maximized if a firm undertakes all investment projects that have a prospect of yielding more than the cost of
capital.

Cheng and Shelton use the following example to illustrate their position.

EXAMPLE: There are two projects both costing $600,000 and returning
respectively perpetuities of $200,000 (a return of .33) and $45,000 (a return
of .075). There are currently 100,000 shares outstanding with a market price
of $60 per share and earnings of $4 per share (price earnings multiple of
15 implying a cost of capital of .067).

If both projects are accepted 20,000 shares will have to be issued (there
will be 120,000 shares outstanding) and the total expected net income will be
$645,000 or $5.375 per share.

If only the better project is approved 10,000 shares will be issued and the
total expected net income will be $600,000 or $5.456 per share.

Cheng and Shelton conclude "The existing owners of the corporation
will be better off if the firm does not undertake the second project... earnings
per share will be maximized if the firm undertakes the second project at a
subsequent time...."

Required: Discuss the problem considered and offer a possible approach
to coping with the problem.

REFERENCES

Barges, A. *The Effect of Capital Structure on the Cost of Capital*, (Prentice-
Hall, Englewood Cliffs, N.J., 1963).

Chen, Houng-Yhi. "Valuation Under Uncertainty," *Journal of Financial and
Quantitative Analysis* (September), 1967.

Durand, D. "The Cost of Capital, Corporation Finance, and the Theory of
Investment: Comment," *The American Economic Review* (September),
1959.

Fisher, I. *The Theory of Interest*, (Macmillan Co., New York, 1930).

Hirshleifer, J. "On the Theory of Optimal Investment Decision," *The Journal
of Political Economy* (August), 1958.

——, DeHaven, J. C., and Milliman, J. W. *Water Supply* (The University
of Chicago Press, Chicago, 1960).

Lerner, E. M., and Carleton, W. T. "The Integration of Capital Budgeting
and Stock Valuation," *The American Economic Review* (September),
1964.

Modigliani, F., and Miller, M. H. "The Cost of Capital, Corporation Finance,
and the Theory of Investment," *The American Economic Review* (June),
1958.

Modigliani, F., and Miller, M. H. "The Cost of Capital, Corporation Finance, and the Theory of Investment: Reply," *The American Economic Review* (September), 1959.

———. "Corporate Income Taxes and the Cost of Capital: A Correction." *The American Economic Review* (June), 1963.

Robichek, A. A., and Myers, S. C. "Conceptual Problems in the Use of Risk-Adjusted Discount Rates," *The Journal of Finance* (December), 1966.

Dividend Policy Decisions

In Part III we will deal with decisions involving the distribution of cash to the common stockholders of a firm. The basic choices involve the size of the cash dividend (dividends versus retention) and the form the distribution will take (a cash dividend versus other forms of cash distribution).

CHAPTER 8

Corporate Dividend Policy[1]

SYMBOLS

P_t	the price per share time t	T_0	equal to $1 - t_0$
D	the earnings per share	D_i	earnings per share of the ith period
α	the percentage of earnings paid as a dividend	r_e	minimum reinvestment rate of the firm and return available to individuals (before tax)
αD	the dividends per share		
$(1 - \alpha)D$	the retained earnings		
V_n	the value per share at time n	r	the after-tax return available to individuals, $r = T r_e$; the discount rate applied by stockholders
C_n	the tax cost basis of the shares at time n		
t_k	capital gains tax rate		
T_k	equal to $1 - t_k$		
t_0	tax rate on ordinary income		

For some time the question of how a firm's dividend policy can be expected to influence the value of its shares has been of interest to businessmen, investors, and economists. And yet, until quite recently there existed no well-developed theory (or theories) of the relationship between dividend policy and share valuation. In the past several years, however, the work of Modigliani and Miller, Gordon, Lintner, and others, has eliminated this deficiency.[2]

Miller and Modigliani argue that with no income taxes and other well-defined assumptions (such as perfect knowledge and certainty) a dollar retained is equal in value to a dollar distributed, thus dividend policy is not a relevant factor in determining the value of a corporation.

Let us define the price (and value) of a share of common stock to be equal

[1] Parts of this chapter are based on an article written jointly with Richard R. West, "Corporate Dividend Policy and Preemptive Security Issues," *The Journal of Business* (January, 1968), pp. 71–75.

[2] See M. H. Miller and F. Modigliani, "Dividend Policy, Growth and the Valuation of Shares," *The Journal of Business* (October, 1961), pp. 411–433, for a good bibliography of the relevant literature. For a recent comprehensive study see J. A. Brittain, *Corporate Dividend Policy* (The Brookings Institution, Washington, 1966).

to the present value of the next dividend (assumed to be declared and paid one period from now) and the price of the share at the time the dividend is paid:

$$P_0 = \frac{\alpha D + P_1}{1 + r}.$$

We will assume P_1, the price at time one, is equal to the initial price P_0 plus the retained earnings $(D - \alpha D)$, where D is the income of the period and αD is the dividend paid. We now have

$$P_0 = \frac{\alpha D + (P_0 + D - \alpha D)}{1 + r} = \frac{P_0 + D}{1 + r}.$$

This relationship shows that P_0 is independent of the size of the dividend αD. Note that we assumed that $(1 - \alpha)D$ measured the increase in the price per share arising from retained earnings. (The actual increase may be more or less than this depending on the market's expectations as to the value of the investments available to the firm.) Also, we assumed no income taxes.

We will consider three different situations modifying the assumption that the change in price will be equal to the retained earnings. The situations are where,

1. A firm only has earning opportunities that are inferior to those external opportunities available to its stockholders.
2. A firm has more desirable earning opportunities than it has cash that it is able and willing to obtain from external sources.
3. A firm has more desirable earning opportunities than it has cash and will obtain the needed cash from its present stockholders.

In the first situation the firm should return the money to the stockholders. The external earning opportunities of the stockholders set a minimum cost that must be earned-internally if the funds are to be retained. Unfortunately with the personal income tax rate structure, it is not clear that the distribution of cash to the stockholders should take the form of a cash dividend.

The second situation is more complex. Every dollar of dividends must be replaced by a dollar of external capital. If the money is obtained from new stockholders the ownership of the present stockholders is being diluted. If the funds are obtained using the debt form, the risk characteristics of the firm are being changed. There is no clearcut guide for decision here. If the present stockholders want cash (and want effectively to reduce their investment compared to what it would be if the funds were retained) then a cash distribution is in order. However, even here it should be noted that the firm could retain and stockholders could obtain cash by selling a portion of their holdings. The advantage of this latter procedure is that the stockholders might be able to convert income taxed as ordinary income into income taxed as capital gains. Also, it is not clear that the distribution should be in the form of a cash dividend. The heavily progressive personal income tax rates give high-income investors an incentive to invest in situations that lead to capital gains rather than ordinary income. Thus the informed investor with a high income is apt to seek out firms with dividend policies that are consistent with this objective.

In the third situation the firm is concurrently paying dividends and obtaining funds from the investors. When firms concurrently pay dividends and raise capital through preemptive security issues to stockholders, there are reasons to believe that a reduction in dividend payments could lead to an increase in share values. The importance of the problem is highlighted by the fact that a significant number of major corporations continue paying dividends while floating preemptive security offerings. Table 8–1 shows a sampling of corporations that have issued securities to stockholders at the same time as dividends were being paid.

TABLE 8–1. Securities Issued to Stockholders by Dividend Paying Corporations[a]

CORPORATION	APPROXIMATE SIZE OF ISSUE (IN MILLIONS)	YEAR	ISSUES ARE GREATER THAN THE TOTAL CASH DIVIDENDS PAID SINCE:
Armour	24	1965	1949
	33	1961	
Boeing	100	1966	1959
Celanese	96	1966	
	79	1965	1954
	45	1963	
Chrysler	280	1965	1954
IBM[b]	370	1966	1964
Riegel Paper	10	1965	1962
Union Electric	28	1965	1965 (one year's dividends)
United Air Lines	70	1966	1954
	67	1965	

[a] The information for this table was obtained by Edward Tauber.
[b] A 1957 issue of $220 million was equivalent to the dividends of the next five years.

Our conclusions relative to the dividend policy of firms that are not anticipating acquiring funds from its stockholders are less easy to prove; nevertheless there is a carry-over from the particular case that is studied in detail. It will become apparent that dividend policy can affect the valuation of stock in the presence of personal income taxes that distinguish between ordinary income and long-term capital gains. The present tax law allows deferral of tax payment (or complete avoidance) on capital gains, and recognized gains may be taxed at different rates than ordinary income.

Dividend policies of firms have relevance for public policy in the areas of taxation of both corporations and individuals. As corporate managers adjust their decision making to include the tax law considerations, the makers of public policy must decide whether the results are beneficial to society. This question is not considered in this chapter.

A Model

Consider a world of certainty, and in that world a corporation with a policy of financing investments either by retaining earnings or through preemptive security offerings to its stockholders. Further, assume that the firm has been in a steady state where it has earned D per period, has not had additional profitable investment opportunities, and has paid out all earnings in dividends.

Now, however, let the corporation be faced at time $i = 0$ with profitable investments of $D(1 + r_e)^n$ per period for the next n periods, where r_e is the return earned per period and D is the current earnings (and equal to the amount that could be paid as dividends without reducing the net assets of the firm below the total at the beginning of the period). How will its choice of financing these investments as between retention (reducing dividends) or preemptive stock issues (while maintaining dividends) affect the value of its shares?

If we assume for simplicity that a dividend has just been received and that investments and dividend payments (if any) will be made at the end of each period, the value of the firm's shares at $i = 0$ (i.e., V_0) can be represented as follows:

$$V_0 = [(V_n - C_n)T_k + C_n](1 + r)^{-n} - \sum_{i=1}^{n} \alpha t D_i (1 + r)^{-i}, \qquad (8\text{-}1)$$

where V_n = the value of the shares at time n

C_n = the tax cost basis of the shares at time n

$T_k = (1 - t_k)$, and t_k is the tax rate on capital gains (assumed to be the same for all investors)

t_0 = the tax rate on ordinary income (assumed to be the same for all investors) $T_0 = 1 - t_0$

α = the percentage of earnings paid out as dividends

D_i = the dividends of the ith period, $D_i = D_1(1 + r_e)^{i-1}$ or $D_i = D_0 (1 + r_e)^i$

r_e = minimum reinvestment rate of firm and before-tax rate of return available to an individual if he invests outside the firm (to simplify the development assume the marginal reinvestment rate for the firm equals the average)

r = the after-tax rate of return available to an individual, where $r = Tr_e$

The firm intends to invest an amount each period equal to D_i. If a dividend of D_i is paid ($\alpha = 1$), an amount equal to D_i will be obtained from the stockholders. If the firm retains D_i and pays no dividends ($\alpha = 0$) then the stockholders do not have to make an explicit investment. The funds retained by the firm earn r_e per year. The stock is presently held by the investors and we want to find the difference in value to the investor of two different dividend policies (1) paying D_i in cash dividends ($\alpha = 1$); (2) paying zero dividends ($\alpha = 0$) for n periods to be followed by a dividend of D_{n+1} for perpetuity.[3]

The value of the firm's shares at $i = 0$ is equal to the present worth of the after-tax value of the shares at time n, less the present worth of taxes on dividends received prior to $i = n$.

From equation 8–1 it can be seen that the firm's payout policy (i.e., the size of α) inversely affects the value of its shares via its effect on tax payments arising from the receipt of dividends. An increase in α leads not only to an increase in dividends (and taxes on dividends), but also to a rise in preemptive security issues, and thus to an expansion of the cost basis of stockholder interests. This can be stated formally as follows:

$$C_n = C_0 + \sum_{i=1}^{n} \alpha D_i, \tag{8–2}$$

where C_0 is the cost basis of shares at $i = 0$. That is, the cost basis of the stockholders' interests at $i = n$ is equal to the cost basis at $i = 0$ plus the value of the preemptive issues sold by the firm.

Substituting $C_0 + \sum_{i=1}^{n} \alpha D_i$ for C_n in Equation 8–1 and simplifying, we obtain:[4]

[3] The assumption that the stock is presently held can be dropped without changing the analysis.

[4] If $\alpha = 1$,

$$V_0 = [V_n(1 - t_k) + C_0 t_k + \sum_{i=1}^{n} t_k D_i](1 + r)^{-n} - \sum_{i=1}^{n} t_0 D_i(1 + r)^{-i}.$$

If $\alpha = 0$,

$$V_0 = [V_n(1 - t_k) + C_0 t_k](1 + r)^{-n}.$$

The advantage of deferring dividends ($\alpha = 0$) compared to current dividends ($\alpha = 1$) is:

$$\sum_{i=1}^{n} t_0 D_i(1 + r)^{-i} - t_k(1 - r)^{-n} \sum_{i=1}^{n} D_i.$$

Note that we do not need to know V_n to compute the advantage of deferring the dividends.

$$V_0 = [V_n(1 - t_k) + C_0 t_k + \sum_{i=1}^{n} \alpha t_k D_i](1 + r)^{-n} - \sum_{i=1}^{n} \alpha t_0 D_i(1 + r)^{-i}.$$

(8–3)

We can now see that the firm's dividend policy affects the value of shares in two ways: by reducing the capital gains tax burden at time n when the shares are sold, and by increasing taxes on dividends.

EXAMPLE: Let

$$r_e = .05$$

$$t_0 = .4, T_0 = .6, t_k = .25$$

$$r = T_0 r_e = .6 \times .05 = .03$$

$$D_1 = \$1.$$

$$D_i = (1 + r_e)^{i-1} = (1.05)^{i-1}$$

The difference in value arising from the dividend policy, assuming we are considering delaying dividends for three years ($n = 3$) so that the first dividend is four years from now, is:

$$P_0 - V_0 = \sum_{i=1}^{n} t_0 D_i(1 + r)^{-i} - t_k(1 + r)^{-n} \sum_{i=1}^{n} D_i.$$

i	D_i	$(1.03)^{-i}$	$D_i(1.03)^{-i}$	$t_0 D_i(1.03)^{-i}$
1	$D_1 = 1$	.9709	.9709	.3884
2	$D_2 = 1.05$	.9426	.9897	.3959
3	$D_3 = 1.1025$	.9151	1.0089	.4036

$\sum_{i=1}^{n} D_i = 3.1525$ 2.9695 $1.1879 = \sum_{i=1}^{n} t_0 D_i(1 + r)^{-i}$

$P_0 - V_0 = 1.1879 - .25 (.9151) 3.1525$

$= 1.1879 - .7212 = .4667$

Delaying the dividend payments for three years has a present value to the investor equivalent to $.4667 of the present dividend of $1.

If the personal income tax rate was .7 we would have

$$P_0 - V_0 = .7 \times 2.9695 - .25(.9151) 3.1525 = 2.0787 - .7212 = 1.3575.$$

The increase in value would be equal to 1.3575 times the current dividend of $1 if we delay the dividend payment for only three years. The amount would increase if we delayed for a longer period of time.

The extent to which the size of α influences share values depends to some extent on the magnitudes of t_o and t_k. If both are assumed to be zero, for example, Equation 8–3 becomes

$$V_0 = V_n(1 + r)^{-n}.$$

This is, of course, as it should be.[5] In a certain no-tax world the value of a firm that finances investments either by retained earnings or preemptive security issues is not influenced by the firm's dividend policy. Once taxes on capital gains and dividends are introduced, however, this is no longer the case. To the contrary, depending on the relative sizes on t_0 and t_k, and the magnitudes of n and r, the firm's dividend policy can have an important effect on share values. If $t_k < t_0$, and a firm has desirable investment opportunities, the value of the firm's shares will be increased by reducing dividends and using

TABLE 8–2[a].　Value of No Dividends ($\alpha = 0$) for N Periods Compared to Dividends Equal to Earnings ($\alpha = 1$)

The advantage of $\alpha = 0$ compared to $\alpha = 1$ is expressed in terms of multiples of a year's dividend of \$1.

n \ r_e	$t_0 = .4$　$t_k = .2$ .05	.10	.15
1	.1942	.1887	.1835
5	1.0654	1.1232	1.1720
20	5.7217	7.4064	9.1469

n \ r_e	$t_0 = .4$　$t_k = .4$ .05	.10	.15
1	0.0	0.0	0.0
5	.1121	.2108	.2956
20	2.0618	3.8345	5.4917

n \ r_e	$t_0 = .7$　$t_k = .25$ .05	.10	.15
1	.4433	.4369	.4306
5	2.4119	2.5757	2.7408
20	13.2625	19.3248	27.9569

[a] The computations for this table were done by Ernest Liu.

[5] See Miller and Modigliani, *ibid.*, for a comprehensive analysis of this situation.

internally generated funds.[6] Under these circumstances the shareholders' tax payments are both reduced and delayed. In the case where $t_k = t_0$, the shareholders' nominal tax payments will be the same regardless of the firm's dividend policy, however, it still pays to reduce present dividends when funds are needed by the firm as a result of the delaying of these payments. Indeed, there is even some range over which t_k can be greater than t_0, and it may still be reasonable to lower α in order to put off tax payments.

Table 8–2 illustrates the significance of the impact of dividend policy on common stock values. The table shows the changes in the value of a firm's shares resulting from a shift from $\alpha = 1$ to $\alpha = 0$; that is, from paying out all earnings to complete retention, for various sizes of n and r_e, t_k, and t_0.

For $r_e = .10$, for example, compared to paying current dividends, delaying dividend payments for five years (i.e., reinvesting earnings) has a present value to shareholders of 1.1232 times the firm's current dividends of $1 when $t_k = .2$ and $t_0 = .4$.[7] If the maximum rate on ordinary income of .7 were assumed, this figure would be 2.5757. With $t_0 = .7$, and delaying dividends for twenty years, the advantage is 19.3248 times the present dividend. With a current dividend of $10 per share the value of following this policy would be $193 per share.[8]

Some Complications

Up to this point we have been operating with a model having rather restrictive assumptions. In particular, we have been assuming that we have a certain world, and that, for tax or other reasons, all stockholders take up preemptive security offerings. Let us now relax these assumptions and see how our conclusions are affected.

Consider first the matter of uncertainty. In many discussions of dividend policy it is argued that under conditions of uncertainty an increase in a firm's dividend payout can be expected to increase share prices. We will not attempt to reproduce these arguments in detail here. In brief, however, they usually begin by assuming (1) that stockholders have risk aversion, and (2) that the uncertainty of a firm's dividends increases as the time of payment lengthens into the future, thus investors discount expected future dividends using higher interest rates. It is thus concluded that if shareholders are faced with the choice of a certain increase in current dividends ΔD or the possibility of an increase in future dividends whose present value is also ΔD, they will choose the former.

[6] We are not predicting the price per share but rather suggesting that the basic value of the stock to an investor will increase.

[7] The weighted average marginal tax rate has been computed to be 40%. See V. Jolivet, "Tax Rate on Dividends," *The American Economic Review* (June, 1966), p. 474.

[8] Compare with Miller and Modigliani, *ibid.*, p. 432.

In the class of cases we are discussing, however, the dividend policy is not altered by the shareholders' preferences for returns as between dividends today or dividends in the future. The dividend policy does affect the magnitude and timing of his tax payments. In particular, decreases in present dividends tend to reduce the size of tax payments. In a world of certainty these benefits permit us to make a strong case in favor of reducing a firm's payout ratio where funds are needed for investment, and if not retained these funds would be obtained from the stockholders. Under uncertainty, this case is if anything strengthened for a decrease in dividends results in a known reduction in current tax payment which is only partially offset by a smaller increase in the present value of a less certain future tax liability.

Some stockholders, however, may not choose to purchase their allotted share of the firm's preemptive issues, preferring instead to pocket current dividends and sell the rights. Retired individuals and tax exempt institutions, such as universities, are apt to eschew plowing back dividends into preemptive issues in favor of current consumption. And thus, they are not likely to appreciate a shift to greater retention of earnings instead of more generous dividends.

However, we do not believe that the presence of dividend preferring shareholders alters our basic conclusion that firms now combining dividends with preemptive security issues ought to consider retaining a greater portion of earnings. There is little reason to believe that these shareholders will lose, as a consequence of a decision to reduce dividend payments. To the contrary, they probably stand to gain. For a large portion of the firm's shareholders as well as other investors not yet holding stock in the firm, who desire to have their earnings reinvested there are good reasons to value shares more highly after dividends have been cut back. The dividend preferring shareholders could quite likely sell their holdings at attractive prices, reinvesting the proceeds in firms that have a high payout ratio.

We are not arguing that all firms should discontinue dividends payments. There is a place for a variety of payout policies. We are suggesting, however, that there may be a high cost for all firms to attempt to cater to the dividend and reinvestment preferences of an average stockholder. The firm that combines dividend payments with the issuance of preemptive securities, for example, is causing some of its stockholders to pay unnecessary taxes. The firm can argue that it gives its investors a choice about whether or not they want to reinvest their earnings, but it does so at a high cost in terms of the additional taxes paid by a large number of its investors as well as the increased underwriting fees incurred by the firm.

To avoid the misleading impression that we are suggesting that all firms should stop paying dividends, we will describe some advantages of cash dividends. The primary advantage is to the stockholder who desires cash. A dividend supplies cash without the investor incurring brokerage expense. If the corporation, in its efforts to obtain additional capital, issues rights, the stockholder desiring cash will incur some transaction cost in selling the rights, but this cost will be smaller than that incurred with the retention of 100% of the earnings. If cash is retained by the corporation the stockholder will have to sell a fraction of his holdings to obtain cash and this process will result in brokerage fees. Retired individuals living off their dividends and tax-free universities are apt to prefer dividend-paying corporations to corporations retaining income. While a 100% cash dividend has the advantage of giving cash to those investors who desire cash, the policy also results in cash being given to those investors who do not desire cash, and who must incur brokerage fees to reinvest the dividends. The retention of earnings gives the stockholders a form of optional dividend in that those desiring cash can sell their stock (incurring brokerage costs). Those wanting further investment merely hold their stock (with no transaction cost).

Our arguments in favor of retention of earnings do not require that all nvestors prefer retention of earnings, but that some fraction of the market has this preference. There is a need for securities that fit the investment preferences for a variety of investors. It would not be desirable for all corporations to pay 100% of their earnings as dividends, or for all corporations to retain 100% of their earnings. It may be desirable for some firms to follow these policies.

Another advantage of paying dividends is that it helps avoid conflict with Section 531 of the Internal Revenue Code. This section provides for penalties if retained earnings are kept by a corporation for the purpose of avoiding personal income taxes. The primary purpose of the retention must be to advance the legitimate objectives of the firm, not to reduce the tax payments of the investors. In this paper we are recommending a dividend policy for firms that have a need for funds to carry out the normal appropriate investment policies of the firm. The result of our suggestion will be to reduce the tax bill of the investors, but this is not the primary purpose of the reinvestment. Nevertheless, it should be recognized that a clearcut 100% payout of dividends is less likely to be questioned by the Internal Revenue Service than 100% retention of earnings.

The third advantage of a high-dividend payout is that it gives the stockholder a choice as to which corporations use his funds without having to sell his stock and incurring transaction costs. A corporation using retained earnings bypasses the market forces and this may not be desirable from the point of view of the economy (assuming a more efficient allocation of resources will result from investors deciding what firms should receive additional investment capital rather than leaving this decision in the hands of the corporate managers). The method of taxing dividends and capital gains plus the presence of the costs of security transactions lead to a tendency for the corporation to retain the capital it needs, rather than for it to go to the market to obtain this capital.

Stock Dividends

With a stock dividend the holders of common stock each receive additional shares equal to a given percentage of the shares currently held (the percentage must be small or the process is described as a stock split). One purpose of a stock dividend is to reduce the market price per share to a level that is more attractive to the market.

Stock dividends are redescriptions of the holdings of the stockholders, but are not distributions of the firm's assets, thus should not be cal'ᵈ ᵈʳidend. With a cash dividend the firm's cash and stockholders' equity are reduced by the amount of the dividend. With a stock dividend the stockholders' equity is not changed in total (individual components may be changed). If a stockholder holds 10% of the company before the stock dividend, he will hold 10% after the dividend. If he wanted to sell 5% of his holdings before the dividend, he could also sell 5% after the dividend. The number of shares involved would change, but not the basi; nature of the transactions.

Conclusions

A board of directors acting in the interests of the stockholders of a corporation must set the dividend policy of the firm. The distinction between ordinary income and capital gains for purpose of income taxation by the federal government accentuates the importance of the investor knowing the dividend policy of the firms whose stock he is considering purchasing or has already purchased. In turn, this means the corporation has a responsibility to announce its dividend policy.

In the particular situation where a firm is expanding its investments rapidly, and is financing this expansion by issuing securities to its stockholders, the payment of cash dividends is especially vulnerable to criticism.

Appendix

Derivation of the Dividend-Capital Gain Models

The symbols to be used are:

V_i value of a share of stock at time i assuming dividends of D_i are paid in all future periods

P_0 value of a share of stock at time zero assuming no dividends are paid until $n + 1$ periods

C_n tax cost basis of a share of stock at time n (C_0 is the cost at time zero and C_n is the cost at time n)

D_i dividend in period i
$$D_i = D_1 (1 + r_e)^{i-1}$$

t_0 tax rate on personal income

T_0 equal to $(1 - t_0)$
t_k capital gains rate
T_k equal to $(i - t_k)$
r_e minimum reinvestment rate of firm and before-tax rate of return available to an individual if he invests outside the firm (to simplify the development assume the marginal reinvestment rate for the firm equals the average)
r the after-tax rate of return available to an individual
$r = T_0 r_e$

Model 1 : Stock Presently Held by Investors

The firm invests an amount each period equal to D_i. If a dividend is paid, an amount equal to D_i will be obtained from the stockholders. If the firm retains D_i and pays no dividends then the stockholders do not have to make an explicit investment. The funds retained by the firm earn r_e. The stock is presently held by the investors, and we want to find the difference in value to the investor of two different dividend policies (1) paying D_i in cash dividends, (2) paying zero dividends for n periods to be followed by a dividend of D_{n+1} for perpetuity.

We will assume that a dividend has just been received and the policy being decided will affect the next dividend to be received one period from now.

If the firm pays dividends of D_i and invests D_i, the value of a share to a stockholder in the t_0 tax bracket is

$$V_0 = - \sum_{i=1}^{n} t_0 D_i (1 + r)^{-i} + [V_n - C_n)T_k + C_n](1 + r)^{-n},$$

where $\sum_{i=n}^{n} t_0 D_i (1 + r)^{-i}$ is the present value of the taxes on the dividends

$(V_n - C_n)$ is the capital gain and $(V_n - C_n)T_k$ is the amount remaining after tax
$(1 + r)^{-n}$ converts the capital gain of the nth period to a present value, assuming an after tax time value of money of r.
C_n is the tax basis of the stock and $C_n = C_0 + \sum_{i=1}^{n} D_i$.

If the firm pays no dividends for n periods and invests D_i each period, the value of a share is

$$P_0 = [(V_n - C_0)T_k + C_0](1 + r)^{-n}.$$

The difference between the values P_0 and V_0 is

$$P_0 - V_0 = [(V_n - C_0)T_k + C_0](1 + r)^{-n}$$
$$- [(V_n - C_n)T_k + C_n](1 + r)^{-n} + \sum_{i=1}^{n} t_0 D_i (1 + r)^{-i}.$$

Simplifying:

$$= t_k C_0 (1 + r)^{-n} - t_k C_n (1 + r)^{-n} + \sum_{i=1}^{n} t_0 D_i (1 + r)^{-i}.$$

Substituting $C_0 + \sum_{i=1}^{n} D_i$ for C_n,

$$P_0 - V_0 = t_k (1 + r)^{-n}(C_0 - C_0 - \sum_{i=1}^{n} D_i) + \sum_{i=1}^{n} t_0 D_i (1 + r)^{-i}$$

$$= \sum_{i=1}^{n} t_0 D_i (1 - r)^{-i} - t_k (1 + r)^{-n} \sum_{i=1}^{n} D_i.$$

An important advantage of this formulation is that V_n washes out when we compute the difference in the two values.

If desired we could estimate V_n assuming the dividend D_{n+1} continued for perpetuity.

$$V_n = \frac{(1 - t_0)D_{n+1}}{(1 - t_0)r_e} = \frac{D_{n+1}}{r_e}.$$

Since $D_{n+1} = D_1(1 + r_e)^n$, we have

$$V_n = \frac{D_1(1 + r_e)^n}{r_e}.$$

Model 2: Stock Not Presently Owned

We will now assume the stock is not presently owned by an investor, but he is considering investing and we want to find the share value, assuming zero dividends will be paid for n periods and assuming D_i dividends will be paid. The market price of a share is now C_0. Again we will assume the firm is investing D_i funds each period where

$$D_i = D_1(1 + r_e)^{i-1}.$$

If the firm pays dividends of D_i and invests D_i, the value of a share is

$$V_0 = [(V_n - C_0 - \sum_{i=1}^{n} D_i)(1 - t_k) + (C_0 + \sum_{i=1}^{n} D_i)](1 + r)^{-n}$$

$$- \sum_{i=1}^{n} t_0 D_i (1 + r)^{-i}.$$

If the firm pays no dividends,

$$P_0 = [(V_n - C_0)T_k + C_0](1 + r)^{-n}.$$

These are the same formulations as we found when the stock was held by investors (C_0 drops out when we find the difference in value). The difference in the value of the stock arising from dividend policy is independent of whether the stock is presently held or is being purchased. The value of a share is affected by the tax base of the share but the improvement in value arising from the dividend policy is not affected by the initial cost.

PROBLEMS

1. Assume you hold 100 shares of common stock in the XYZ Company. The company is considering paying you a $10 per share extra dividend or reinvesting the funds in the firm. If the funds are invested in the firm you can expect (based on expert analysis) an increase in the price per share of $10.

   Required: What would *you* want the firm to do?

2. The ABC Company is currently paying $10 per share cash dividends. The firm can reinvest funds internally to earn .10 after tax. The personal tax rate is .4 for ordinary income and .25 for capital gains. If the stockholders receive back the funds they can be reinvested to yield .10 (before tax). The company is considering postponing its $10 dividend due one year from now for two years and reinvesting the funds internally. Assume the stockholders' time value of money is .06.

   Required: (a) Compute the value to a stockholder of receiving $10 (1.10)^{i-1}$ dividends for the next three years ($i = 1, 2, 3$) using a .06 discount factor.

   (b) Compute the value to a stockholder of receiving a capital gain (assume the gain is taxed at .25; ignore the fact that this will not happen unless the stock is sold).

   (c) Compute the value of delaying the dividends for three years compared to obtaining the funds ($10, $11, and $12.10) for reinvestment from the present stockholders.

   (d) Compute the present value to the stockholders if the dividends are paid and amounts are obtained from the investors equal to $10 in year one, $11 in year two, 12.10 in year three.

3. Assume a company is currently paying $10 annually of dividends per share and taking $10 per year back from its stockholders for reinvestment. Assume the personal tax rate is .7 and the capital gains tax rate is .25. The firm and stockholders can earn .10 on invested funds.

   Required: What is the advantage per share of delaying dividends: one year, five years, and twenty years?

4. The United States Government has offered to assist a foreign government. It will lend $20 million for the construction of roads. The $20 million will be repaid forty years from now. For the first twenty years no interest will be paid; thereafter .03 interest will be paid per year (first payment twenty-one years from today). The long-term borrowing rate for the United States Government is .05. A Senate committee is investigating the cost of foreign aid. Prepare a statement for the committee.

REFERENCES

Brittain, J. A. *Corporate Dividend Policy* (The Brookings Institution, Washington, 1966).

Friend, I., and Puckett, M. "Dividends and Stock Prices," *American Economic Review* (September), 1964.

Gordon, M. J. "Dividend, Earnings and Stock Prices," *Review of Economics and Statistics* (August), 1962.

————. *The Investment, Financing, and Valuation of the Corporation* (Irwin, Homewood, Ill., 1962).

————. "Optimal Investment and Financing Policy," *Journal of Finance* (May), 1963.

Joliet, V. "Tax Rate on Dividends," *American Economic Review* (June), 1966.

Lintner, J. "Dividends, Earnings, Leverage, Stock Prices, and the Supply of Capital to Corporations," *Review of Economics and Statistics* (August), 1962.

Modigliani, F., and Miller, M. H. "Dividend Policy, Growth and the Valuation of Shares," *Journal of Business* (October), 1961.

Walter, J. "Dividend Policies and Common Stock Prices," *Journal of Finance* (March), 1956.

————. *Dividend Policy and Enterprise Valuation* (Wadsworth Publishing Co., Belmont, Calif., 1967).

CHAPTER 9

The Acquisition of Common Stock by the Corporate Issuer[1]

SYMBOLS

t_0	tax rate on ordinary income
α	the percentage of earnings paid as a dividend
D	earnings and dividends (if α is equal to 1)
r	discount rate
c_i	the cost of a share in the ith period
p	the price at which a share is repurchased

m	the number of shares retired in each period
n	the number of shares outstanding
t_k	the capital gains tax rate
V_0	the value of the firm at time zero
K	the tax basis of the stock

In the past decade major U.S. corporations have increasingly repurchased significant amounts of their own common shares. The reasons for this development and its implications for the theory of share valuation and for public policy, however, have been subject to numerous, and often conflicting, interpretations. This chapter presents a theoretical analysis of the economics of share repurchasing which leads to some fairly definite conclusions concerning the questions of share valuation and public policy.

The Background

It is not difficult to illustrate the dimensions to which corporate share repurchasing has recently grown. A survey of the repurchasing activities of companies listed on the New York Stock Exchange revealed that in 1963, for example, 132 firms "repurchased enough of their own common shares to account for 5% or more of the total trading in their securities."[2] Share re-

---

[1] This chapter is based on an article with the same title by Harold Bierman, Jr., and Richard West published in the December, 1966, issue of *The Journal of Finance*, pp. 687–696.

[2] Leo Guthart. "More Companies are Buying Back Their Stock," *Harvard Business Review*, Vol. 43, No. 2 (March–April, 1965), p. 40.

purchasing was, in fact, such a popular corporate activity in 1963 that "the total dollars spent by companies to buy back their common shares was 30% greater than the amount which they raised through (new) equity issues."[3] Moreover, in both 1964 and 1965 manufacturing, commercial and transportation corporations continued to be net purchasers of stock.[4]

The growth of corporate share repurchasing has aroused considerable interest, and a number of explanations of the motivation behind this activity have been suggested. It has been argued, for example, that firms sometimes buy back their own shares to have them available to acquire other companies or to fulfill the obligations of stock option plans.[5] Unquestionably, some repurchasing has been done for these reasons. Income tax considerations may make it possible for firms to acquire other companies more cheaply for stock than for cash, and use of stock options as a form of executive compensation has been widespread. However, it seems quite unlikely that the rapid growth of share repurchasing in recent years can be explained by merger and stock option plans. Most importantly, there is no essential reason why shares used for these purposes should be repurchased, rather than newly issued. Also, the chronologies of merger and stock option activities have not paralleled the growth of share repurchasing with sufficient regularity to indicate a causal relationship between these developments. The postwar merger movement was in full swing long before corporations began buying back their own shares in significant amounts, and the decline in the attractiveness of stock option plans because of the changes in the tax code has not been accompanied by a reduction in the amount of repurchasing.[6]

Corporations also repurchase shares with the intention of retiring them, or, at least, holding them indefinitely in the treasury. Several motives for such repurchasing activities have been suggested, virtually all relating the repurchase of the shares to the generation of liquid assets which cannot be profitably invested by the firm in the foreseeable future. In particular, it has been suggested that firms with "redundant" liquid assets have one or more of the following motives to repurchase shares:

1. Repurchasing shares is the best investment that can be made with these assets.[7]

[3] James Fleck. "Corporate Share Repurchasing: An Informal Discussion," *Harvard Business School Bulletin,* Vol. 41, No. 1 (January–February, 1965), p. 10.

[4] The net change for all corporations during these years, however, was positive due to the sales of new securities by public utilities and real estate and investment companies. For more detail on this point, see the *Federal Reserve Bulletin* (May, 1966), p. 716.

[5] Eugene Brigham. "The Profitability of a Firm's Repurchase of Its Own Common Stock," *California Management Review,* Vol. VII, No. 2 (Winter, 1964), p. 69, and Charles Ellis. "Repurchase Shares to Revitalize Equity," *Harvard Business Review,* Vol. 43, No. 4 (July–August, 1965), p. 120.

[6] On these points see, *The Wall Street Journal,* August 10, 1964, p. 1, *Business Week,* January 11, 1964, p. 104.

[7] Brigham, *op cit.*, p. 69.

2. Repurchasing shares has beneficial leverage effects which cannot be obtained by distributing these assets to stockholders in another form, such as dividends.[8]

3. Repurchasing shares, rather than paying dividends, has significant tax advantages for stockholders.[9]

In view of the fact that U.S. corporations have experienced an unprecedented growth in liquidity over roughly the same period that stock repurchasing has flourished,[10] the explanations listed above merit consideration. Is a firm's purchase of its own common stock an investment? Does a firm repurchase stock to produce leverage effects not otherwise attainable? What are the tax advantages associated with buying back shares?

The next section is devoted to a discussion of the investment and leverage questions. In brief, we shall argue that repurchasing is *not* an investment and does not produce "special" leverage effects. We then shall consider the argument that repurchasing shares can have beneficial tax effects for stockholders. After explaining why the tax benefits are great, we shall consider the implications of share repurchasing for the theory of share valuation and for public policy.

Share Repurchasing as an Investment and as a Means of Influencing Capital Structure

In this section we shall examine the logic underlying the arguments that when a firm is generating more cash than it can profitably invest internally, share repurchasing (a) is itself a good investment, and (b) can have beneficial leverage effects.

1. *The Investment Question.* The argument that share repurchasing involves some sort of investment seems widely held. The following statements, for example, have recently been made:

1. "The repurchase of its own stock by a company is an investment decision—plain and simple."[11]

---

[8] *Ibid.*

[9] Alexander Robichek and Stewart Myers. *Optimal Financing Decisions*, Prentice-Hall, 1966, p. 133.

[10] Ernest Bloch. "Short Cycles in Corporate Demand for Government Securities," *American Economic Review*, Vol. LIII, No. 5 (December, 1963), pp. 1058–1077. William Frazer. "Large Manufacturing Corporations as Suppliers of Funds to the Government Securities Market," *Journal of Finance*, Vol. XIII, No. 4 (December, 1958), pp. 499–509. Donald Jacobs. "The Marketable Securities Portfolios of Nonfinancial Corporations: Investment Practices and Trends," *Journal of Finance*, Vol. XV, No. 3 (September, 1960), pp. 340–355.

[11] C. A. Rundell. "From the Thoughtful Businessman," *Harvard Business Review*, Vol. 43, No. 6 (November–December, 1965), p. 39.

2. "It is apparent that the *investment* of substantial sums in a company's own stock, beyond the amount required for stock options or acquisitions, is essentially a negative act which is inconsistent with constructive and aggressive management."[12]

3. "One of the clearest signals the management could give to him (the shareholder) is 'We think this (share repurchasing) is the best *investment* we can make. We have no other alternative investments for our cash.'"[13]

Share repurchasing does not possess the same general characteristics as other acts of investment, e.g., purchasing plant and equipment. Normal investments keep the size of the firm intact or increase it, and either have no effect on the stockholders' equity balance or the number of shares outstanding, or increase them. A firm's acquisition of its own common stock, on the other hand, reduces the size of the enterprise. In particular, the cash balance is decreased, the stockholders' equity balance is reduced, and the number of shares outstanding is cut back. In short, repurchasing shares has few characteristics which identify it as a normal investment.

2. Repurchasing and Leverage. In a recent article, Charles Ellis argued that firms with redundant liquid assets should "Repurchase Stock to Revitalize Equity." Ellis noted that over the past decade a growing number of major U.S. companies have replaced cheap senior capital with expensive equity funds. This development, he stated, has created "unused debt capacity" and higher than necessary capital costs. His solution was for firms to regain an "optimal capital structure" by buying back their own shares and retiring them.[14]

If we accept the argument that with the present tax code there is an optimal capital structure, we are still faced with the question: why repurchase shares to change the debt/equity ratio, rather than pay dividends? Buying back stock involves no changes in capital structure that could not also be obtained by combining a dividend payment with a reverse stock split.[15] Both procedures have the effect of distributing cash to stockholders, reducing the firm's capitalization, and the number of outstanding shares, increasing its earnings per share, and thereby raising stock price per share (compared to what it would have been if the number of shares had not been reduced).[16]

[12] Gordon Donaldson. "From the Thoughtful Businessman," *Harvard Business Review*, Vol. 43, No. 4 (July–August, 1965), p. 31.

[13] Warren Law as quoted in Fleck, *op. cit.*, p. 13.

[14] Ellis, *ibid.*, pp. 119–128.

[15] To be sure, the repurchase eliminates the need to make the reverse stock split. However, in view of the fact that there is little evidence to suggest that simply changing the number of shares outstanding has a significant effect on the real value of the firm, this point seems somewhat trivial.

[16] Ellis, *ibid.*, p. 122, states "while higher dividends probably are the most attractive method for distributing a moderately and consistently increasing surplus of cash flow, they are not always appropriate when the surplus arises in a sporadic pattern of large amounts." This position, however, ignores the possibility of firms paying "special" or "extra" dividends, a possibility that some firms, such as General Motors, use on occasion.

Summing up, our analysis thus far suggests it is unlikely the recent growth in share repurchasing can be accounted for on the grounds that it has been done (a) to provide shares to be used for mergers or stock options, (b) to "invest" redundant liquid assets, or (c) to produce changes in leverage.[17]

Taxes and Share Repurchasing

In several recent publications it has been suggested that the current tax laws provide powerful incentives for firms with redundant liquid assets to repurchase shares, rather than pay dividends.[18] However, these arguments and their implications for the theory of share valuation and public policy have not been fully developed.

1. *Tax Benefits to Shareholders.* Under the present tax structure many persons prefer capital gains to ordinary income. The reason for their preference is that the marginal rate of taxation on ordinary income can range as high as 70%, while the rate on long-term capital gains is only one-half that on ordinary income, up to a maximum of 25%.[19]

Consider now a corporation with excess liquid assets that it desires to pay out in the form most attractive from its shareholders' point of view. If it distributes them as dividends, they will represent ordinary income to shareholders, and will be taxed accordingly. If, on the other hand, the corporation buys back shares, a portion of its distribution will be regarded as a return to the shareholders' capital and will not be taxed at all, while that portion of the return which is taxed, i.e., the capital gain, will be subject to a lower rate than ordinary income. In addition, the investor who merely wants to reinvest is not taxed at all since he does not sell his stock.

Given these incentives for returning cash to stockholders by repurchasing shares, a relevant question would seem to be: Why do firms ever pay dividends? We suspect that the answer is related to the attitude of the Internal Revenue Service toward share repurchasing. The current Internal Revenue Code clearly seeks to prohibit firms from disguising dividends in the form of share repurchases.[20] Proportional repurchases, for example, are treated the same as dividends for tax purposes. Thus, if firms began to make all distribu-

---

[17] It is highly likely that some purchases take place in order for one group of investors to take advantage of insider information. Lacking the resources to buy the stock themselves they use the corporation as the vehicle for making their investment. Another reason for purchase is that one group of stockholders currently controlling the corporation may seek to retain control. Again, lacking the financial resources as individuals they use the corporation's resources to attain their own objective. We consider both of these reasons for purchase to result in improper activities by a corporation. The possibility of these situations developing is a cost of allowing corporations to repurchase their own shares.

[18] Brigham, *op. cit.*, pp. 69–75, and Robichek and Myers, *op. cit.*, p. 133.

[19] Dividends and capital gains accruing to some stockholders are not taxed at all.

[20] On this point see Internal Revenue Code, Sec. 302.

tions in the form of share repurchases, they would almost certainly bring forth a response from the IRS.

But, why then have firms begun to repurchase shares in increasing amounts? One possible rationalization is that they feel they can defend their recent activities on non-tax grounds, e.g., on the grounds that they are making investments or simply adjusting leverage.

2. *Repurchasing and Share Valuation.* We have argued that tax considerations are an important explanation of corporate repurchasing of stock. It is desirable for us to attempt to specify how a firm's decision to repurchase stock rather than pay dividends might be expected to influence share prices.

We shall now consider how the choice of the form of a company's cash distribution (as between dividends and share repurchasing) influences stock valuation in a world where ordinary personal income and capital gains are both taxed. Assume that all individuals are subject to a personal income tax rate of t_0, and that our firm distributes earnings of αD dollars per period as dividends. If $\alpha = 1$ the dividends equal the earnings and the value of the firm's common stock at the beginning of the current period will be

$$V_0 = \sum_{i=0}^{\infty} (1 - t_0)D(1 + r)^{-(i+1)} = \frac{(1 - t_0)D}{r}. \qquad (9\text{--}1)$$

Now assume that the firm announces it will distribute its earnings by repurchasing stock rather than paying dividends. Furthermore, let us assume (1) present shareholders desire to keep their percentage ownership interest in the firm intact over time, and thus, each period sell a proportion of their holdings equal to the proportion of the total shares retired; and (2) immediately following its share repurchasing, the firm declares a stock dividend large enough to replace the shares retired; that is, the number of shares outstanding at the beginning of any period n is constant.

Given these assumptions, we can now write[21]

$$V_0 = \sum_{i=0}^{\infty} [c_i + (p - c_i)(1 - t_k)]m(1 + r)^{-(1+i)}, \qquad (9\text{--}2)$$

where t_k = the tax rate on capital gains

$\quad c_i$ = the cost basis of a share retired in the ith period (i.e., the return of capital implicit in the share retired)

$\quad p$ = the price at which a share is repurchased (the same in all periods due to the assumptions of constant earnings per period, and of the declaration of a stock dividend to replace repurchased shares)

---

[21] Derivations of the equations in this section can be found in the Appendix 1 at the end of this chapter.

$m =$ the number of shares retired each period (also the same for all periods)

Substituting $p\left(1 - \dfrac{m}{n}\right)^i$ for c_i in Equation 9–2, we have

$$V_0 = \sum_{i=0}^{\infty} \left[p\left(1 - \frac{m}{n}\right)^i + p\left[1 - \left(1 - \frac{m}{n}\right)^i\right](1 - t_k)\right] m(1 + r)^{-(1+i)}.$$

$$(9\text{--}3)$$

Further substitutions, summing of several infinite series, and simplification yields

$$V_0 = \frac{D}{2} \left[\left(1 + \frac{4(1 + r - t_k)}{r^2}\right)^{1/2} - 1\right] \qquad (9\text{--}4)$$

A comparison of Equations 9–1 and 9–4 reveals that in a world in which capital gains and ordinary income are accorded different tax treatment, the value of the firm's stock is influenced by the form of its cash distribution. A better idea of how the form of the distribution affects share valuation can be obtained by assuming a constant capital gains tax rate and computing the breakeven rate on ordinary income (i.e., the rate at which investors would be indifferent between having the firm pay dividends or repurchase shares). Assuming that capital gains are taxed at a rate of .25, the break-even rate of taxation on ordinary income (dividends) would approximate .15. In other words, given a .25 tax rate on capital gains, investors would prefer to have firms repurchase shares as long as ordinary income was taxed at more than .15.[22] The higher tax rate on capital gains is preferred since part of the cash distribution (equal to the tax basis) is not taxed at all. It should be noted that the models presented above could be adjusted to include fluctuating corporate earnings, various payout ratios, a progressive income tax, uncertainty, etc. Naturally, such adjustments would significantly complicate the mathematical statement of the problem and alter somewhat the relative attractiveness of share repurchasing and dividend payments. There are two factors at work, however, that cause buying back shares to be more profitable than dividend payments (from the stockholders' point of view) under any reasonable set of assumptions that includes taxation of income. For one thing, part of the distribution under the share repurchasing arrangement is considered a return of capital and is not taxed at all. Second, that part of the distribution subject to tax (i.e., the capital gain) is generally taxed at a lower rate than ordinary income.

Let $t_0 = .7$, $t_k = .25$, and $r = .04$.

---

[22] A stronger statement could be made since only .5 of long-term capital gains are taxed (with a maximum rate of .25 on the total gain).

Assume constant dividends (cash distributions) of $1 million per year, the first distribution being due one period from now.

Assuming cash dividends:

$$V_0 = \frac{(1 - .7)}{.04} (1,000,000) = \$7,500,000.$$

If shares are reacquired, instead of a cash dividend:

$$V_0 = \frac{1,000,000}{2} \left[\left[1 + \frac{4(1.04 - .25)}{.04^2} \right]^{1/2} - 1 \right]$$

$$= 500,000 \ [(2226)^{1/2} - 1] = 500,000 \times 46.2$$

$$= \$23,000,000.$$

Stock Acquisitions: A Flexible Dividend

One real tax advantage of stock acquisitions in lieu of cash dividends is that an investor who does not want to convert his investment into cash does not sell his stock back to the corporation. By not selling he avoids realization of the capital gain and does not have any taxation on the increment to the value of his wealth (he also avoids transaction costs).

The investor who wants to receive cash sells a portion of his holdings, and even though he pays tax on his gain it is apt to be less than if the cash distribution was taxed as ordinary income. By using stock acquisition as the means of the cash distribution the company tends to direct the cash to those investors who want the cash and bypass the investors who do not need cash at the present time.

Conclusions

Two public policy questions concerning corporate share repurchasing become apparent. First, should firms be allowed to buy back their own shares, and, if so, should they be required to give stockholders advance notice of their intentions for the future?

We have shown that repurchasing shares can have a significant impact on the after-tax returns of stockholders. Should the form of the firm's distribution, rather than its substance, influence the amount of taxes paid by stockholders? It seems clear that as more and more firms become aware of the advantages of repurchasing shares compared with paying dividends, this issue will have to be faced.

Should corporations that decide to repurchase shares be required to notify stockholders of their intentions? We have shown that the value of the firm's stock is a function of the form of its cash distributions. Thus it seems reasonable that shareholders should be advised of a company's distribution policy, and of changes in that policy. The corporation that repurchases shares without giving its stockholders advance notice is implicitly, if not explicitly, penalizing those who sell their shares without this information.

Appendix 1

The Valuation of a Firm Using Share Reacquisition

Consider a corporation that has D dollars per period available for distribution, has no profitable internal investment opportunities, and must decide whether to pay out all of D as dividends, or use some of it to buy shares. How will its decision affect the value of the firm's shares? Let us assume that (1) all shareholders are subject to the same tax rates on ordinary income and capital gains, (2) the firm makes known its intentions concerning paying dividends and repurchasing shares, and (3) the value of the common stock is equal to the present value of the firm's total cash distributions (after taxes). If we assume further that immediately following repurchasing, the firm declares a stock dividend large enough to replace the shares bought back, we can write

$$V_0 = \sum_{i=0}^{\infty} [c_i + (p - c_i)(1 - t_k)]m(1 + r)^{-(1+i)}$$

$$+ \sum_{i=0}^{\infty} (1 - t_0)\alpha D(1 + r)^{-(1+i)}, \quad (A-1)$$

where D = dollars available for distribution

V_0 = value of the firm's shares at the beginning of any period

c_i = cost basis of the shares retired in the ith period (i.e., the return of capital associated with the shares retired)

p = price per share at the time of share repurchasing (i.e., at the end of every period)

t_k = rate of taxation on capital gains

t_0 = rate of taxation on ordinary income

m = number of shares retired in each period

α = percentage of the company's earnings paid out as dividends, thus $(1 - \alpha)$ is percentage used to repurchase shares

r = rate of interest

We also can write

$$c_1 = c_0 - c_0 \frac{m}{n} = c_0\left(1 - \frac{m}{n}\right), \qquad \text{(A–2)}$$

where, n = number of shares at the beginning of any period.
   Continuing,

$$c_2 = c_1 - c_1 \frac{m}{n} = c_1\left(1 - \frac{m}{n}\right). \qquad \text{(A–3)}$$

Substituting,

$$c_2 = c_0\left(1 - \frac{m}{n}\right) - c_0\left(1 - \frac{m}{n}\right)\frac{m}{n} = c_0\left(1 - \frac{m}{n}\right)^2. \qquad \text{(A–4)}$$

Once more,

$$c_3 = c_2 - c_2\frac{m}{n} - c_0\left(1 - \frac{m}{n}\right)^2 - c_0\left(1 - \frac{m}{n}\right)^2\frac{m}{n} = c_0\left(1 - \frac{m}{n}\right)^3. \qquad \text{(A–5)}$$

To generalize,

$$c_i = c_0\left(1 - \frac{m}{n}\right)^i. \qquad \text{(A–6)}$$

If we assume

$$c_0 = p,$$

$$c_i = p\left(1 - \frac{m}{n}\right)^i. \qquad \text{(A–7)}$$

Substituting $p(1 - m/n)^i$ for c_i in Equation (A–1) yields,

$$V_0 = \sum_{i=0}^{\infty} \left[p\left(1 - \frac{m}{n}\right)^i + p\left(1 - \left(1 - \frac{m}{n}\right)^i\right)(1 - t_k)\right]m(1 + r)^{-(1+i)}$$

$$+ \sum_{i=0}^{\infty} (1 - t_0)\alpha D(1 + r)^{-(1+i)}. \qquad \text{(A–8)}$$

If we let $s = (1 - m/n)$,

$$V_0 = mp \sum_{i=0}^{\infty} [s^i + (1 - s^i)(1 - t_k)](1 + r)^{-(1+i)}$$

$$+ \sum_{i=0}^{\infty} (1 - t_0)\alpha D(1 + r)^{-(1+i)}. \qquad \text{(A–9)}$$

Since $D(1 - \alpha) = mp$, we have

$$V_0 = D(1 - \alpha) \sum_{i=0}^{\infty} [s^i + (1 - s^i)(1 - t_k)](1 + r)^{-(1+i)}$$

$$+ \sum_{i=0}^{\infty} (1 - t_0)\alpha D(1 + r)^{-(1+i)}. \quad \text{(A–10)}$$

Summing the infinite series[23] yields

$$V_0 = D(1 - \alpha)\left[\frac{1}{1 + r - s} + \frac{1 - t_k}{r} - \frac{1 - t_k}{1 + r - s}\right] + \frac{(1 - t_0)\alpha D}{r}$$

$$= D(1 - \alpha)\left[\frac{1 - t_k}{r} + \frac{t_k}{1 + r - s}\right] + \frac{(1 - t_0)\alpha D}{r}. \quad \text{(A–11)}$$

We can illustrate the effect of varying the size of α by referring to Equation A–11. As this equation makes clear, the size of α affects the value of shares in two conflicting ways—directly via its impact on the dividend component, $[(1 - t_0)D\alpha]/r$, and inversely via its influence on the repurchasing component, $D(1 - \alpha)[(1 - t_k)/r + t_k/(1 + r - s)]$. If the firm chooses to pay out a smaller proportion of its earnings in the form of dividends, how will share values be affected? The answer depends on the relationship between t_k and t_0. If $t_k \leqslant t_0$, and assuming perfect information and capital markets, the value of the firm's shares will be increased by having a policy of reducing α (i.e., by paying smaller dividends in the future and increasing the number of shares repur-

---

[23] We have to sum the several infinite series:

$$s^i(1 + r)^{-(1+i)} = s^i\left(\frac{1}{1 + r}\right)^i\left(\frac{1}{1 + r}\right) = \left(\frac{s}{1 + r}\right)^i\left(\frac{1}{1 + r}\right),$$

$$\sum_{i=0}^{\infty} \left(\frac{s}{1 - r}\right)^i\left(\frac{1}{1 + r}\right) = \frac{1}{1 + r}\left[\frac{1}{1 - (s/(1 + r))}\right] = \frac{1}{1 + r - s}.$$

Also

$$(1 - t_k) \sum_{i=0}^{\infty} (1 - s^i)(1 + r)^{-(1+i)}$$

$$= (1 - t_k)\left[\sum_{i=0}^{\infty} (1 + r)^{-(1+i)} - \sum_{i=0}^{\infty} s^i(1 + r)^{-(1+i)}\right]$$

$$= \left[\frac{(1 - t_k)}{(1 + r)} \times \frac{1}{1 - (1/(1 + r))}\right] - \frac{1 - t_k}{1 + r}\left[\frac{1}{1 - s/(1 + r)}\right]$$

$$= \left(\frac{1 - t_k}{1 + r - 1}\right) - \left(\frac{1 - t_k}{1 + r - s}\right)$$

$$= \frac{1 - t_k}{r} - \frac{1 - t_k}{1 + r - s}.$$

Finally,

$$\sum_{i=0}^{\infty} (1 - t_0)\alpha D(1 + r)^{-(1+i)} = \frac{(1 - t_0)\alpha D}{r}.$$

chased). Even if the tax rate on capital gains were greater than the rate on ordinary income, it may pay to repurchase shares, since the stockholders' return of capital is not taxed at all.

Letting $\alpha = 0$ substituting $V_0/(V_0 + D)$ for s and simplifying, we have the quadratic equation:[24]

$$r^2 V_0^2 + r^2 D V_0 + (t - r - 1)D^2 = 0 \qquad \text{(A-12)}$$

Solving for V_0:

$$V_0 = \frac{D}{2}\left[\left(1 + \frac{4(1 + r - t_k)}{r^2}\right)^{1/2} - 1\right]. \qquad \text{(A-13)}$$

On the other hand, if $\alpha = 1$, we have,

$$V_0 = \frac{D(1 - t_0)}{r}. \qquad \text{(A-14)}$$

As an examination of Equations (A-13 and A-14) reveals, the value of the firm's shares is a function of the amount of the earnings available for distribution, the rate of interest, the form in which earnings are distributed (i.e., the breakdown between dividends and share repurchasing), and the rates of taxation on ordinary income and capital gains.

If we assume that there are no taxes on either ordinary income or capital gains, Equations A-13 and A-14 become $V_0 = D/r$.

In other words, in a no-tax world the value of the firm's shares is not influenced by the way in which returns are distributed to shareholders (i.e., by the size of α). Without taxes, share values are a function of the stream of earnings available for distribution and the rate of interest at which those earnings are capitalized. Since the policy of repurchasing stock rather than paying dividends influences neither of these factors, it would not affect share valuation in the absence of taxation. As Miller and Modigliani observed several years ago, "There are no financial illusions in a rational and perfect economic environment. Values there are determined solely by real considerations... and not by how the fruits of the (firm's) earning power are 'packaged' for distribution."[25] Once taxes on ordinary income and capital gains are introduced, however, the value of α has a significant influence on share valuation.

[24] We know from equation (9) that $s = (1 - m/n)$. Since $mp = D(1 - \alpha)$, $m = D(1 - \alpha)/p$. Let V be the value of the stock at the end of the period. $V = np$ and $p = V/n$. Substituting for $p: m = nD(1 - \alpha)/V$. And if we assume $V = V_0 + D$, $m = nD(1 - \alpha)/(V_0 + D)$; substituting $nD(1 - \alpha)/(V_0 + D)$ for m in the expression $s = (1 - m/n)$ yields, $s = (V_0 + \alpha D)/(V_0 + D)$. If $\alpha = 0$ we have $s = V_0/(V_0 + D)$. The assumption that $V = V_0 + D$ is a simplification. In fact, the value should not rise by the exact amount that is paid out, but rather should be closer to:

$$V = V_0 + D(1 - \alpha)(1 - t_k) + D(1 - t_0)\alpha.$$

[25] Modigliani and Miller, "Dividend Policy, Growth and the Valuation of Shares," *Journal of Business*, Vol. XXXIV, No. 4 (October, 1961), p. 413.

Appendix 2

The Acquisition of Common Stock: Other Models

We have assumed the cost base of the stock is p (the price immediately before a cash distribution) with n shares outstanding, where $p = V/n$ and $V = V_0 + D$. The next cash distribution is one period from the moment of valuation.

An alternative interpretation is to assume that we will buy immediately before their next cash distribution one period from now. Thus we are computing the value one period prior to purchase.

The first model assumed that $V = V_0 + D$. We will now assume that $V = V_0 + D(1 - t_k)$, where t_k is the capital gains tax rate:

$$V_0 = D\left[\frac{1 - t_k}{r} + \frac{t_k}{1 + r - s}\right]$$

$$mp = D \qquad np = V$$

$$m = D/p \qquad n = V/p$$

$$s = (1 - m/n) = (1 - D/V)$$

$$1 + r - s = 1 + r - 1 + \frac{D}{V} = r + \frac{D}{V} = \frac{rV + D}{V}$$

$$V_0 = D\left[\frac{(1 - t_k)\dfrac{(rV + D)}{V} + t_k r}{r\left(\dfrac{rV + D}{V}\right)}\right]$$

$$r\left(\frac{rV + D}{V}\right)V_0 = D\left[(1 - t_k)\frac{(rV + D)}{V} + t_k r\right]$$

$$(r^2 V + rD)V_0 = D[(1 - t_k)(rV + D) + t_k rV]$$

$$= DrV + D^2 - Drt_k V - t_k D^2 + Drt_k V$$

$$= DrV + D^2 - t_k D^2.$$

We are assuming that $V = V_0 + D(1 - t_k)$.

$$r^2 V_0^2 + r^2 DV_0 - r^2 t_k DV_0 + rDV_0 = rDV_0 + D^2 r - D^2 t_k r + D^2 - t_k D^2$$

$$r^2 V_0^2 + r^2 D(1 - t_k)V_0 + D^2(rt_k - r + t_k - 1) = 0$$

$$V_0^2 + D(1 - t_k)V_0 + \frac{D^2}{r^2}(rt_k - r + t_k - 1) = 0$$

$$V_0 = \frac{-D(1 - t_k) + \left[D^2(1 - t_k)^2 - 4\dfrac{D^2}{r^2}(t_k - 1)(r + 1)\right]^{1/2}}{2}$$

If $t_k = 0$ (no taxes):

$$V_0 = \frac{-D}{2} + \frac{1}{2}\left[D^2 + 4\frac{D^2}{r^2}(r+1)\right]^{1/2}$$

$$= \frac{-D}{2} + \frac{D}{2r}[r^2 + 4r + 4]^{1/2} = \frac{-D}{2} + \frac{D}{2r}(r+2) = \frac{-rD + Dr + 2D}{2r}$$

$$= \frac{D}{r}.$$

EXAMPLE: $D = \$1,000,000$; $r = .04$; $t_k = .25$

$$V_0 = \frac{-750,000 + 1,000,000\left[.5625 - \frac{1}{.0004}(-.75 \times 1.04)\right]^{1/2}}{2}$$

$$= \frac{-750,000 + 10^6}{2}[.5625 - 1950]^{1/2}$$

$$= \frac{-750,000 + 10^0}{2}[44.16]$$

$$= (-750,000 + 44,160,000)\tfrac{1}{2} = \tfrac{1}{2}(43,410,000)$$

$$= \$21,700,000.$$

The Cost Basis Is p_0

Assume the cost basis of the stock being acquired is p_0 (the value immediately after a cash dividend). We must wait one period for the next cash distribution.

$$V_0 = \sum_{i=0}^{\infty}[p_0 s^i + (p - p_0 s^i)(1 - t_k)]m(1 + r)^{-(1+i)}$$

$$= \sum_{i=0}^{\infty}[p(1 - t_k) + p_0 s^i t_k]m(1 + r)^{-(1+i)}$$

$$= m(1 - t_k)\sum_{i=0}^{\infty}p(1 + r)^{-(1+i)} + mt_k\sum_{i=0}^{\infty}p_0 s^i(1 + r)^{-(1+i)}$$

$$= \frac{m(1 - t_k)p}{(1 + r)} \times \left(\frac{1}{1 - \frac{1}{1+r}}\right) + mt_k p_0\sum_{i=0}^{\infty}\left(\frac{s}{1+r}\right)^i\left(\frac{1}{1+r}\right)$$

$$= \frac{m(1 - t_k)p}{1 + r} \times \frac{1 + r}{r} + mtp_0\frac{1}{1 + r - s}$$

$$= \frac{m(1 - t_k)p}{r} + \frac{mt_kp_0}{1 + r - s}$$

$$= m \left[\frac{(1 - t_k)p}{r} + \frac{t_kp_0}{1 + r - s} \right].$$

Assume $p = p_0 + D/n(1 - t_k)$ $V = V_0 + D(1 - t_k)$

$$s = \left(\frac{1 - D}{V} \right)$$

$$1 + r - s = 1 + r - 1 + \frac{D}{V} = r + \frac{D}{V} = \frac{rV + D}{V}$$

$$p = \frac{V}{n} \quad \text{and} \quad p_0 = \frac{V_0}{n}.$$

$$V_0 = m \left[\frac{(1 - t_k)V}{nr} + \frac{t_kV_0}{n(r + D/V)} \right]$$

$$= \frac{m}{n} \left[\frac{(1 - t_k)V}{r} + \frac{t_kV_0}{(r + D/V)} \right]$$

$$V_0 = \frac{D}{V} \left[\frac{(1 - t_k)V\left(r + \dfrac{D}{V}\right) + rt_kV_0}{r\left(r + \dfrac{D}{V}\right)} \right]$$

$$r\left(r + \frac{D}{V}\right)V_0 = \frac{D}{V} \left[(1 - t_k)V\left(r + \frac{D}{V}\right) + rt_kV_0 \right]$$

$$(r^2V + rD)V_0 = D \left[(1 - t_k)V\left(r + \frac{D}{V}\right) + rt_kV_0 \right]$$

$$(r^2V_0 + r^2D(1 - t_k) + rD)V_0 = D[rV + D - trV - Dt_k + rt_kV_0]$$

$$r^2V_0^2 + r^2D(1 - t_k)V_0 + rDV_0$$
$$= D[(r - t_kr)(V_0 + D(1 - t_k)) + D - Dt_k + rt_kV_0]$$

$$r^2V_0^2 + r^2DV_0 - r^2Dt_kV_0 + \underline{\underline{rDV_0}} = \underline{\underline{rDV_0}} - t_krDV_0 + rD^2(1 - t_k)$$
$$- t_krD^2(1 - t_k) + D^2 - D^2t_k + \underline{rDt_kV_0}$$

$$r^2V_0^2 + r^2D(1 - t_k)V_0 = D^2[r(1 - t_k) - tr(1 - t_k) + (1 - t_k)]$$

$$r^2V_0^2 + r^2D(1 - t_k)V_0 - D^2(1 - t_k)(r - t_kr + 1) = 0$$

$$V_0^2 + D(1 - t_k)V_0 - \frac{D^2}{r^2}(1 - t_k)(r - t_kr + 1) = 0$$

$$V_0 = \frac{-D(1 - t_k) + \left[D^2(1 - t_k)^2 + 4\frac{D^2}{r^2}(1 - t_k)(r - t_k r + 1)\right]^{1/2}}{2}.$$

If $t_k = 0$ (no taxes),

$$V_0 = \frac{-D + [D^2 + 4(D^2/r^2)(1)(r + 1)]^{1/2}}{2}$$

$$= \frac{-D}{2} + \frac{D}{2r}[r^2 + 4r + 4]^{1/2} = \frac{-rD + D(r + 2)}{2r}$$

$$= \frac{D}{r}.$$

EXAMPLE: $D = \$1,000,000$; $r = .04$; $t_k = .25$

$$V_0 = \frac{-D(1 - t_k)}{2} + \frac{D}{2}\left[(1 - t_k)^2 + \frac{4}{r^2}(1 - t_k)(r - t_k r + 1)\right]^{1/2}$$

$$= -500,000\,(.75) + 500,000\left[.75^2 + \frac{1}{.0004}(.75)(1.04 - .01)\right]^{1/2}$$

$$= -375,000 + 500,000\,[.75(.75 + 2,575)]^{1/2}$$

$$= -375,000 + 500,000\,[1,931.81]^{1/2}$$

$$= -375,000 + 500,000\,(43.9)$$

$$= -375,000 + 21,950,000 = \$21,575,000.$$

The General Case

Instead of assuming that the cost basis is p where $p = V/n$ and $V = V_0 + D(1 - t)$, we will now generalize the solution and assume the cost basis is K. We are valuing the stock immediately after a cash distribution.

$$V_0 = \sum_{i=0}^{\infty} \left[K\left(1 - \frac{m}{n}\right)^i + \left(p - K\left(1 - \frac{m}{n}\right)^i\right)(1 - t_k)\right]m(1 + r)^{-(1+i)}$$

$$= \sum_{i=0}^{\infty} \left[p(1 - t_k) + Kt\left(1 - \frac{m}{n}\right)^i\right]m(1 + r)^{-(1+i)}.$$

The actual value of V_0 would depend on observed values of K, m, n, and p. The larger the value of K the larger the value of V_0.

However, remember that a person purchasing the stock would be interested in the net value of the investment. Thus K, the cost of the stock, would have to be subtracted from V_0.

PROBLEMS

1. Assume the ABC Company has $10 per share per year available for distribution to its stockholders. The tax rate on ordinary income for investors is .6 and on capital gains is .25. The time value of money is .05.

   Required: (a) Compute the per share value of a perpetual cash dividend of $10.

   (b) Compute the per share value of a systematic acquisition of shares of stock using the following relationship:

   $$V_0 = \frac{D}{2}\left[\left(1 + \frac{4(1 + r - t_k)}{r^2}\right)^{1/2} - 1\right].$$

   (c) Repeat (b) using:

   $$V_0 = \frac{-D(1 - t_k) + [D^2(1 - t_k)^2 - 4(D^2/r^2)(t_k - 1)(r + 1)]^{1/2}}{2}.$$

   (d) Repeat (b) using:

   $$V_0 = \frac{-D(1 - t_k) + [D^2(1 - t_k)^2 + 4\,(D^2/r^2)(1 - t_k)(r - t_k r + 1)]^{1/2}}{2}.$$

   (e) What are the assumptions of Parts (b), (c), and (d)?

2. Assume the tax basis of the common stock of ABC Company is $100 per share. There are one million shares outstanding. The company will be able to distribute $10 million per year ($10 per share). The current market price is $200 per share. If the company purchases its own shares it will be able to purchase 50,000 shares per year. It will issue a stock dividend of 50,000 shares to keep the number of shares constant.

   The tax rate on ordinary income is .7. The tax rate on capital gains is .25. The time value of money is .05.

   Required: (a) What is the value of the firm's common stock if a dividend is paid annually?

   (b) What is the value of the firm's common stock if shares of stock are acquired?

3. Continue Problem 2. Assume the cost basis is $200 per share instead of $100. Compute the value using the relationship:

   $$V_0 = \frac{D}{2}\left[\left(\frac{1 + 4(1 + r - t_k)}{r^2}\right)^{1/2} - 1\right].$$

4. Should a corporation be allowed to acquire its own shares of common stock?

REFERENCES

See also References for Chapter 8.

Bierman, H., Jr., and West, R. "The Effect of Share Repurchase on the Value of the Firm; Some Further Comments," *The Journal of Finance* (December), 1968.

Bloch, Ernest. "Short Cycles in Corporate Demand for Government Securities," *American Economic Review* (December), 1963.

Brigham, Eugene. "The Profitability of a Firm's Repurchase of Its Own Common Stock," *California Management Review* (Winter), 1964.

Donaldson, Gordon. "From the Thoughtful Businessman," *Harvard Business Review* (July–August), 1965.

Ellis, Charles. "Repurchase Shares to Revitalize Equity," *Harvard Business Review* (July–August), 1965.

Elton, E., and Gruber, M. "The Effect of Share Repurchase on the Value of the Firm," *Journal of Finance* (March), 1968.

———. "Reply," *Journal of Finance* (December), 1968.

Fleck, James. "Corporate Share Repurchasing: An Informal Discussion," *Harvard Business School Bulletin* (January–February), 1965.

Frazer, William. "Large Manufacturing Corporations as Suppliers of Funds to the Government Securities Market," *Journal of Finance* (December), 1958.

Guthart, Leo. "More Companies are Buying Back Their Stock," *Harvard Business Review* (March–April), 1965.

Jacobs, Donald. "The Marketable Securities Portfolios of Nonfinancial Corporations: Investment Practices and Trends," *Journal of Finance* (September), 1960.

Kaplan, A. D. "The Current Merger Movement," *Harvard Business Review* (May–June), 1955.

Modigliani, Franco, and Miller, Merton. "Corporate Income Taxes and the Cost of Capital: A Correction," *American Economic Review* (June), 1963.

———. "Dividend Policy, Growth and the Valuation of Shares," *Journal of Business* (October), 1961.

Robichek, Alexander, and Myers, Stewart. *Optimal Financing Decisions* (Prentice-Hall, Englewood Cliffs, N.J., 1966).

CHAPTER 10

Dividend Policy and Taxes

SYMBOLS

D the amount available for dividends (earnings)

t_0 tax rate on ordinary income

r the return available if the funds are invested internally

i the return to individuals external to the firm

I_n the value n periods from now of an investment if a dividend of D is paid immediately

V_n the value n periods from now if the dividend is paid one period from now

t_k the capital gains tax rate

The manner in which the tax structure affects the optimum financial decisions of corporations is of continuing interest. In this chapter we shall consider how the dividend policy of a corporation is affected by taxes and the investment objectives of the stockholders. Initially we shall assume that capital gains do not receive special tax treatment. In all the examples we shall assume that the stockholders have instantaneous and perfect knowledge of the investments of the firm.

In the first situation we will assume that all the earnings are paid as dividends and the only difference between the two alternatives offered is that in one alternative there is no initial dividend and only one final dividend, and with the other alternative dividends are paid as they are earned. Dividends are taxed and then invested in dividend paying stock.

In the second situation we will investigate the possibility of an initial dividend, enabling the owner to move to more desirable investments, *and then* *retention* at the higher earning rate. It does not make a difference as to whether or not there is a final dividend, but the length of the planning horizon (the length of time considered) is very relevant.

Reinvested in Dividend-Paying Stock

Consider the situation where a firm has $\$D$ available for dividends and where the firm allows itself to have a choice as to whether the funds are invested for one period or given to the stockholders. The stockholders are all assumed to have a tax rate of t_0. After a dividend of $\$D$ and the recognition of the liability to the tax authorities the stockholder will have

$$(1 - t_0)D.$$

The stockholders can earn i per dollar of investment if they are given the dividend.[1] At the end of the one period all funds are distributed to the stock-holders, and the stockholders will have

$$(1 - t_0)D + (1 - t_0)Di(1 - t_0).$$

Now assume that instead of paying an immediate dividend of $\$D$, the firm reinvests the $\$D$ for one time period to earn r, and the corporation then pays a dividend of $(1 + r)D$. After tax, the stockholder will have

$$(1 + r)D(1 - t_0).$$

We want to find the internal rate r that will give the stockholder the same benefits after one period as if he invested the funds externally to earn i. Setting the two values equal to each other and solving for r:

$$(1 + r)D(1 - t_0) = (1 - t_0)D + (1 - t_0)Di(1 - t_0)$$
$$1 + r = 1 + i(1 - t_0)$$
$$r = (1 - t_0)i.$$

An equivalent approach would be to analyze the situation as follows. The firm can retain D and pay a dividend of rD one period from now, and the stock holder will have $rD(1 - t_0)$ after tax. Alternatively the firm can pay a dividend of D now and the individual will have $D(1 - t_0)$ to reinvest. The investor will receive a dividend of $D(1 - t_0)i$ one period from now and will have $D(1 - t_0)i(1 - t_0)$ after tax. Equating the consequences of the two alternatives:

$$rD(1 - t_0) = D(1 - t_0)i(1 - t_0)$$
$$r = (1 - t_0)i.$$

A third equivalent approach is to compare rD/i, the present value of the dividends assuming retention of $\$D$ with the present value $[(1 - t_0)Di]/i$, assuming an immediate dividend of D.

$$\frac{rD}{i} = \frac{(1 - t_0)Di}{i}$$
$$r = (1 - t_0)i.$$

---

[1] We are assuming that the funds from dividends (after tax) are invested in dividend-paying stocks yielding i.

EXAMPLE:

$$i = .10 \qquad D = \$100$$

$$t_0 = .4$$

Solving for r, we obtain:

$$r = (1 - .4).10 = .06$$

If the funds are invested internally to earn .06 for one period and then distributed the investor will have \$63.60 at the end of one period.

$$(1 + r)D(1 - t_0) = 1.06 \times 100 \times .6 = \$63.60$$

If the dividend of $\$D$ is declared immediately, and the funds reinvested to earn a .10 dividend, the investor will again have \$63.60 at the end of one period.

$$(1 - t_0)D + (1 - t_0)^2 Di = .6 \times 100 + .36 \times 100 \times .10 = \$63.60$$

Assuming the firm can earn a return in excess of .06, the stockholder is better off with the firm retaining income rather than distributing it, if the stockholder has a tax rate equal to or greater than .4.[2] This bias does not require an assumption of a special capital gains tax rate. It occurs because we can defer the payment of taxes by the individual taxpayer.

Instead of assuming that the firm invests at r for one period, we could assume that the firm invests for n periods and then pays a dividend. This new assumption would not change the value of r in terms of i if we continue to assume that the dividends are paid as earned with the alternative being an initial dividend (assuming the dividends are reinvested in dividend paying stocks thus the earnings of the new investment are taxed currently).

EXAMPLE: Assume funds are reinvested to earn r for two periods. If the funds are retained and distributed after two periods we will have

$$D(1 + r)^2(1 - t_0).$$

If the earnings of each year are paid as a dividend, the net after-tax amounts reinvested to earn i for two years, and then distributed we will have

$$D(1 - t_0) + D(1 - t_0)^2 i + i[D(1 - t_0) + D(1 - t_0)^2 i](1 - t_0)$$

or

$$D(1 - t_0)[1 + 2(1 - t_0)i + (i - t_0)^2 i^2] = D(1 - t_0)[1 + (1 - t_0)i]^2.$$

---

[2] At this point we are assuming the firm cannot invest externally. If the firm invested externally it presumably could earn i.

Equating the two values and solving for r:

$$D(1 + r)^2(1 - t_0)$$
$$= D(1 - t_0) + D(1 - t_0)^2 i + i[D(1 - t_0) + D(1 - t_0)^2 i][(1 - t_0)]$$
$$= D(1 - t_0)[1 + (1 - t_0)i]^2;$$
$$(1 + r)^2 = [1 + (1 - t_0)i]^2$$
$$r = (1 - t_0)i.$$

We would obtain the same results for n periods if we continue the same assumptions.

Instead of assuming that the internal rate of return differs from the market return let us assume that the firm can earn a return of .10 (equal to the market rate). If the $100 is reinvested at the end of the year the firm will have $110 and the investor will have $66 after tax compared to an after-tax return of $63.60 if the funds are distributed as they are earned. The $2.40 increase can be explained by noting that the firm has $40 more to invest if the initial dividend is not paid. The $40 earns $4 during the one period. This $4 on an after tax basis increases the well being of the taxpayer by $2.40.

Let I_1 be the value one period from now of an investment if a dividend of D is paid immediately. We have

$$I_1 = (1 - t_0)D + (1 - t_0)Di(1 - t_0)$$
$$= (1 - t_0)(1 + i(1 - t_0))D$$
$$= [1 - t_0)(1 + i) - it_0(1 - t_0)]D.$$

If the dividend is paid one period from now, the value one period from now will be V_1:

$$V_1 = (1 - t_0)(1 + i)D.$$

It follows that

$$I_1 = V_1 - it_0(1 - t_0)D.$$

For example,

$$V_1 = (1 - t_0)(1 + i)D = .6(1.10)100 = 66,$$
$$it_0(1 - t_0)D = .10 \times .4 - .6 \times 100 = 2.40,$$
$$I_1 = 66.00 - 2.40 = 63.60$$

Thus the deferral of taxes accomplished by the retention of earnings may be said to reduce the required return (assuming the firm cannot invest externally) or to increase the present value of the dividend stream available to the stockholders if we assume investments are yielding the same return as the market rate of return available to the firm. The option of deferring taxes is valuable to a stockholder.

Reinvested in Stock Retaining Earnings[3]

We will now assume that the funds obtained from the dividends are invested in companies that retain their earnings for n periods and are able to earn i per year (the price of the common shares will increase i per year). The firm can earn r internally compared to the market return of i (where r is less than i). With no initial dividend (the funds are retained and paid after n periods) a larger amount (D) is earning a lower return (r). If the initial dividend is paid, the smaller sum $D(1 - t_0)$ is earning a higher return (i). At some (n periods) we would be indifferent between the two alternatives, but if the funds are distributed before n periods the investing of $\$D$ at a return of r is better than paying a $\$D$ dividend and reinvesting $D(1 - t_0)$ to earn i.

EXAMPLE:[4] Assuming no dividend until n periods and that the value after n periods is $D(1 + r)^n$, the after-tax value will be

$$D(1 + r)^n(1 - t_0).$$

Assuming an initial dividend and $D(1 - t_0)(1 + i)^n$ value after n periods the after-tax value will be

$$[D(1 - t_0)(1 + i)^n - D(1 - t_0)](1 - t_0) + D(1 - t_0).$$

Equating the two values at time n:

$$(1 - t_0)D(1 + r)^n = [D(1 - t_0)(1 + i)^n - D(1 - t_0)](1 - t_0) + D(1 - t_0);$$

$$(1 + r)^n = (1 - t_0)(1 + i)^n + t_0 = (1 + i)^n + t_0(1 - (1 + i)^n).$$

If $t = .40$, $i = .10$, we can determine the break-even r for $n = 20$.

$$(1 + r)^{20} = \frac{.6}{.1486} + .4 = 4.44$$

$$(1 + r)^{-20} = .225$$

$$r = .08 \text{ (approximately)}$$

---

[3] This section evolved from classroom discussion led by graduate students at Cornell, Neil Houghton and Robert Earl.

[4] The illustration assumes the increments in value are taxed at ordinary rates. This is reasonable if the increments are ultimately distributed in the form of a cash dividend. Later the capital gains tax rates will be introduced. Also, it is possible for an estate to avoid a tax on the increment completely (e.g., by holding until death).

The break-even r for $n = 3$ is

$$(1 + r)^3 = .6(1.331) + .4 = .80 + .4 = 1.199$$

$$(1 + r)^{-3} = .834$$

$$r = .06 \text{ (approximately)}.$$

If we can invest internally to earn .08 then it takes the initial dividend alternative 20 years to catch up assuming the funds from the initial dividend alternative earn .10 on investment in a company that reinvests its earnings. If the firm can only earn .06 internally the 'pay a dividend now' procedure can catch up to full retention in three years.

If a $100 dividend is paid now there would be $60 after tax. After three years this would grow to $60 \times 1.331 = \$79.86$.

The tax on sale is $.4(79.86 - 60)$ or $7.94. The after-tax proceeds are $71.92.

If the $100 is reinvested to earn .06 the firm will have $100 \times (1.06)^3 = \$118.10$. The after-tax proceeds are $.6 \times \$118.10$ or $71 (there is $1 rounding-off error arising from the fact that the break-even interest rate is not exactly .06).

If the planning horizon is long enough and if investments are available when tax deferment is possible, we would conclude that the firm should not accept a lower yield than the investor can earn by placing his funds in other investments. Note that to reach this conclusion it required a policy of retention on the part of the firm which received the investment after the initial dividend. If $r = .09$ for the example being considered, it requires in excess of fifty years for the dividend alternative to catch-up. In such a situation a person may well prefer the return of .09 on the larger initial amount since for over fifty years this investment will have a higher value than the .10 return on the small investment resulting from the initial dividend.

We can also compare the increase in present values arising from deferral of dividends assuming the firm can earn i by investing internally or externally. Let I_n be the value of n periods from now of a policy of paying an immediate dividend of $1:

$$I_n = [(1 - t_0)(1 + i)^n - (1 - t_0)](1 - t_0) + (1 - t_0).$$

The value of a deferred dividend is

$$V_n = (1 - t_0)(1 + i)^n.$$

I_n in terms of V_n is

$$I_n = [V_n(1 - t_0) - (1 - t_0)^2 + (1 - t_0)] = (1 - t_0)[V_n + t_0].$$

EXAMPLE:

$$t_0 = .40 \qquad i = .10, \qquad n = 3$$

$$V_n = (1 - t_0)(1 + i)^n = .6 \times 1.331 = .7986$$

$$I_n = (1 - t_0)[V_n + t_0] = .6[.7986 + .4] = .7192.$$

The improvement arising from deferral of dividends is $.0794 per dollar of dividend.

If we compare an immediate dividend and reinvestment to earn i (but no second dividend) with a process of reinvestment (but no initial dividend) to earn r and then a dividend, we have

$$D(1 - t)(1 + i) = D(1 + r)(1 - t)$$

$$1 + i = 1 + r$$

$$i = r.$$

The equality of i and r results because of the assumption that the retained earnings are paid as a dividend (where there was no initial dividend) but that the retained earnings resulting from the reinvestment of the initial dividend are not paid as a dividend.

Even without the capital gains option we find that the ability to defer taxes by retention of earnings is valuable to a corporation and its stockholders. When the internal rate of return of the corporation is equal to the market return, the ability to defer taxes increases the present value of the future dividend stream. If only investments inferior to the market are available it may be desirable to accept these investments rather than pay a dividend. The possible desirability of such investments will depend on the period of time until the accumulated earnings are paid as dividends and the attitudes toward risk of the investors.

Capital Gains

We will now assume that capital gains are taxed at a rate of t_k. The possibility of capital gains taxation requires that we consider the option of the stockholder selling the portion of his investment representing the reinvested earnings and having the gain taxed at a rate of t_k.

Let us assume that if D is retained it will earn r per period (rD in terms of dollars and this amount is paid as a dividend. With a time value of money $i(1 - t_0)$ these dividends will have a capitalized value of $[rD(1 - t_0)]/[i(1 - t_0)] = rD/i$ to the stockholders holding for the dividends. If the value of the stock increases by rD/i and the future earnings are realized by the stockholder selling part of his holdings, the net after tax value is: $rD(1 - t_k)/i$.

If the dividend of D is paid immediately the investor will have

$$D(1 - t_0).$$

Equating the latter two values and solving for r:

$$\frac{rD(1 - t_k)}{i} = D(1 - t_0),$$

$$r = \frac{(1 - t_0)i}{(1 - t_k)}.$$

EXAMPLE

$$t_0 = .4, \qquad t_k = .25, \qquad i = .10,$$

$$r = \frac{.6 \times .10}{.75} = .08.$$

If the firm is able to reinvest and earn i (instead of r), the after tax value of reinvesting would be

$$\frac{iD(1 - t_0)(1 - t_k)}{i(1 - t_0)} = D(1 - t_k).$$

If the dividend of D is paid immediately the after-tax value is

$$D(1 - t_0).$$

The improvement in value arising from reinvestment is

$$D(t_0 - t_k).$$

For the example being considered we would have

$$D = 1, t_0 - .4, \quad t_k = .25$$

$$D(t_0 - t_k = 1)(.4 - .25) = \$.15 \text{ per dollar of dividend.}$$

The above model assumed the stock was sold immediately after the retention of the earnings of D; thus the investor fails to take advantage of tax deferral opportunities. An alternative approach for the no-dividend situation would explicitly include the possibility of holding the stock for n periods rather than selling immediately if the cash is retained. Also, if there is an immediate dividend it could consider the possibility of reinvesting the cash dividend in another company and then selling the appreciation n periods from now. Assume the new stock acquired would increase in value i per year and would pay no dividends during the twenty-year period. This model would be as follows:

NO DIVIDEND FOR n PERIODS	DIVIDEND NOW AND SELLING n PERIODS FROM NOW

$$D(1 + r)^n(1 - t_k) = [D(1 - t_0)(1 + i)^n - D(1 - t_0)](1 - t_k) + D(1 - t_0)$$
$$(1 + r)^n(1 - t_k) = [(1 + i)^n - 1](1 - t_k)(1 - t_0) + (1 - t_0)$$
$$= \{[(1 + i)^n - 1](1 - t_k) + 1\}(1 - t_0)$$
$$= [(1 + i)^n(1 - t_k) + t_k](1 - t_0).$$

For the above example, for a period of 20 years, we would now have:[5]

$$(1 + r)^n = \frac{(1 - t_0)}{(1 - t_k)} [(1 + i)^n(1 - t_k) + t_k]$$

$$\frac{(1 - .4)}{(1 - .25)} [1.10^{20}(.75) + .25]$$

$$= .8(5.04 + .25] = 4.232$$

$$(1 + r)^{-20} = .236\%$$

$$r = .075.$$

If the firm uses .08 as its cut-off, an investment of $100 will earn $8 at the margin. Since the investor, with an immediate dividend of $100, will only have $60 after taxes and will earn $6, he is better off with the retention (indicating that the cut-off rate of .08 is too high from the point of view of an investor intending to hold the investment). Assuming the firm has accepted an investment yielding .08, an investor who sells will net $60 after taxes and will be in the same position as if the firm had paid a $100 dividend immediately. Thus the .08 cut-off determined previously applies to an investor who intends to sell.

When we consider the capital gains opportunity, the required return for the corporation is less than the return that the stockholder has available if he invests funds external to the firm, since ordinary income is being converted into capital gains.[6]

---

[5] We could also compute the improvement in present value assuming the funds could be invested internally to earn $i = .10$. Also, if we compared an immediate taxable dividend with a deferral taxable capital gain (say for one period) we would find that return required for reinvestment would be very low (it could be negative). That is not to say that an investment yielding a negative return should be accepted.

[6] The investment opportunities available to the firm have been assumed to be less desirable than the market alternatives. Now assume the firm can earn .10 (r is equal to i) on incremental investments. A $100 investment now earns $10 per period and the present value of the investment to the market is $100. If the stockholder sells he will realize $75 (assuming a .25 capital gains rate). With an ordinary income tax rate of .7 he would only realize $30. If the internal return were greater than .10, the advantage of the capital gains treatment would become even more dramatic.

Conclusion

We have divided the stockholders into several groups. For example:

1. Those intending to hold and invest in dividend paying firms (thus preferring that the firm use a .06 cut-off rate).
2. Those intending to sell immediately (thus preferring that the firm use a .08 cut-off rate).

We can subdivide these two groups further by allowing the ordinary tax rates and capital gains rates to take on different values. Since the ordinary income tax rates may vary from 0% to 70% and the capital gains rate from 0% to 25% we would have the minimum value of r ranging from .04 to .10. Let $t_0 = .7$ and $t_c = .25$, using the simpler of the two relationships illustrated for capital gains:

$$r = \frac{(1 - t_0)i}{(1 - t_k)} = \frac{(1 - .7).10}{.75} = .04.$$

If the tax rates t_0 and t_k are zero, r will be equal to .10.

These examples assume there are external investments available to the stockholders yielding .10, and we conclude that it might be worthwhile for the firm to invest internally to earn something less than .10 in order to assist the stockholders in their efforts to avoid or postpone personal income taxes. However, it is not necessary or desirable for the firm to invest internally in such a situation and accept inferior investments. The same investments are available to the firm with excess cash as to the individual. Let us assume that the ABC Company has taken all internal investments yielding .10 or better and still has excess cash. At this point it can consider investing in other enterprises where the expected yield is .10. The stockholders subject to personal income taxes may be better off if the ABC Company makes the investment than if they receive dividend and make it. To avoid an intermediate tax on dividends transferred between the two companies the ABC Company might want to acquire 100% of the company in which it is investing and file consolidated income tax returns. There is a significant tax incentive for corporations to acquire other corporations rather than distributing the funds in the form of dividends to their stockholders.

If an investor in a high tax bracket expects the price of a stock to increase because of improved earnings (and a higher level of future dividends) he is willing to pay more for the stock knowing that if his expectations are realized he can sell the stock and be taxed at only a .25 rate on the capital gain. While the capital gains tax treatment tends to increase the value of a share of stock (thus decreasing the cost of raising funds), we have shown that another powerful factor arises from the ability of the individual stockholder to defer paying taxes if the corporation retains income rather than paying dividends.

PROBLEMS

1. The ABC Company intends to pay out all its earnings as dividends, how-
    ever, it wants to choose between a policy of paying out dividends as the
    income is earned (now and for the next three years) or alternatively pay
    one dividend three years from now. With no additional retained earnings
    the firm can maintain a dividend of $100 per share.

    Stockholders can earn dividends of .10 of investment by investing in
    other firms of comparable risk. We will assume that these firms are divi-
    dend paying, thus the entire .10 yield is subject to tax.

    Assume capital gains and ordinary income are both taxed at a rate of
    .6.

    Required: (a) The firm has many investments that yield .08. Should the
    firm invest or pay a current dividend?
    (b) How low a yield can an investment have and still be accept-
    able to the firm?
    (c) Is the answer to (a) or (b) affected by the time horizon con-
    sidered?
    (d) Assume the firm has investments yielding .10. What is the
    improvement in value arising from retaining for one year
    compared with a $100 dividend?

2. Continue Problem 1. Assume that the stockholders can also invest in a
    firm that is earning .10 on its investments and is retaining its earnings (the
    price of a share of stock is increasing .10 per year and is expected to continue
    to increase at the same rate). The stockholder will either sell his present
    stock or the stock he acquires with the dividend proceeds at the end of the
    designated time (or alternatively the amounts accumulated will be paid as
    dividends).

    Required: Determine the break-even return between a policy of paying
    an immediate dividend and paying a dividend at the end of:

    (a) Three years (show that the investor will break even).
    (b) Ten years.
    (c) Twenty years.
    (d) What is the improvement in value twenty years from now
    of a policy of deferring dividends for twenty years com-
    pared to a policy of paying an immediate dividend?

3. It has been argued that it makes no difference whether or not a firm pays
    dividends or retains the earnings, since the value to the stockholder is the
    same for both.

    For example, assuming a .4 tax rate and an ability to find a stock that is growing at a value of .10, if $100 is paid as a dividend, the investor will have after one period:

$$100(.6)(1.10) = \$66.$$

If the funds are retained and invested internally to earn .10, and then paid as a dividend after one period, the investor will again have

$$100(1.10)(.6) = \$66.$$

Required: Comment on the illustration.

4. Continue Problem 1. Assume that capital gains are taxed at a rate of .25. We will assume that investors will hold the stock for twenty years and then sell. If a dividend is paid the investors will reinvest and hold that stock for twenty years. The firm purchased will reinvest its earnings for twenty years.

Required: (a) Assume the ABC Company can invest to earn .08. Should it pay a dividend or reinvest?

(b) Determine the break-even internal rate if we compare the after-tax cash proceeds from a dividend and the proceeds from selling the capital appreciation that would occur if the funds from a dividend are reinvested to earn the market return of (.10) per year in the form of dividends.

5. The tax court decided several years ago that increases in the value of endowment policies under certain circumstances are income. The court drew a distinction between endowment policies and other assets such as stock whose appreciation reflects price changes over time. The gain in value of an endowment policy results from the annual addition to the investment fund of the earnings on the investments and the gain is not directly related to price changes.

Required: Comment on the distinction.

REFERENCES

See References for Chapters 8 and 9.

Long-Term Debt

In Part IV we will investigate the nature of long-term debt and the costs of various characteristics. The basic cost of debt and the effect of the introduction of more debt were discussed in Part II. In this section other factors affecting the cost of debt will be discussed.

CHAPTER 11

Measuring Debt[1]

Accounts implicitly or explicitly make use of the present value principles in the measurement of long term debt.[2] However, they have done so incompletely and inexactly. For example, when the bond is issued the liability is recorded at the amount received from the creditors; for a bond with a maturity value of $1000 the liability is measured by the amount of cash received. This eliminates the need for the firm to compute explicitly the present value of the future payments. When the effective interest rate is equal to the contractual rate of the debt, the amount received at time of issue is equal to the amount to be paid at maturity, assuming the interest is paid periodically. That is, the cash received is equal to both the maturity amount and the present value of the debt using the current effective interest rate. Thus the accountant can avoid asking himself whether the cash received or the present value of the debt is a better measure of the liability.[3]

Comparing Firms

An important operational weakness of this practice is that it complicates interfirm comparisons since the debt-type cash flows are implicitly discounted using different discount rates. Consider the following example:

Company A issues $10 million of twenty-year 5% bonds at 5%, its effective rate of interest, and the debt is recorded at $10 million. Company X issues $10 million of twenty-year 10% bonds at 10%, its effective rate of interest, and its debt is recorded at $10 million.[4]

We argue that, in an important sense, the two companies have different amounts of debt outstanding, and that conventional accounting fails to note this. Company A has promised to pay only $500,000 of interest per year for twenty years; Company X has promised to pay $1 million a year

---

[1] Parts of this chapter have appeared in an article written with Seymour Smidt, "Accounting for Debt and Costs of Liquidity under Conditions of Uncertainty," *Journal of Accounting Research* (Autumn, 1967), pp. 144–153.

[2] See, for example, W. A. Paton, *Advanced Accounting* (Macmillan, N.Y., 1947), pp. 604–629; or H. R. Anton, "Accounting for Bond Liabilities," *The Journal of Accountancy*, Vol. 102, No. 3 (September, 1956), pp. 53–56.

[3] While the liability may be equal to the maturity amount, the maturity amount cannot be assumed to be an estimator of the liability.

[4] Both Paton and Anton, *op. cit.*, would agree that the debts are $10,000,000.

interest for the same period. Both companies have promised to pay $10 million at maturity.

We will review (a) the factors that required Company X to promise to pay the larger interest payments in order to receive the same amount of cash as Company A, and (b) the reasons Company X might have been willing to enter into this debt contract.

Explaining Differences in Bond Interest Rates

In the example, we assume that both sets of bonds were issued at par and at the same time. Therefore the difference in the quoted yields (which are equal to the contractual rates in this case) must be due to differences in risk in the two firms and not to differences in general economic conditions.

Since we conclude that the yield differences result mainly from investors' evaluation of and reaction to the risk of default (assuming the bonds have similar call protection and other such contract provisions), we examine how this reaction may lead to the observed differences. Potential investors may not analyse default risk in the manner here adopted.

If there were no risk of default it would be possible to obtain a reliable predictor of the value of the bonds of Company A and of Company X (and therefore a predictor of how much the companies would obtain by selling them) using the yield on U.S. government bonds of similar maturity. Suppose that when the bonds were issued, U.S. government bonds of the same maturity has a 4% yield. The present values of the liabilities of Companies A and X using a 4% interest are computed in Table 11–1. These present values are predictions of the value of the bonds if they were default free. We cannot assume there is no risk of default for the securities of A and X. Investors do not expect to receive the amounts listed above, because they do not consider the bonds to be default free. Although there is no objective means of determining the probabilities of default that investors actually assign, we will consider two sets of investors' beliefs about the probability

TABLE 11–1. Present Value Computations with Default-Free Assumption

DOLLAR AMOUNTS	PRESENT VALUE FACTORS (.04)	COMPANY A	COMPANY X
$10,000,000	.4564	$4,564,000	$4,564,000
500,000 per year	13.5903	6,795,000	
1,000,000 per year	13.5903		13,590,000
Present value of the liabilities		$11,359,000	$18,154,000

of default. We sacrifice realism in order to simplify the explanations and computations; for example, we assume that investors believe receiving the principal is certain but the interest payments are uncertain.

First assume that investors believe that there is a .8 probability of prompt receipt of all the interest payments from Company A's bond, and a .2 probability that no interest payments will be made. For Company X, there is a .4 probability of receiving and .6 probability of not receiving the interest payments. The expected present values of the cash receipts under these assumptions are given in Table 11–2.

TABLE 11–2. Computation of Expected Present Values

AMOUNTS	PRESENT VALUE FACTORS (.04)	PRESENT VALUE	PROBABILITY OF PRESENT VALUE	EXPECTED VALUES COMPANY A	COMPANY X
$10,000,000	.4564	$4,564,000	1.0	$4,564,000	$4,564,000
500,000	13.5903	6,795,000	.8	5,436,000	
1,000,000	13.5903	13,590,000	.4		5,436,000
Expected net present value				$10,000,000	$10,000,000

Table 11–2 illustrates one explanation for the amounts investors were willing to pay for the two bond issues. The bonds were described as having coupon rates (and effective yields) of 5 and 10%. But bond yields are conventionally quoted on the basis of contractual obligations, not investors' expectations. Investors in fixed income securities should expect to receive less than the amount to which they are legally entitled. If the probabilities given in Table 11–2 apply, we could say that investors' expected annual interest receipts for both bond issues were only $400,000 ($500,000 × .8 from Company A, and $1 million × .4 from Company X).

If we knew that the probabilities given in Table 11–2 were correct, the fact that both sets of bonds sold for $10 million would indicate that investors are willing to buy bonds on the basis of the expected present value of the cash flows.

In this example the probability of default affects the amount of the expected cash flow; the twenty-year bonds of Company A, Company X, and the U.S. government all yield an expected $400,000 per year. The example uses probabilities to compute the expected monetary value, but there is no adjustment for possible risk aversions of investors. We now change the probability of interest payment assumption, but will continue to assume that payment at maturity is certain for both companies. Now Company A bondholders have a .9 probability of promptly receiving all interest payments and Company X bondholders have a .6 probability.

TABLE 11–3. Computation of Expected Present Values

DOLLAR AMOUNTS	PRESENT VALUE FACTORS (.04)	PRESENT VALUE	PROBABILITY	EXPECTED VALUES COMPANY A	EXPECTED VALUES COMPANY X
$10,000,000	.4564	$4,564,000	1.0	$4,564,000	$4,564,000
500,000	13.5903	6,795,000	0.9	6,116,000	
1,000,000	13.5903	13,590,000	0.6		8,154,000
Expected net present value				$10,680,000	$12,718,000

The expected net present values of the proceeds of both bonds (shown in Table 11–3) are more than the amounts paid for the bonds ($10 million). We will use the term risk premium to describe the difference between the expected net present value of a bond and its issue price. The risk premiums are $680,000 for Company A and $2,718,000 for Company B. These risk premiums are the expected amounts (in present value terms) necessary to compensate investors for holding these securities rather than default-free government bonds.

We explain the difference between the present value of the bond's promised payments, using the default-free interest rate, and its market value by two sets of deductions: there is a deduction from the present value (computed using the default-free rate) to reduce the amount of debt to the expected monetary value of the debt (the amount expected to be received by the investors); from the expected present value we subtract an expected risk premium to obtain the market value of the bond. The calculations are illustrated for Company X using the investors' expectations from 11–2 and 11–3.

Objective estimates of items 1 and 5 of Table 11–4 are typically available. The difference between these two items is the excess of the present value of the liability (using the default-free rates) over the amount of cash received for the promises to pay. This difference is an operationally useful concept that can be measured fairly accurately. However, there is no objective means of dividing this difference into the expected amount of default and the risk premium.[5] To divide the difference into these two components, we need investors' beliefs about the probability of default.

---

[5] The difference between items 1 and 3 arises because the future payments are not certain (there is some probability of nonpayment). The difference between items 3 and 5 arises because of a psychological aversion to the possibility of loss.

TABLE 11–4. Reconciliation of Present Value Using the Default-Free
Rate and the Market Price of Company X Bonds

	ASSUMPTIONS:	
ITEM	.4 PROBABILITY OF PAYMENT OF INTEREST	.6 PROBABILITY OF PAYMENT OF INTEREST
1. Present value of liability at default-free rates (.04)	$18,154,000[a]	$18,154,000[a]
2. Less: Present value of expected amount of default	8,154,000	5,436,000
3. Equals: Present value of expected receipts	10,000,000[b]	12,718,000[c]
4. Less: Expected risk premium	0	2,718,000
5. Equals: Market value of bond	$10,000,000	$10,000,000

[a] From Table 11–1.
[b] From Table 11–2.
[c] From Table 11–3.

Why Firms Borrow

Consider the situations for Company X that are described in Tables 11–1 and 11–3. The most likely amounts to be paid have a present value of $18,154,000 and the expected value of the debt (using the investors' expectations) is $12,718,000. The simplest situation warranting the issuance of the debt occurs when the funds are invested in an asset that costs $10 million and where the present value of the investment's cash flows (using .04) exceeds $18,154,000 and are known with certainty. If the cash flows of the investment are not known with certainty, the willingness to undertake the investment (and issue the debt) is less easily explained.

We have not considered the merits of issuing common stock rather than debt. We have shown that borrowing was desirable where the investment's cash flows were known with certainty, and had a present value in excess of $18,154,000. Further analysis might show that the capital should be obtained by issuing common stock, but at least we have shown that it may be desirable to accept $10 million of cash in return for a promise to pay $18,154,000.

Consider the situation of Company A at the time of issuance of the debt yielding .05. At the time of issue there was a risk of default associated with the firm's bonds, otherwise the interest rate of the industrial bond would have been equal to the interest rate on the government bond. The market rate of interest of .05 on the industrial bonds reflects a fear of default if other securities of the same maturity issued by the federal government are yielding .04. Thus the investor purchasing a $1000 bond is taking into consideration the fact that the $50 of interest per year is not certain (an investor expects to receive on the average something less than $50). The investor's willingness to pay $1000 for the bond does not reflect a time value of money of .05, but rather a time value of money of less than .05 since the amount the investor expects to receive is less than $50.

Let us return to the situation (Table 11–2) where the investor considers his time value of money to be .04 (the default-free rate) and expects to receive $50 with .8 probability or $0 with .2 probability, and expects to receive the $1000 at maturity with probability of one. This investor, basing his decision on expected monetary value, would be willing to pay $1000 for the bond and would seem to have a time value of money of .05, but actually has a time value of money of .04. However, even with the given probabilities and a .04 discount rate, an individual with an aversion to risk would pay less than $1000 for one of the bonds. We have described three factors affecting the price of the bonds, namely, the time value of money, the expectations of the several possible events including nonpayment of interest or principal, and the aversion of the investing community to investments with risk.

The borrowing corporation should indicate the present value of the debt using the default-free interest rate of .04. With twenty year bonds and a .05 contractual interest rate this would result in a $1000 face value bond being recorded at $1,135.90. The liability to the corporation using the present value of the contractual flows (the most likely amount of payment) is $11,359,000.

Despite the incurrence of a liability with a most likely amount of payment that exceeds the cash received, the contract is not necessarily disadvantageous to the borrowing corporation. First, the expected (mean) payments are less than the most likely payments. With a positive probability of default, if the expected cash flow is used, the present value of the debt is less than the most likely amount of $1136. If the expected interest is $40 a year because of a .2 probability of not receiving any interest, and the expected maturity amount is $1000, the debt would have an expected present value of $1000, even though the contractual rate is .05 and we used a .04 discount rate.

The debt could be shown as follows on the balance sheet:

Present value of contractual payments	$11,359,000
Less: Expected monetary value adjustment	1,359,000
Market value of debt at time of issue	$10,000,000

Now assume the bonds have been outstanding one year and are still selling for $10 million. The default-free interest rate is still .04, and the market value of the debt is $10 million. The present value of the contractual stream and the expected value of the debt is given in Table 11–5.

There would be $500,000 interest cost for the year and a $46,000 gain resulting from adjusting the debt.

•

TABLE 11–5

AMOUNT OF PAYMENTS	PRESENT VALUE FACTORS (.04) FOR 19 YEARS	PRESENT VALUE OF CONTRACTUAL STREAM	PROBABILITY	EXPECTED VALUE
$10,000,000	.474642	$4,746,000	1.0	$4,746,000
500,000/yr	13.13394	6,567,000	.8	5,254,000
		$11,313,000		$10,000,000

TABLE 11–6

	PRESENT VALUE	PROBABILITY	EXPECTED VALUE
$50 × 13.5903	$679.50	.9	$611.60
1000 × .4564	456.40	1.0	456.40
			$1068.00

Any change in the market rates of interest can be handled by loss or gain accounts. These changes should be labeled as realized or unrealized depending on the definition of "realization"; with reliable market quotations of bond prices we would consider the gains or losses realized.

In addition, the risk preferences of the investors may be of such a nature that they will be unwilling to pay an amount equal to the expected monetary value of the debt. In this situation a risk adjustment may have to be subtracted from the expected monetary value. Assume there is a .9 probability of collecting the .05 interest (the situation illustrated in Table 11–3). The expected monetary value of the bond at the time of issue is given in Table 11–6.

Assume 10,000 of the bonds described were sold in the market for $10 million. There is a $680,000 risk adjustment (the expected monetary value of the debt is $10,680,000 and the market price is $10 million.)

The accountant would be presenting three measures of debt:

1. The most likely amount of payments $11,359,000.
2. The expected monetary value of the payments $10,680,000.
3. The market value of the debt $10 million.

In answer to the question "What is the liability?" we could answer with the three-component vector (11,359,000; 10,680,000; 10,000,000).

The debt could be shown as follows on the balance sheet:

Present value of contractual payments	$11,359,000
Less: Expected monetary value adjustment	679,000
Expected monetary value of the debt	10,680,000
less: Risk adjustment	680,000
Market value of debt at time of issue	$10,000,000

Since we generally know (1) and (3), but not (2), we have to be satisfied with the present value of the most likely payments using the default-free rate ($11,359,000) and the market value of the debt ($10 million). The present value of the contractual payments should be computed each year using the default-free rate. The combined expected value and risk adjustments should be subtracted to obtain the market value of the corporation's debt.

EXAMPLE:

Assume that after one year the default-free interest rate is .051 and the bonds are selling for a market value of $8,884,000 (yielding .06). The present value of the contractual payments is $9,880,000 (Table 11–7).

The corporation's evaluation of its financial position might differ from that of the market. For example, the corporation might consider the probability of meeting the legal obligations to be 1.0. In that case, the most relevant amount associated with the debt, from the point of view of the corporation, is the $11,359,000. The corporation is willing to give the bond holders a bargain to take advantage of earning opportunities available to it. The journal entries for the transaction might be as follows:

Cash	$10,000,000	
Cost of liquidity (an asset)	1,359,000	
Bonds payable		$11,359,000

The liability could be described as $11,359,000, despite the fact that the market value of the liability is $10 million.[6] The "cost of liquidity" is an asset account to be written off as a cost of acquiring assets.

[6] The liability of $11,359,000 could be shown to equal the sum of the market value of $10 million plus an adjustment for expectations and risk aversion of $1,359,000.

TABLE 11–7

DOLLAR AMOUNTS	PRESENT VALUE FACTORS FOR 19 YEARS (.051)	PRESENT VALUE OF CONTRACTUAL PAYMENTS
$10,000,000	.388641	$3,886,000
500,000	11.98744	5,994,000
		$9,880,000

The journal entries would be:

Interest charges	$500,000	
Cash		$500,000

Bonds payable	1,479,000	
Expected monetary value and risk adjustment		363,000
Gain on interest rate increase		1,116,000

(to reduce the bonds payable to the new present value of the contractual payments)

EXPLANATIONS:

$11,359,000	present value of contractual payments at beginning of period
− 9,880,000	present value of contractual payments at end of period
$1,479,000	reduction in present value

$9,880,000	present value of contractual payments at end of period
− 8,884,000	market value of debt at the end of period
$996,000	desired balance in the adjustment account

$1,359,000	present balance in the adjustment account
− 996,000	desired balance
$363,000	necessary adjustment (a credit to reduce the account)

$10,000,000	market value of debt at the beginning of period
− 8,884,000	market value of debt at the end of period
$1,116,000	market gain

For uniformity and elimination of judgment the above transaction might be recorded with the $1,359,000 classified as a contra-liability account. The journal entry to record the issue would be:

Cash	$10,000,000	
Expected monetary value and risk adjustments	1,359,000	
Bonds payable		$11,359,000

The presentation on the balance sheet might be as follows:

Bonds payable (present value of the most likely amount to be paid)	11,359,000
Less: Expected monetary value and risk adjustments	1,359,000
Estimate of market value of debt	$10,000,000

Conclusions

When the discounting process and decision making under uncertainty is better understood we may expect a series of suggestions similar to the above. These suggestions may require the accountant to modify or discard old rules and to supply more information. The suggested procedure enables us to evaluate more effectively different debt contracts. The information given by the market value of the debt or, equivalently, by the cash received is less useful than the more complete description of the liability using the present value of the contractual payments adjusted for the possibility of no payment and the risk attitudes of the investors.

PROBLEMS

1. The ABC Company has just issued (at par) $10,000,000 of twenty year 6% bonds. There is a .9 probability of the investors receiving all the interest payments and .1 probability of receiving none. There is 1.0 probability of the investors receiving the principle at maturity. The interest rate on default-free bonds is .04.

   Required: (a) Compute the present value of the most likely amount to be paid.
   (b) What is the yield of the bonds (computed conventionally)?
   (c) Compute the expected present value of the bonds.
   (d) Prepare a table showing the information about the liability for the bond.
   (e) What would be the expected present value of the debt if the principle as well as the interest had a .9 probability of collection?

2. The XYZ Company had just issued (at par) $10 million of twenty year 10% bonds. There is a .6 probability of the investors receiving all the interest payments and .4 probability of receiving none. There is 1.0 probability of receiving the principle at maturity. The interest rate on default-free bonds is .04.

Required: (a) Compute the present value of the most likely amount to be paid.
　　　　　 (b) Compute the expected present value of the bonds.
　　　　　 (c) Prepare a table showing the information about the liability for the bond.
　　　　　 (d) Compare the liability of the XYZ Company and ABC Company of Problem 1.

3. The RST Company has signed a lease agreement whereby it promises to pay $1 million a year for the use of computer equipment for twenty years. If the company fails to pay it can be forced into bankruptcy by the computer company.

　　The RST Company has recently borrowed funds for twenty years at a cost of .07 (bonds with .07 coupons were sold at par) and could borrow considerably more at that rate. Default-free bonds of twenty year maturity are currently being issued by the government to yield .04. The life of the equipment is twenty years. There are zero taxes.

Required: (a) Compute the present value of the lease payments using .07.
　　　　　 (b) Compute the present value of the lease payments using .04.
　　　　　 (c) Assume you could purchase the computer equipment at a cost of $10 million, would you buy or lease? Assume the financing would be accomplished with debt-type securities repaid by equal payments if the equipment is purchased.

4. Continue Problem 3. Assume the RST Company could borrow at a cost of .10 per year, and that the equipment could be purchased at a cost of $10 million. Would you buy or lease? What is the present value of leasing?

REFERENCES

Anton, H. R. "Accounting for Bond Liabilities," *The Journal of Accountancy* (September), 1956.

Everett, E. "Subordinated Debt—Nature and Enforcement," *Business Lawyer* (July), 1965.

Hicks, J. R. *Value and Capital*, Second Edition (Oxford University Press, Oxford, 1940).

Modigliani, F., and Miller, M. H. "The Cost of Capital, Corporation Finance and the Theory of Investment," *American Economic Review* (June), 1958.

Paton, W. A. *Advanced Accounting* (Macmillan, New York, 1947).
Robichek, A. A., and Myers, S. C. "Problems in the Theory of Optimal Capital Structure," *Journal of Financial and Quantitative Analysis* (June), 1966.
Schwartz, Eli. "Theory of the Capital Structure of the Firm," *Journal of Finance* (March), 1959.

CHAPTER 12

Subordination, Potential Subordination, and the Cost of Debt[1]

SYMBOLS

$i(\alpha)$ the average return demanded by debtholders where α is a measure of the amount of fully protected outstanding

debt $\alpha = \left(\dfrac{\text{Debt}}{\text{Debt} + \text{Stock}}\right)$

$m(\alpha)$ marginal cost of issuing more debt when there is α debt outstanding

I interest payment per year

Assume a new firm has assets that have been acquired and financed with common stock, and now it is possible to substitute some debt for common stock.[2] Furthermore, the firm may wish to issue additional debt in the future. This additional debt may or may not be identical to the original debt with respect to its priority in case of bankruptcy. The primary question we will consider is how the cost of present and future issues of debt will be influenced by the number of different categories of debt used, and by the protection that may or may not be given the holders of a particular category against the possibility that additional debt of an equal or higher priority may be issued in the future.

In practice the situation is complicated by a number of considerations, including the possibility that the value of the assets securing a particular category of debt will change through time. To simplify the exposition we will assume that the assets of the firm are replaced as they wear out as long as the firm is not bankrupt. There is no likelihood that the quantity of assets owned by the firm will increase.

In this chapter, debt category A will be defined to be senior to debt category

[1] The ideas of this chapter were formulated jointly with my colleagues Seymour Smidt and Richard West.
[2] Assume the lenders do not object to the utilization of funds for this purpose. We are holding everything constant except capital structure. In a realistic dynamic situation, the size of the firm would also be changing.

B if all the claims of A's contract must be fully satisfied before any assets can be applied to satisfy the claims in B's contract. If A is senior to B then we can say B is subordinate to A. We will assume (for simplicity) that the only possibilities are that A is senior to B, or A is subordinate to B, or A is equal to B.[3]

A bond category will be said to be protected against senior issues if during the life of the given category, the firm cannot have outstanding a larger quantity of senior debt than was outstanding at the time the given category was issued. Similarly, a bond category will be said to be protected against equal issues if during the life of the given category the firm cannot issue additional debt that is equal in priority to the given category. If a bond category is protected against both senior and equal issues, the category will be described as fully protected. A bond category will be said to have limited protection against senior (equal) categories if the firm is allowed to issue a specified amount of additional senior (equal) debt.

Given the assumptions we are making about the possible types of relative priority, there is no logical reason for the potential purchaser of a given category of debt to be concerned about the amount of subordinate debt that is currently outstanding or that may be issued in the future.

In borrowing for the first time, the firm has a number of options available to it that are within the scope of this chapter. First, it must decide the number categories of debt (one or more) to issue simultaneously. Second, it must decide, for each category, whether the category is to be given full protection or only limited protection, and if the latter, how large the limits should be. The firm will be concerned with how these decisions influence the current cost of borrowing and the cost of future borrowing.

Costs of One Issue of One Category of Fully Protected Debt

First consider how the cost of debt is affected by the quantity of debt outstanding if all the debt issued at one moment in time is in one category, there is only one issue (the size of which is not yet determined), and it is fully protected against additional debt of equal or higher priority. (Thus any subsequent issues of debt must be of lower priority.) As we increase the amount of debt issued, the return demanded by the purchasers of the debt will increase. In Fig. 12–1, $i(\alpha)$ represents the average return demanded by debtholders, where α is a measure of the amount of fully protected debt outstanding (there is only one issue). Specifically α is the ratio of the market value of the debt issued to the sum of the market values of the total debt plus the stock equity.

[3] In practice, relationships may be more complicated; for example, if A is senior to B with respect to the disposition of certain assets, but A is subordinate to B with respect to other assets.

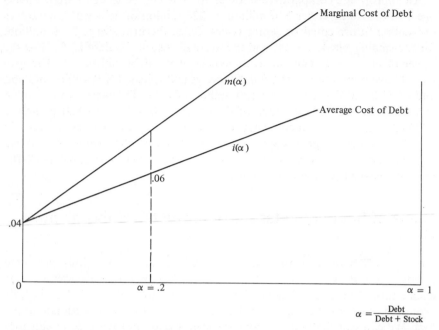

FIGURE 12-1   Average and marginal costs of one issue of fully protected debt.

Assume the firm has a total capital of $100 million of common stock and that all debt issued will be in the form of perpetuities. Suppose that r increases as α increases according to the following relationship:

$$i(\alpha) = .04 + .1\alpha.$$

The curve $i(\alpha)$ is a curve measuring the cost of debt capital offered to the firm for the conditions described.

The return or cost of debt can be measured in several ways. One measure is the coupon rate. Another is the yield to maturity. (For perpetuities, this is the ratio of the annual interest payment to the market value of the debt.) If the debt is issued at par, the coupon rate and the yield to maturity will be identical at the time of issue. Assume that this is the case. Another measure is the yield bondholders *expect* to earn if they hold the debt to maturity. This expected yield will be less than the quoted yield to maturity if bondholders believe there is a positive probability of default. Since the expected yield cannot be observed directly we assume the return to bondholders is measured by the quoted yield. However it is important to remember that the quoted yield to maturity is a biased estimator (biased upward) of the expected yield. The increased probability of default as more bonds are issued is the main reason why the $i(\alpha)$ function rises to the right.

An appropriate comparative static analysis would be to compare the average cost of issuing either $10 million or $20 million of debt with guarantees preventing future equal or senior issues. Since the firm size is $100 million, for the smaller block $\alpha = .1$, and the average cost of the debt is .05. For the larger block, $\alpha = .2$, and the average cost of the debt will be .06. The firm would have interest costs of $500,000 per year if it issued $10 million of debt, and of $1,200,000 per year for $20 million of debt. The incremental cost of increasing the size of the block of debt from $10 million to $20 million is $700,000 per year, an incremental cost of .07 per year. The curve $m(\alpha)$ in Fig. 12–1 is the marginal cost curve associated with the average cost curve $i(\alpha)$. The equation for m is $m(\alpha) = .04 + (.2)\alpha$. When α is equal to .2 the marginal cost of issuing more debt is .08.[4]

Costs of Sequential Issues of Protected Subordinated Debt

Suppose that the firm first issued $10,000,000 ($\alpha = .1$) of fully protected bonds at a cost of 5%, and then later (or at the same time) decided to issue an additional amount of debt. Since the first $10 million of debt is fully protected, the second category of debt must necessarily be subordinate to the first. We can call the first category the senior debt and the second category the junior debt. Suppose the amount of junior debt is $10 million and is fully protected with respect to any issues of debt in the future.

Conceivably some financial analysts might feel that the assets of this company are relatively secure, the risk of default is slight, and that the fact that the second block of debt is subordinated to the first is of minor importance. They might be willing to recommend purchase of this block of junior debt if it were priced to yield slightly more than 6%. It would, however, be inconsistent with the previous assumption to suggest that the junior debt could be priced to yield an amount equal to 6%, since in this case the second block of $10 million is subordinate, whereas we have previously assumed that the average cost of a single $20 million issue of fully protected senior debt would be 6% and the incremental cost of the second $10 million would be 7%.

We would expect many financial analysts to be apprehensive about the security of the assets, and thus be more concerned about the fact that the debt is subordinated. They would be unwilling to recommend purchase unless the junior debt were priced above 7%.

It might be argued that if the firm set out to raise $20 million by debt, two separate issues of $10 million each (one subordinated to the other) might be more or less expensive than one $20 million issue of nonsubordinated

---

[4] It should be remembered that the .08 marginal cost applies only to the next dollar of debt issued; it does not apply to the next $10 million.

debt.[5] The one large issue would be more or less expensive, depending on whether the subordinated $10 million issue would require a quoted yield of more or less than 7%.

We suggest that the cost to the firm will tend to be the same regardless of which choice it makes. We will use an argument analogous to the now-familiar argument advanced initially by Modigliani and Miller to support the proposition that the average cost of capital of a firm is independent of its capital structure.[6] In essence, the argument, as it applies to the present problem, is that if the firm issued two blocks of bonds, one subordinate to the other, and both fully protected, an investor could buy a proportion of both blocks of bonds and have the same risk as if the firm had issued one large block, and the investor had invested the same total amount in that block. Assuming that there are some potential investors willing to switch, and that bonds of the same risk class are available as substitutes elsewhere, we expect the average return on the two blocks taken together to be equal to the average return on the large block.

Now assume that potential investors, because of preferences or legal restrictions, are unable to switch from one type of debt to another. The conclusion may still hold that a large issue of nonsubordinated debt will cost the firm the same amount as two separate issues, one senior to the other. Suppose the conclusion were not true, and two separate issues, one subordinate to the other, cost the firm less than a single large issue. Other firms would observe the lower cost and would also issue new debt in the form of separate categories. The firm would refund old debt (in the form of more expensive large blocks) into the less expensive separate issues with different seniorities. Over time the supply of the relatively expensive debt would decrease and the supply of relatively inexpensive types of debt would increase. This shift would continue until the alternatives of one large issue or several smaller issues (with the different issues having different priorities) were equally expensive.[7]

[5] For a discussion of the possible profitability of having categories of debt, see Eli Schwartz "Theory of the Capital Structure of the Firm," *The Journal of Finance* (March, 1959), pp. 18–39. Schwartz uses the term "discrimination" to describe the situation where the debt is not all of equal priority. Since the different issues are not equivalent he would expect them to appeal to different buyers at different prices (and costs). He describes the necessary graphical conditions for the superiority of the discriminating procedure. He does not argue that these conditions will hold, though he does give a mathematical example illustrating a situation where they do hold. For an argument that the structure of debt obligations should be irrelevant see A. A. Robichek and S. C. Myers, "Problems in the Theory of Optimal Capital Structure," *Journal of Financial and Quantitative Analysis* (June, 1966), pp. 1–35.

[6] F. Modigliani and M. Miller. "The Cost of Capital, Corporation Finance and the Theory of Investment," *The American Economic Review* (June, 1958), pp. 261–297.

[7] J. R. Hicks, in *Value and Capital*, Second Edition (Oxford University Press, Oxford, 1940), p. 144n, states "Thus the complications of the financial structure of firms seem to be largely due to attempts at discrimination on the capital market." There is little question that lenders (and other supplies of capital) have different investment objectives and are apt to value different characteristics of securities differently. Thus the more complex the security the more likely it is that different buyers will place different prices on the security. By adding special features attractive to a fraction of the market it may be possible in the

If this argument is accepted, then the $i(\alpha)$ curve in Fig. 12–1 represents the average cost of issuing a given quantity of debt protected against subordinate future issues. This debt might consist of one large fully protected issue, or of two (or more) issues of unequal priority, as long as each issue is fully protected against future issues.

The argument also implies that the marginal cost of an additional quantity of debt (protected against future subordination) is given by the $m(\alpha)$ curve in Fig. 12–1, where α measures the quantity of debt already outstanding.

We conclude that the firm, considering the costs of servicing the debt, should be indifferent as to whether it raises a given amount of debt by making one large issue or several smaller issues, of unequal priority, as long as each issue is protected.[8]

We now turn our attention to the cost effects of issuing debt that has partial protection.

The Costs of Partial Protection

Suppose that the firm, at the beginning of its life, issues $90 million common stock and $10 million debt on terms that allow the firm to raise in the future an additional $10 million debt that could have equal rights with the first issue. The first issue of debt could be sold at a yield of 5% if it were protected against equal or senior issues. If a full $20 million debt, wholly protected, against future subordination had been issued in one block, the average cost would be 6%. To sell the first block of $10 million under the circumstances described will require a quoted yield of more than 5%, but no larger than 6%.

If at the time the first $10 million debt is issued, the date at which the second $10 million is going to be issued is known with certainty, then it is possible to calculate exactly the yield that is required (theoretically) on the first block of debt. A specific example will be helpful to illustrate the calculations. Suppose it is known that the second $10 million debt will be issued exactly one year after the first block is issued.

Let I equal the annual interest payment, in millions of dollars, to be made in perpetuity on the first block of debt. In one year, the market value of that debt will be $(I/.06)$, since after the second block is issued, the market will want

---

short run to get a higher price (and pay a lower cost) than if these features were not included in the security. This implies the value to the investor of the total sum of the gingerbread added to the security is less than the cost to the firm.

[8] Before making a decision as to the relative desirability of different sized issues the firm must consider the costs of issuing the debt and carrying the extra cash. See Chapter 2. In addition one would want to consider future interest rate changes and allow for the possibility (in the case of marketable debt) that a large issue may be preferred because it may be more liquid.

a 6% return. During the first year, the $10 million debt will have a higher level of security than in later years and the debtholders should be satisfied to earn 5% on their investment during that one year.

At the end of the first year proceeds to the bondholders will be the interest payment of I plus the value of a bond equal to $I/.06$. The present value of

$$\left(I + \frac{I}{.06}\right) \quad \text{is} \quad \left(I + \frac{I}{.06}\right)(1 + .05)^{-1}.$$

If this present value is to equal $10 million, I must satisfy the following equation:

$$\left(I + \frac{I}{.06}\right)(1 + .05)^{-1} = \$10,000,000.$$

Solving for I gives

$$I = \$594,000.$$

The market value of the initial block of debt in one year will be $594,000/ .06 = $9,906,000. If at time one the firm borrows as planned an additional $10 million at a quoted yield of 6% its total interest payments after year two will be $594,000 + $600,000 = $1,194,000 per year.

The market value of its outstanding debt at that time will be

$$\frac{\$1,194,000}{.06} = \$19,906,000.$$

The debt at the beginning of the second year will be $19,906,000, not $20 million. The $594,000 cash payment made at the end of the first year is made up of $500,000 interest on the initial $10,000,000 borrowed, and a $94,000 repayment of capital. Thus the firm in effect has only $9,906,000 of the old debt outstanding at the beginning of the second year after it has issued $10 million new debt.

If the firm wanted to have $20 million debt capital at the beginning of the second year it would need to borrow $10,094,000 at that time. The interest on $10,094,000 at 6% would be $606,000. This amount, added to the interest of $594,000 on the original debt, makes a total of $1,200,000 annual interest from year two on. Notice that $1,200,000 per year interest is equal to the total interest the firm would have to pay if it issued one block of fully protected debt for $10 million and later borrowed a block of $10 million of subordinated debt, fully protected against future issues on which it would need to pay 7%.

Under these conditions, a firm that wanted to borrow $10 million immediately, and an additional $10 million a year later, would have two alternatives available to it.[9] One alternative is to borrow $10 million on a fully protected basis with a 5% coupon, and a year later borrow another $10 million of debt subordinate to the first issue but fully protected with respect to future issues.

[9] It could also borrow the entire $20 million immediately.

This issue would yield 7%. A second alternative is to borrow $10 million now, with a coupon of 5.94%, and borrow slightly more than $10 million with a coupon of 6.0% a year later. Both issues would have equal rights. Under the assumption made, the real costs of the two alternatives are identical. A firm concerned only with the real costs of borrowing might be indifferent between the two alternatives. However a firm that had a preference for mini- mizing the maximum cost that it paid for debt would prefer to issue the first debt with only limited protection, so that the coupon rate on its second borrowing would be 6% rather than 7%. (The second block has equal rights with the first thus its cost is less than if it were subordinate.)

In practice, the firm does not know with certainty when future loans will be made. If a debt issue does not carry protection against the issue of future debt of equal or higher priority, then lenders will need to be compensated by a higher yield than the interest rate associated with fully protected debt to offset the capital loss they will suffer if additional debt is issued. Lenders may, in addition, require compensation for the risk they bear because of uncer- tainty about when this capital loss will occur.

For example, assume the firm wanted to borrow $10 million now and have the right to issue an additional $10 million of equal priority debt at a later date. If the lenders did not know exactly when this second issue would be made, conservative (risk-averting) lenders would most probably require a coupon of nearly 6.0% on the initial debt. If there was a good chance that the firm would not borrow the second $10 million for several years, the total real cost of borrowing would be higher than if the firm had given full protec- tion on its initial debt.

It would appear that a firm might gain a reduction in the costs of borrowing through issuing debt that allowed future issues of equal priority to be made only after the passage of a given amount of time or after satisfying of a given set of conditions. The conditions could be of such a nature that when satisfied the firm was essentially in the same position as it was when the initial debt was issued. Thus another issue of debt would merely move the risk situation from a very safe level back down to a level that the bondholders of the initial issue find acceptable. The addition of the new debt should result in the lenders desiring the same yield as when the initial debt was originally issued. For example, one condition could be the addition of the same proportion of stock equity capital so that α remained unchanged from its initial value.[10]

Instead of having some form of protection the debt might carry no restric- tions as to the characteristics or the amount of future issues of debt. The lack of any protection would cause lenders to demand high interest rates. The investors would tend to fear the worse and anticipate a flood of future debt (some of which might have prior claims). The advantage of this type of un-

[10] This statement implies relaxing the assumption that the size of the firm stays con- stant.

protected debt is that it gives management a maximum flexibility. However, we would expect that unprotected debt would tend to increase the average cost of borrowing because of the risk-aversions tendencies of the investors in bonds.[11]

Conclusions

In evaluating the cost of borrowing one must consider both the priority status of a debt issue compared with other existing issues, and the type of protection the debt carries against the possibility of subsequent issues of debt with equal or higher priority.

We doubt that a firm can lower its real cost of borrowing by issuing at the same moment-in-time debt in many priority categories. Such attempted discrimination can be expected to be effective only if potential lenders were restricted to a narrow range of securities and if a limited group of corporations were able to issue their securities. These limitations are not characteristic of modern capital markets.

By contrast we believe that whether or not debt issues are protected against future issues can make a difference in the firm's real cost of borrowing. A firm that has a preference for minimizing the maximum interest rate on its debt can achieve this goal by issuing debt carrying no protection or only limited protection to lenders against future issues of the same or higher priority. However, the lower maximum interest rate achieved this way is likely to lead to a higher average real cost of borrowing.

The types of subordination and protection against subsequent issues are only two of the many ways in which a debt issue can be characterized. However, an understanding of how these characteristics affect the cost of debt is necessary to an understanding of the overall cost of raising capital.

PROBLEMS

1. The average return (i) demanded by debtholders (and potential buyers of bonds) is estimated to be

$$i = .05 + .08\frac{D}{D + S},$$

where D is the fully protected debt and S is the market value of the common stock. Assume the debt is a perpetuity and the company is going to make one issue of fully protected debt. The firm size will be $50 million. If debt is added it will replace common stock.

Required: (a) Compute the average and marginal cost of $10 million of fully protected debt.

---

[11] If the expected yields of the unprotected bonds were the same as the expected yields of protected bonds we would expect the market to prefer the protected bonds.

   (b) Compute the average and marginal cost of $20 million of fully protected debt.
   (c) What is the annual interest cost of adding another $10 million of debt to the first $10 million?

2. Continue Problem 1. Assume that the initial block of $10 million debt (fully protected) was issued to yield .066. After one year it was decided to issue a second $10 million debt. This second debt would be junior to the first issue but senior to any debt issued subsequently.

   Required: Based on the information presented in Problem 1 and in this problem, at what yield might you expect the second issue of $10 million to sell?

3. Continue Problem 1. Assume the firm has just issued $10 million debt (at perpetuity) that was not fully protected and that an additional $10 million debt could be issued with equal rights (but no more than $10 million could be so issued).

   Required: (a) What is the minimum yield that you would expect for the first issue of $10 million? The maximum yield?
   (b) Assume that it is expected that the second debt will be issued three years from now. What interest payment would you expect on the first issue? What yield for the second issue when it is issued? What yield would you expect for the first issue after the issuance of the second issue?
   (c) What will be the market value of the first debt after the issue of the second $10 million?

4. The $113,921 annual benefits from an investment have a present value of $700,000 using a .10 cost of capital and a 10-year life. The cost of the investment is $1,200,000. The firm has an opportunity to lease at a cost of $100,000 a year for ten years.[12]

   Required: (a) Assuming the firm has a borrowing cost of .05, should the firm lease?
   (b) The firm believes that its cost of capital will not change as more debt is borrowed but that the borrowing rate will increase. Assume the firm changes its capital structure so that the borrowing rate goes up to .10 (the cost of capital stays at .10). Should the firm lease?

REFERENCES

See References for Chapter 11.

[12] This question is based on comments by Neil Houghton and Jack Amon, former Cornell students.

CHAPTER 13

Income Bonds[1]

Finance officers are constantly seeking cheaper sources of capital. The income bond is a form of security that has not been used to a large extent, but its use is likely to increase in the future. A discussion of income bonds is particularly useful as a learning device since it helps open our imagination to the possibility of new types of securities. On the spectrum of securities ranked according to riskiness to investors income bonds would lie between subordinated debentures and preferred stock.

In 1955 Sidney M. Robbins wrote a comprehensive article urging a bigger role for income bonds.[2] In a book published in 1966 Robbins and Cohen wrote, "Were it not for the continuing stigma attached to the income bond as a result of its emergence from railroad reorganizations, it would undoubtedly be used more widely since there is an evident tendency for a corporation's bonds to cost less than its preferred shares."[3]

This chapter will review some of the primary points made by Robbins in his 1955 article and will attempt to define somewhat more exactly the economic advantages of income bonds compared to preferred stock.

Income bonds are not easy to define since they come in a variety of forms. They have many characteristics found in regular bonds or preferred stock, thus may be said to be merely variations on bonds or preferred stock. But if income bonds have essentially the qualities of preferred stock, they would seem to warrant consideration by prospective issuers of securities as a way to avoid income tax; however, if income bonds had the same characteristics as preferred stock there would be no reason to expect special treatment under the tax code as compared to preferred stock. If income bonds are essentially like regular bonds, there would be little reason for using them because they sell at a premium over straight bonds and are not as easily marketable. We will attempt to define income bonds so that they find acceptance by both the taxpayer and tax collector. They are a hybrid combining the characteristics of

---

[1] This chapter is based on an article written with Bowman Brown, "Why Corporations Should Consider Income Bonds," *Financial Executive* (October, 1967), pp. 74–78.

[2] Sidney M. Robbins, "A Bigger Role for Income Bonds," *Harvard Business Review* (November–December, 1955).

[3] Jerome B. Cohen and Sidney M. Robbins, *The Financial Manager* (Harper and Row, New York, 1966), p. 600.

both their parents; a new variety of security with characteristics that none of the traditional securities capture as well.[4]

Gordon Donaldson in an article defending preferred stock uses the following differences between an income bond and preferred stock to reach the conclusion that "the income bond is not a direct substitute for preferred stock from the risk standpoint."[5]

1. The interest *plus sinking fund* on the bond may equal or exceed dividend payments on the preferred stock.
2. There is a difference between earned income and cash flow, so that a company might be liable for income bond interest at a time of zero or negative cash flows.[6]

We shall show that while the first point *may be* true for some finite time period, for some large part of the firm's life, the dividends of the preferred stock *will be* larger than interest and sinking funds. Also, the sinking fund plus interest do not have to be larger than the preferred dividends, it can be less. Third, cash flow from operations will frequently be larger than the income of the period, thus if the firm has income for the period, it is also very likely to have a net positive cash flow from operations. Donaldson is correct that the total cash flow may be negative, but the relationship of income and cash flow is of such a nature (especially during a period of business contraction) that the second type of difference is not of major importance.

However, a disagreement with Donaldson's analysis does not mean that there is total disagreement with his basic conclusions. Income bonds and preferred stock are not perfect substitutes for one another. On the other hand, the risk differences to the issuing corporation are much less than implied, in fact we conclude that the risk differences between income bond and preferred stock are not material. Because they can be retired with the tax savings we can argue that income bonds have a less risk than preferred stock.

Characteristics of Income Bonds

Income bonds have a set rate of interest, but the interest has to be paid only if earned. The interest may be cumulative to give the investor more

---

[4] There are two requirements necessary for us to have a tax deduction for interest on income bonds; first there must be some reason for allowing a deduction for interest even though dividends are not deductible, and second income bonds must be enough like debt so that the deduction of interest on income bonds is included in the government's definition of interest on debt.

[5] Gordon Donaldson. "In Defense of Preferred Stock," *Harvard Business Review* (July–August, 1962), reprinted in James Van Horne, *Foundations for Financial Management* (Irwin, Homewood, Ill., 1966), p. 213.

[6] Donaldson, *ibid.*, p. 213. He lists a third reason. A period of loss may be followed by a profit but the corporation may still not be in a position to pay interest. While this is true, it does not substantiate a clearcut superiority of preferred stock over income bonds.

security.[7] The interest features of income bonds are not greatly different from the dividend features of preferred stock. The most significant difference is that the payment of dividends on preferred stock is more discretionary, it is usually mandatory to pay interest on income bonds if income is earned. The interest payment on an income bond is substantially different from that on straight bonds since there is no obligation on the part of the corporation to pay interest when it has not earned an amount equal to the interest. Consequently income bondholders cannot force a corporation, which has a loss period, into receivership.

Income bonds may give their holders a position preferred to that of general business creditors in the hierarchy of creditor's rights, but below other bondholders. Preferred stockholders are placed below the general business creditors and would be below the income bondholders. The effect of this arrangement, where it exists, would make credit a little more difficult to secure with income bonds outstanding than with preferred stock. If the income bonds were made junior to the general business creditors it would increase the risk of the income bondholders getting nothing in the event of liquidation, but the investors would still be in a better position than the preferred stockholders.

Income bonds must have a maturity date and in this respect differ from preferred stock. A maturity date is considered by the tax courts to be a necessary condition for there to be debt (though there is no essential reason for this requirement). If there is a maturity date, there must be some provision for retiring debt. Provision is commonly made in the form of a sinking fund. A maturity date imposes more risk on the borrower. If he does not have the funds for repayment at the maturity date he may be forced into receivership. Preferred stock has no such risk since no provision must be made for retirement, and there is no way the preferred shareholder can force the issuing firm into bankruptcy. There have been issues of preferred stock with provision for repurchase each year or with provision for mandatory redemption, but these issues are rare.

To reduce the risk associated with meeting the retirement payments several steps could be taken. The bonds could be made callable past a certain date, with the firm required to call a given percentage of the bonds if an amount of funds equal to or greater than some given amount is earned.[8] Thus not only would the firm unconditionally have to retire bonds at given moments in time, but the firm would be given the opportunity to meet this requirement in advance (in fact to some extent the firm would be required to do this) if the funds were available.

In summary, income bondholders generally have substantially greater rights against the corporation than holders of preferred stock and less rights than

---

[7] In practice the period of cumulation varies considerably, but there is no reason why the interest cannot accumulate without limit.

[8] The corporation would also want to be able to call the bonds in the event the revenue code were changed.

bondholders. Income bondholders have the right to demand their money at maturity, and the right to interest if earned. They may also have senior liquidation claims compared to general creditors thus making it somewhat more difficult for the firm to secure credit. As compared with regular bonds, income bonds are less risky to the corporation because the holders do not have the right to demand interest as it falls due. The risk associated with income bonds are between the risk normally associated with preferred stock and that associated with bonds.[9] What is the optimum mix of securities (from the point of view of the issuing corporation)?[10] A fund raiser can probably get the same degree of risk by using preferred stocks and bonds as he can by using these securities with income bonds. This may be demonstrated by arbitrarily assigning risk factors of 0 to preferred stock, 1 to income bonds, and 2 to bonds. Risk in the middle ranges may be achieved with or without the use of income bonds.[11] The important question is whether income bonds can be used to achieve certain levels of risk more cheaply than combinations of other securities.

Comparing the Cost of Preferred Stock and Income Bonds

There is little question that income bonds can be used to raise funds more cheaply than preferred stock. We will illustrate this in a situation where we roughly equate the risk of the two types of securities and thus reduce the importance of this factor. This may be done by: (1) assuming an issue of preferred stock with the same dividend rate as the interest rate of an issue of income bonds, (2) stripping the securities of their differences in creditor's rights, and (3) eliminating the discretion in the payment of dividends if the income is earned. What is left are identical issues of preferred stock and income bonds with the exception that there is a maturity date attached to the income bonds.[12]

The differences in the cash outlays to the issuer of the income bonds resulting from the maturity date can be eliminated by applying the tax savings generated by the use of income bonds instead of preferred stock to provide for

[9] Empirical evidence of the difference in prices associated with preferred stocks, income bonds, and bonds has been noted by Sidney M. Robbins in his 1955 *Harvard Business Review* article (*op. cit.*). He says investment bankers place a .21 to 1.00 percentage point interest premium on income bonds over comparable bonds, and that they sell at less than comparable preferred stock.

[10] For one position see F. Modigliani and M. H. Miller, "The Cost of Capital, Corporation Finance and the Theory of Investment," *The American Economic Review* (July, 1958), pp. 261–297.

[11] We should consider the relevance of the fact that preferred stock would not be included as debt but income bonds would be included.

[12] It should be realized that with the given assumptions the maturity provision of the bonds would make them less risky to prospective purchasers and thus would allow the issuer to pay a lower interest rate on the bonds, thus the equality of dividends and interest introduces a bias in favor of preferred stock.

repayment of the bonds through a sinking fund. When this is done the bonds will have the same cash outlay as preferred stock during the period in which the payments to the sinking fund are made, and at the end of that period the bonds will be retired. With preferred stock the obligation represented by the preferred stock will still be outstanding. We will define the disutility of having the preferred stock outstanding compared to retiring the bonds to be the extra cost of using preferred stock instead of income bonds.

EXAMPLE: Compare the use of $1 million of income bonds with $1 million of preferred stock, both paying .05. The corporate tax rate is assumed to be .4.

Comparison of Annual Cash Outlays to Corporation

	INCOME BONDS	PREFERRED STOCK
Interest	50,000	50,000
Tax saved	20,000	0
Net cost to corporation	30,000	50,000

Assume the $20,000 annual saving from the income bonds (50,000 − 30,000) are applied to a sinking fund earning .03 after taxes. The income bonds will be retired in 31 years. The $1 million of preferred stock would still be outstanding.

These computations assume a corporate tax rate of .40. If the tax rate were greater, the savings would be greater to the corporation issuing income bonds and the income bonds would be paid off sooner. If the rate were lower, it would take longer to pay off the income bonds.

If the sinking fund earned a higher return (or if the firm had opportunities to earn an excess of .03) the duration of repayment would be reduced. For example, if the firm's true value of money were .10 it would require only 18 years (plus a fraction) of interest payments before the bonds could be retired with the tax savings.

If the securities are held by a corporate investor, preferred stock has the advantage of a .85 dividend received credit. This characteristic would narrow the gap between preferred stock and bonds, but would not change the fact that debt has a less total after-tax cost to the issuer—investor combination.[13]

This above analysis indicates that savings can be achieved through the use of income bonds instead of preferred stock.

[13] Preferred stock issued prior to 1942 by a public utility is a special situation because there is an additional deduction to the issuing company of 29.166% (at 1967 tax rates).

Use of Income Bonds

If income bonds can provide a large degree of risk avoidance compared to bonds and cost less than preferred stock, why are they not used more? One reason is that income bonds have been used extensively in connection with reorganizations, and thus they tend to be associated with weak corporations. Recently income bonds have been issued by strong corporations but the historical association with weakness seems to be fading slowly.

A second reason offered is that strong companies do not need to issue income bonds because they can bear the burden of fixed charges on bonds. While this argument is superficially attractive, it should be noted that even a strong corporation can issue only a limited amount of low-cost debt with low risk. It may be more logical for such a corporation to pay the interest premium income bonds would cost compared to the interest cost of regular debt when the choice may actually be between income bonds and an equity type of security (whose dividends are not deductible for tax purposes).

One fear of financial officers that is preventing the widespread use of income bonds may be that if many corporations used this type of security to raise capital the government would react and change the internal revenue code and disallow the deduction. This is a somewhat confused and incomplete analysis. The present code has a bias in favor of fixed-payment type of securities (interest payments being deductible and dividends not). This is undesirable from the point of view of the economy since it leads to corporations being more unstable. Corporations are more susceptible to ruin if business activity slackens. Income bonds used instead of regular debt adds to the surviving rather than reducing power of a corporation, and as such should be welcomed by government decision makers. This is not to say that the bias in favor of debt will not be reviewed by the government in the future (it is a questionable arrangement). But this possible review does not currently prevent the issuance of long-term debt. Income bonds may be slightly more risk-producing than preferred stock, but the relative riskiness of the two types of securities is not clear since the retirement of the income bonds tends to be risk-reducing.

We conclude that none of these difficulties are sufficient to preclude the use of income bonds. The benefits of income bonds arising from the tax structure are too great. However, it may be that innovating firms will find the bond market unreceptive to income bonds.

The market may have to be educated as to the nature and advantages of income bonds. Maybe a new title is needed such as "preferred income bonds." In any event, given the present tax code, it is apparent that there is a place in the capital structure of a corporation for income bonds. The corporate financial officer who does not investigate the possibility of their use is giving up the opportunity for tax savings (where the income bonds are used instead of equity-type securities) or reducing risk (where the income bonds are used instead of pure debt).

PROBLEMS

1. The ABC Company is either going to issue $10 million of preferred stock yielding .08 or income bonds yielding .08. The bonds would have a life of five years and would be characterized by payments of $2 million of principal each year through their five year life (the annual payment would be $2 million plus interest). Assume a .4 tax rate will be in effect throughout the five-year period and that the firm is a profitable firm with little chance of not having significant taxable income. The company uses a .08 time-discount factor.

   Required: Should the company issue the preferred stock or the bonds?

2. Continue Problem 1. Assume the bonds are twenty-year income bonds repayable at maturity and paying .08 interest annually.

   Required: (a) Compute the present value of debt using .08 as the discount rate.
   (b) Compute the present value of the debt using .08 assuming a .6 tax rate and thirty years until maturity.
   (c) Assume the bonds are perpetuities. What is the present value of the debt assuming a tax rate of .6?

3. The XYZ Company is either going to issue $10 million of preferred stock yielding .10 or income bonds yielding .10 with a maturity of 30 years (the bonds will be repaid at maturity).

   Assume a .6 income tax rate. The company uses a .10 time discount factor (it can invest additional funds to earn .10).

   Required: (a) Assuming the tax savings are invested to earn .10, in how many years would the tax savings arising from using bonds instead of preferred stock accumulate sufficiently to pay the $10 million debt?
   (b) Why might one want to use income bonds rather than conventional debt?

REFERENCES

Childs, J. F. *Long-term Financing* (Prentice-Hall, Englewood Cliffs, N.J., 1961).

Cohen, Jerome B., and Robbins, Sidney M. *The Financial Manager* (Harper & Row, New York, 1966).

Donaldson, Gordon. "In Defense of Preferred Stock," *Harvard Business Review* (July–August), 1962.

Halford, F. A. "Income Bonds," *Financial Analysts Journal* (January–February), 1964.

Johnson, R. W. "Subordinated Debt: Debt that Serves as Equity," *Journal of Finance* (March), 1955.

Robbins, Sidney M. "A Bigger Role for Income Bonds," *Harvard Business Review* (November–December), 1955.

CHAPTER 14

The Bond-Refunding Decision as a Markov Process[1]

SYMBOLS

p_{ij} probability of moving from state i to state j in the next move

$\pi(n)$ the state vector at time n. This is a row vector.

P the transition probability matrix

$P(A \mid B)$ The conditional probability of A given event B

$P(A, B)$ the joint probability of events A and B (both A and B occurring)

There are four basic steps in the analysis of the decision whether or not to refund a currently outstanding bond issue prior to its maturity date. These steps are:

1. The computation of the relevant cash flows (or the relevant costs).
2. The choice of the rate of discount to be used in making the analysis.
3. The treatment of uncertainty.
4. The incorporation of qualitative factors.

Computation of the Relevant Cash Flows

Errors have been made in analyzing the bond refunding decision by incorporating in the analysis sunk costs, for example, the discount associated with the currently outstanding bonds. Except as they might affect the income tax computation, these costs are not relevant to the decision. The call premiums and call expenses, the issue costs of the new bonds, duplicate interest payments during the period of issue (taking into account the return earned by investing the excess funds in short term securities), and the savings in interest resulting

[1] A large part of this chapter was originally published as an article in *Management Science* (August, 1966).

from the new issue, are relevant factors. The cash flows should be on an after tax basis.

The Choice of the Rate of Interest

The choice of the rate of interest to be used in discounting the future cash flows has been at issue for many years and remains unresolved. There are essentially three choices:

1. The cost of capital.
2. The rate of interest on the new securities.
3. The rate of interest on default-free securities.

Assume a situation where the possible interest saving associated with refunding is $100,000 a year and the life of the current bonds is ten years. Using a .10 cost of capital as the rate of discount the present value of this saving is $641,770. Using a .05 discount rate (the interest rate of the new issue) the present value of the saving is $772,170. If the cost of the refunding is $650,000 should the refunding be made? Using the interest rate on default free securities would make the present value of the saving even larger than $772,170.

Many firms would reject the refunding using the argument that the funds can earn .10 elsewhere in the firm. However, the risks associated with the refunding are much less than with the normal investment (the cash outlays for incremental interest on the present debt are certain from the viewpoint of the corporation's treasurer) and the firm is better off accepting the investment. An accept decision is indicated if we take only the time value of money into account, and leave out the risk premium incorporated in the cost of capital.

In the discussion which follows we will assume that the savings have been computed using the appropriate rate of discount. For some this will mean the cost of capital, but the author prefers a measure that does not incorporate a risk premium (for the possibility of default) in the discount rate being used to adjust for the time value of money.

Uncertainty

The usual analysis for bond refunding takes the cash flows which would result from an immediate refunding and the decision is based on this computation. There might also be included qualitative factors such as the reaction of the present holders of the bonds to the refunding, or the effect of the additional workload on the treasurers' staff. The primary purpose of this chapter is to suggest that the more interesting task is not to answer the question whether or not to refund now, but to prepare decision rules as to the correct interest rate to trigger the refunding, taking uncertainties relative to the future into account.

Let us assume the ABC Company has issued a .06 bond. After issue the treasurer may compute the interest rate which is required to make refunding desirable (a breakeven interest rate). Each moment of time requires a different breakeven rate since the bond is continuously approaching maturity. Fortunately the changes in the breakeven rate will be slight and for practical purposes the same rate may be used for several time periods. The treasurer will watch the bond market and when the market rate of interest for bonds of comparable firms (or for its own bonds) reaches the breakeven rate of interest the firm has its first decision. Let us assume the current interest rate is a shade below the breakeven rate. Should the refunding take place? Ignoring possible future changes the analysis would indicate that it should. However, a more complete analysis suggests we should be interested in the question as to whether the interest rate will soon be going lower than the current rate. If the rate is expected to decrease then maybe we should wait for the reduction. Now assume the rate has actually decreased. Should we wait further, or should we refund now? Obviously the refunding problem has become complex. We must know not only what the future interest rates will be but also when the changes in rates will occur. The present value of the saving which will occur if we refund at a given interest rate will be a function of when the refunding takes place, which in turn will be a function of when the interest rate that triggers the refunding is encountered.

A Markov Process

A Markov process is a mathematical system which has stochastic elements. If we are in state i then we can describe the probability of being in state j after the next move for all possible states. In fact we can describe the probabilities of being in any state after any number of moves. An important characteristic of the Markov process is that in general the probability of moving to any state j is only dependent on where we are moving from, that is, where the move originates. We can prepare a transition matrix, that is, a matrix of the probabilities of moving from state i to state j.

Table of p_{ij}'s				Transition Matrix

$i \backslash j$	1	2	3
1	p_{11}	p_{12}	p_{13}
2	p_{21}	p_{22}	p_{23}
3	p_{31}	p_{32}	p_{33}

$$\begin{bmatrix} p_{11} & p_{12} & p_{13} \\ p_{21} & p_{22} & p_{23} \\ p_{31} & p_{32} & p_{33} \end{bmatrix}$$

In the matrix, p_{21} is the probability of moving from State 2 to State 1; p_{12} is the probability of moving from State 1 to State 2.[2] The letter P will be used to represent the transition matrix.

Let $\pi(n)$ be the state vector or the vector of probabilities at time n. Thus $\pi(0) = (1, 0, 0)$ would mean that the probability of being in State 1 at time zero is one (we are now in State 1). The probabilities of being in States 2 or 3 are zero. $\pi(1) = (.5, .4, .1)$ means that after one time period (or after one trial) the probability of being in State 1 is .5, in State 2 is .4, and State 3 is .1.

The following important relationship holds the key to the computations that follow:

$$\pi(n + 1) = \pi(n)P$$

where $\pi(n + 1)$ and $\pi(n)$ are row vectors and P is a matrix.

Bond Refunding as a Markov Process

We will assume that interest rates follow a Markov process. The assumption that interest rates follow a Markov process will not be completely valid as a bond approaches maturity if the term structure of interest rates is not flat.[3] Also, interest rates may be subject to changing probabilities as world economic events change, thus not be a Markov process. Despite these limitations we will assume a Markov process applies.

Each interest rate in each time period is defined as a possible state. Let us assume that we are currently at time zero and have an interest rate of .05. We can compute the probability of different interest rates one time period from now. The interest rates of two periods from now will depend on where we are at the end of the first period. At time zero we can consider the future changes in interest rates to be a Markov process. For each time period we want to know the probability of the different interest rates. Once we have established the transition matrix the computations of the state vectors $\pi(n)$ are not difficult. To illustrate the process we will use an artifically simplified example. Expand-

Table of p_{ij}'s

i \ j	5.0	4.9	4.8%
5.0%	.7	.2	.1
4.9	.2	.5	.3
4.8	.0	.3	.7

[2] For a very fine description of Markov processes see R. A. Howard, *Dynamic Programming and Markov Processes* (Technology Press and Wiley, 1960). This section is based on material from that book.

[3] This observation was made to the author by Stewart G. Myers.

ing it to a realistic situation would increase the amount of pencil pushing (or computer time) but it would not change the basic approach.

We will assume the transition matrix on page 224 applies.

It should be noted that the sum of the probabilities of each row add up to 1. This is a necessary condition since we are summing the probabilities of the possible outcomes arising from a trial and have partitioned the sample space (i.e., fully described the possible outcomes so that there are no overlaps).

Assume the current rate of interest is 5.0% and that this is the break-even interest rate.

The example is artificial since we are not allowing the interest rate to go above the current rate of 5.0% nor below 4.8%; thus we are allowing only three possible interest rates. The .7 in the northwest box means that if we are in State 5.0 there is a .7 probability of staying at 5.0 in the next time period. However, there is a .2 probability of moving to State 4.9 and a .1 probability of moving to 4.8.

The initial state vector is

$$\pi(o) = (1\ 0\ 0)$$

That is, we are currently in State one and the interest rate is 5.0%.

Next we want to obtain the state vector after one time period.

$$\pi(1) = \pi(o)P$$

$$= (1\ 0\ 0) \begin{bmatrix} .7 & .2 & .1 \\ .2 & .5 & .3 \\ .0 & .3 & .7 \end{bmatrix}$$

$$= (.7\ .2\ .1)$$

Starting from a 5.0% interest rate after one time period we have the following probabilities for the three possible states:

STATE	PROBABILITY
5.0	.7
4.9	.2
4.8	.1

The state vectors for time periods 2 and 3 are

$$\pi(2) = \pi(1)P = [.7\ .2\ .1] \begin{bmatrix} .7 & .2 & .1 \\ .2 & .5 & .3 \\ .0 & .3 & .7 \end{bmatrix} = [.53\ .27\ .20]$$

$$\pi(3) = \pi(2)P = [.53\ .27\ .20] \begin{bmatrix} .7 & .2 & .1 \\ .2 & .5 & .3 \\ .0 & .3 & .7 \end{bmatrix} = [.43\ .30\ .27].$$

We could continue the computations and determine the probabilities of the different states for each of the future time periods. For simplification of presentation we will assume that we are only concerned with a three-period situation.

The Reward Matrix

Before proceeding further we need a reward or payoff matrix. We want to know the net present value arising from each state for each time period. This requires a computation of the savings from refunding for each interest rate below the break-even rate of interest for each time period. The feasibility of making these computations has been illustrated elsewhere.[4]

The following table shows the present values assumed for the different states and different time periods. We are assuming that the firm breaks even refunding at 5.0%.

Payoff Table (the net present value of the savings)

STATE	TIME PERIOD		
	1	2	3
5.0	0	0	0
4.9	100	70	40
4.8	200	150	60

The second line (opposite State 4.9) indicates that if the refunding takes place in Time period 1 (that is one time period from now) when the interest rate is 4.9 the present value of the saving is 100. If the refunding takes place in the second period the present value of the saving is 70. If the refunding takes place in Period 3 the present value of the saving is 40. These numbers are used for illustrative purposes only (they are not derived).

Testing Two Decision Rules

To test the decision rules "refund when the interest rate reaches 4.9" and "refund when the interest rate reaches 4.8" we will revise the transition matrix. We will now assume that the interest rate can only change by .1 a period

---

[4] R. H. Berglund. "A Practical Application of the Revenue Requirement Technique as an Aid in Decision Making," an unpublished paper presented by Mr. Berglund of Northern States Power at the Iowa State Conference on Public Utility Valuation and the Rate Making Process (April 30–May 2, 1963).

and that we will refund at the first encounter with the interest rate of the decision rule; thus the path will end when that interest rate is first encountered. We handle this requirement by making the transition probability equal to 1 when the desired interest rate is encountered. To test the 4.9 rule the new transition matrix with the 4.9 as a trapping state, becomes:

i \ j	5.0	4.9
5.0	.7	.3
4.9	0	1.0

The computation of the state vectors for the different time periods using the new transition matrix for the decision rule "refund when the rate is 4.9" is as follows:

$$\pi(0) = (1 \ 0)$$

$$\pi(1) = \pi(0)P = (1 \ 0) \begin{bmatrix} .7 & .3 \\ .0 & 1.0 \end{bmatrix} = (.7 \ .3)$$

$$\pi(2) = \pi(1)P = (.7 \ .3) \begin{bmatrix} .7 & .3 \\ 0 & 1.0 \end{bmatrix} = (.49 \ .51)$$

$$\pi(3) = \pi(2)P = (.49 \ .51) \begin{bmatrix} .7 & .3 \\ 0 & 1.0 \end{bmatrix} = (.34 \ .66)$$

We cannot use the probabilities as presented since this would include some double counting of probabilities. We are interested in the changes in the probabilities which occur each time period. For example, in time period 1 there is a .30 probability of the rate being 4.9 and in time period 2 there is a .51 probability. But this .51 probability includes the .30 probability of time period 1, thus we want to measure the increment in the probability for the second time period. The following table shows the computation of the expected value of the decision rule "refund when the interest rate is 4.9."

PERIOD	PROBABILITY OF 4.9	CHANGE OF PROBABILITY	PAYOFF	EXPECTATION
1	.30	.30	$100	$30
2	.51	.21	70	15
3	.66	.15	40	6
		.66		$51

There is an alternative (and equivalent) method of computation. The probability of refunding in any period, *given* that we have not previously refunded, is .3 (i.e., the probability of moving from the State 5.0 to the State 4.9 in the next period is .3. Let this probability be $P(A \mid B)$. $P(B)$ is the probability of not refunding in a previous period. In Period 1 this probability is 1. In the second period it is 1 times .7 (there is a .3 probability of refunding in Period 1). For Period 3 $P(B)$ is $1 \times .7 \times .7$ (this is the probability that we did not refund in the previous periods).

We want to obtain the joint probabilities for each time period of having the interest rate 4.9 and not having previously refunded. In terms of the formula relating joint and conditional probabilities:

$$P(A, B) = P(B)\, P(A \mid B)$$

PERIOD	$P(B)$	$P(A\mid B)$	$P(A, B)$
1	1.	.30	.30
2	$1 \times .7 = .7$	.30	.21
3	$1 \times .7 \times .7 = .49$	.30	.147

We can now compute the expected monetary value of the decision rule "refund when the interest rate is 4.9."

PERIOD	PROBABILITY OF 4.9 AND THIS IS FIRST OCCURRENCE	PAYOFF	EXPECTATION
1	.300	100	30
2	.210	70	15
3	.147	40	6
			$51

Next we have to determine the transition matrix for the decision rule "refund when the interest rate is 4.8." The trapping state is now 4.8 (the probability is one that if the interest rate is 4.8 we do not leave that state, that is, the decision is made).

$$P = \begin{bmatrix} .7 & .3 & .0 \\ .2 & .5 & .3 \\ 0 & 0 & 1.0 \end{bmatrix}$$

The state vectors are

$$\pi(0) = (1\ 0\ 0)$$

$$\pi(1) = \pi(0)P = (1\ 0\ 0) \begin{bmatrix} .7 & .3 & .0 \\ .2 & .5 & .3 \\ 0 & 0 & 1.5 \end{bmatrix} = (.7\ .3\ .0)$$

$$\pi(2) = \pi(1)P = (.7\ .3\ .0) \begin{bmatrix} .7 & .3 & .0 \\ .2 & .5 & .3 \\ 0 & 0 & 1.0 \end{bmatrix} = (.55\ .36\ .09)$$

$$\pi(3) = \pi(2)P = (.55\ .36\ .09) \begin{bmatrix} .7 & .3 & .0 \\ .2 & .5 & .3 \\ 0 & 0 & 1.0 \end{bmatrix} = (.457\ .345\ .198)$$

The computation of the expected value of the decision rule "refund when the interest rate is 4.8" is:

PERIOD	PROBABILITY OF 4.8 OR LESS	CHANGE IN PROBABILITY	PAYOFF	EXPECTATION
1	.00	.00	$200	0
2	.09	.09	150	13.50
3	.198	.108	60	6.78
		.198		19.98

The computations indicate that we should refund at 4.9 with an expected gain of $51 and not wait for the interest rate to decrease to 4.8. A change in the transition matrix or the reward matrix might result in a different decision. For example, subtract 40 from the 4.9 line in the reward matrix and the decision to wait until the interest rate reaches 4.8 becomes more desirable.

Evaluation of the Procedure

The suggested procedure omits making a valuation of the advantage of reducing the degree of uncertainty by refunding when the interest rate is 4.9 rather than waiting for the rate to sink to 4.8. It assumes that it is appropriate to use monetary expectation as the basis of the decision. It is well known that monetary expectations may not be a reliable guide for making decisions. Finally, in computing the expected value of each decision rule it assumes the same rule is being used for each time period. The optimum decision rate may change as we draw closer to the maturity date of the debt. We should also test other decision rules such as "refund in Period 1 at 4.9 and 4.8 in period 2."

Each of these assumptions can be modified to obtain a more refined analysis of the problem. However, one should not lose sight of one of the main difficulties, the obtaining of the transition matrix.

If the matrix is based on the subjective beliefs of management we can use the suggested procedure to enable management to make the decisions consistent with these beliefs. There is no reason why the matrix cannot be based on a combination of historical evidence of changes in interest rates and the judgment of management relative to what is expected to happen in the coming periods.

Conclusions

The first step in the bond refunding decision must be the recognition that a decision exists. If the current interest rate is below the break-even rate then refunding now is in a sense desirable. It may, however, be more desirable to wait for a further reduction in interest rates. Hopefully the procedure suggested in this chapter, or a variant of it, can lead to a systemic quantitative evaluation of the merits of the many alternatives available to management.

PROBLEMS

1. The ABC Company has $10 million bonds outstanding paying .07 interest; the bonds have twenty years until maturity and can be called at $1050 per bond. The face value of the bond is $1000. The expense of obtaining $10 million to accomplish a refunding would be $400,000. New twenty-year bonds issued at par would bear an interest rate of .06. The default-free interest rate is .05. The firm's cost of capital is .10.

   Required: Should the ABC Company refund?

2. Continue Problem 1. Assume a study of interest rates indicate that the following transition probabilities apply:

	.062	.061	.060	.059	.058
.062	.8	.2	.0	0	0
.061	.1	.4	.3	.2	0
.060	0	.3	.5	.2	0
.059	0	0	.1	.7	.2
.058	0	0	0	.1	.9

We will assume that the probabilities apply to the move from the present time to the interest rate at the next feasible moment for a bond issue by this company. The current interest rate is .06.

Required: Assume there are only two alternatives: refund now or wait one period. The time between feasible refunding periods is so short that if we wait we can still use twenty years until maturity. To simplify the analysis assume it is appropriate to use a default-free rate of .05 to accomplish all the time discounting. Assume $10 million will be borrowed to accomplish the refunding.

3. Continue Problems 1 and 2. Assume that it is feasible for the company to wait two periods. If it waits two periods that will mean that there are only nineteen years until maturity.

Required: Determine whether the company should refund now or wait for two periods. Make the assumption that the company will refund in period one if the interest rate is either .060 or .059 and will refund in Period 2 if not refunded in Period 1.

REFERENCES

Berglund, R. H. "A Practical Application of the Revenue Requirement Technique as an Aid in Decision Making," an unpublished paper presented by Mr. Berglund of Northern States Power at the Iowa State Conference on Public Utility Valuation and the Rate Making Process (April 30–May 2, 1963).

Bowein, O. D. "The Refunding Decision," *Journal of Finance* (March), 1966.

Howard, R. A. *Dynamic Programming and Markov Processes* (The Technology Press of the Massachusetts Institute of Technology and John Wiley, New York, 1960).

Spiller, E. A. "Time Adjusted Breakeven Rate for Refunding," *Financial Executive* (July), 1963.

Weingartner, H. M. "Optimal Timing of Bond Refunding," *Management Science* (March), 1967.

CHAPTER 15

The Call Provision

SYMBOLS

r_i the interest rate in time period i

$\bar{B}(n)$ the expected price of the bond at time n

$B(t)$ the price of the noncallable bond at time t

C_t or $C(t)$ the call price at time t

V the value of the call provision

$B^*(t)$ the value of the callable bond

p_{ij} the probability of the interest rate moving to r_j when it is currently r_i

$V_t(r_i)$ the maximum expected present value at time t when the interest rate at time t is r_i

$B_t(r_i)$ the price of the bond at time t when the interest rate is r_i

Most corporate bonds have provisions that allow the corporation to "call" or retire the bond before maturity. The call price is generally above the face or maturity value at the time that the bonds may be first called. (The time of first call may be some reasonably long period, such as five years, after issue.) In this chapter we will discuss the reasons why corporations attach call provisions to bonds; we will also discuss some approaches to placing a value on the call provision.[1]

The Motivation for Call Provisions

Basically a call provision enables a corporation to retire before maturity the debt that is presently outstanding. The call provision gives management flexibility to retire the present debt, to replace it with cheaper or less restrictive debt, to replace it with common stock, or to shrink the size of the corporation.

---

[1] For many of the concepts developed in this chapter the author is indebted to an article by G. Pye, "The Value of the Call Option of a Bond," *The Journal of Political Economy* (April, 1966), pp. 200–205.

The price at which the debt can be retired is well defined by the call provision.[2] Without a call provision the firm would likely have to pay higher amounts to retire the bonds. With a call provision the firm probably has to pay higher interest rates than it would pay without the provision.

Valuation of the Call: Certainty

Assuming certainty, a call option has value to the corporation if interest rates are going down in the future.[3] However, the investors have the same information as the corporation and would adjust the amount they are willing to pay for the debt if there is a call provision. Assuming perfect certainty the firm does not benefit nor is the investor harmed by the inclusion of a call provision, since the price of the bond adjusts to take the prospect of the call into consideration.[4]

EXAMPLE: Assume we have a $1000 three-year .08 bond. The projected interest rates for each of the next three periods are

$$r_1 = .10, \qquad r_2 = .08, \qquad r_3 = .06.$$

The expected prices at three different moments in time, assuming the bond is not callable, are

$$\bar{B}(0) = \frac{80}{1.10} + \frac{80}{1.10 \times 1.08} + \frac{1080}{1.10 \times 1.08 \times 1.06} = 997.70,$$

$$\bar{B}(1) = \frac{80}{1.08} + \frac{1080}{1.08 \times 1.06} = 1017.47,$$

$$\bar{B}(2) = \frac{1080}{1.06} = 1018.87.$$

If the bond is not callable it can be sold at a price of $997.70. Now assume the bond is callable at any time at a price of $1005 but that the market has not adjusted to the call provision and the bond is again issued at $997.70. One period from now the bond will have (ignoring the call feature) a value of $1017.47. But the firm can call at $1005 and issue new noncallable bonds with

---

[2] Some corporate financial officers follow a policy of not calling bonds since they want the lenders to be friendly. While this seems to be a naive policy, it tends to diminish the threat of call thus making the bonds more valuable to the lender, and increasing the amount they are willing to pay.

[3] A complexity arises here since the corporation might not issue long term bonds if it knew interest rates were going to go down. The certainty example illustrates the basic features of a call provision, but is artificially simplified.

[4] In addition to perfect certainty the borrowing corporation must have the same time value of money as the investor in each time period.

exactly the same terms (except for the call feature) for $1017.47, making $12.47 profit per bond by calling and reissuing.

It is not realistic to expect the $12.47 profit actually to occur. The market would recognize the likelihood of the bonds being called and would only be willing to pay a maximum price of ($1005 + 80)/1.10 = $986.36 for the bonds at time 0. It would not pay $1000 for the bonds since it could invest elsewhere, earn .10, and have $1100 at the end of the first period rather than $1085 ($80 interest plus the $1005 call price). Without the call feature the bond would be worth $1017.47 at time one but with the call feature the bond will only be worth $1005. The present value of the "profit" resulting from the call is $12.44/1.10 = $11.34.

The present value of the debt without the call is $997.70 and with the call is $986.36. The decrease in the present value of the debt is $11.34 which is exactly equal to the present value of the profit resulting from the call. Since the firm will receive $11.34 less on issuing the bonds we can say that the cost of call to the firm is $11.34.

Let us now consider the determination of the optimum time to refund and the resulting value of the call provision under conditions of certainty.[5]

Let $B(t)$ be the price at time t of a noncallable bond that is otherwise equivalent to the present bond. Assume there are no costs of issue.

$C(t)$ be the call price of the present bond at time t.

e^{-rt} be the time discount factor (r is the interest rate).

V be the value of the call premium.

$$V = [B(t) - C(t)]e^{-rt}. \tag{15-1}$$

The value of the call option is highest when[6]

$$r = \frac{B'(t) - C'(t)}{B(t) - C(t)}. \tag{15-2}$$

The additional gain from deferring the call divided by the net investment (the amount a new noncallable issue exceeds the call price) must be greater than the value of money for the deferral to be worthwhile.

---

[5] See Pye, *op. cit.*, pp. 200–201, for basically similar but a more sophisticated development.

[6] The first derivative of V with respect to t is:

$$\frac{dV}{dt} = [B(t) - C(t)](-r)e^{-r} + e^{-r}[B'(t) - C'(t)].$$

Setting this equal to zero:

$$r[B(t) - C(t)] = B'(t) - C'(t).$$

EXAMPLE: Assume the time value of money is .05. A firm has a new twenty-year outstanding bond with a call price of $1050. The market price of an equivalent noncallable bond is currently $1000. Assume the following:

$$B(t) = 1000 + 5t - .25t^2$$

$$B'(t) = 5 - .5t$$

$$C(t) = 1050 - 2.5t$$

$$C'(t) = -2.5$$

$$r = \frac{B'(t) - C'(t)}{B(t) - C(t)}$$

$$.05 = \frac{(5 - .5t) - (-2.5)}{(1000 + 5t - .25t^2) - (1050 - 2.5t)} = \frac{7.5 - .5t}{-.25t^2 + 7.5t - 50}$$

$$.25t^2 - 17.5t + 200 = 0$$

$$t^2 - 70t + 800 = 0$$

$$t = 14.4 \text{ and } 55.6.$$

The call should be exercised in 14.4 years (55.6 years is beyond maturity). The value of the call provision is:

$$V = [B(t) - C(t)]e^{-rt} \qquad (15\text{--}3)$$

$$B(14.4) = 1000 + 5 \times 14.4 - .25(14.4)^2 = 1000 + 72 - 51.6 = 1020$$

$$C(14.4) = 1050 - 2.5(14.4) = 1050 - 36 = 1014$$

$$V = (1020 - 1014)e^{-.05 \times 10}$$

$$= (6)e^{-.5} = 6 \times .6065 = \$3.64.$$

The value of the option to the firm is $3.64, but assume that it is expected that if issued the bonds will sell for $994; the market will place a cost of $6 (i.e., $1000 - 994$) on the call. Since the value of the call, if exercised at the optimum time, is less than its "cost," in this case it would not be desirable for the firm to use the call provision.

Instead of approaching the call valuation as above (using the call price and the price of noncallable bonds) we could use the market price of an otherwise comparable callable bond. The market price of a noncallable bond is equal to the sum of the value of the callable bond $B^*(t)$ plus the value of the call, that is:

$$B(t) = B^*(t) + V,$$

or

$$V = B(t) - B^*(t). \qquad (15\text{--}4)$$

This approach would use the present market prices of the callable and non-callable bonds to measure the market value of the call provision.

To this point we have assumed that both the firm and investor had perfect knowledge of the future. It is of course possible that the expectations of the firm will be different than those of the investor, or more generally we can describe the situation as being one of uncertainty.

Valuation of the Call: Uncertainty[7]

Let $r_1, r_2, \ldots, r_n$ be the different possible values of interest rate

p_{ij} be the probability of the interest rate moving to r_j given that it is currently r_i.

$V_t(r_i)$ be the maximum expected present value of the call option at time t when the interest rate is r_i.

$B_t(r_i)$ be the price of the bond at time t when the interest rate is r_i.

C_t be the call price of the bond at time t.

Assume that at time t we know that the interest rate is r_i. The value of the option $V_t(r_i)$ is the higher of the values of exercising the option now $B_t(r_i) - C_t$ or of the value of waiting one period, discounted back to the present, $(1 + r_j)V_{t+1}(r_j)$. (See Fig. 15–1.)

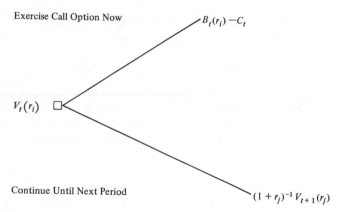

Exercise Call Option Now

$B_t(r_i) - C_t$

$V_t(r_i)$ □

Continue Until Next Period

$(1 + r_j)^{-1}V_{t+1}(r_j)$

FIGURE 15–1

The □ in Fig. 15–1 indicates a decision is being made; we can exercise the call option or continue with the bonds outstanding. We have

$$V_t(r_i) = \max\ [B_t(r_i) - C_t;\ (1 + r_j)^{-1}V_{t+1}(r_j)].$$

[7] This parallels Pye's development, but some changes have been made. It is somewhat more difficult than the previous part of this chapter and may be omitted.

Instead of assuming the interest rate the next period is r_j, assume the value of the interest rate in the next period is a random variable such as r_i or r_k (see Fig. 15–2).

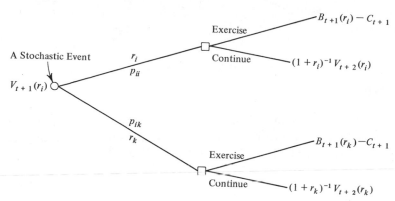

FIGURE 15–2

$$V_{t+i}(r_i) = p_{ii} \max [B_{t+1}(r_i) - C_{t+1}; (1 + r_i)^{-1}V_{t+2}(r_i)] +$$
$$p_{ik} \max [B_{t+1}(r_k) - C_{t+1}; (1 + r_k)^{-1}V_{t+2}(r_k)].$$

At maturity (say time T) the value of V_T, will be equal to zero. We can work backward from the maturity value to compute the value of $V_0(r_i)$.

EXAMPLE: Assume two interest rates are possible (.04, .03) and the transition matrix is as follows:

Probabilities

$i \setminus j$	.03	.04
.03	.3	.7
.04	.6	.4

The interest rate is now .04 and the call price is $1030. The call price will decrease $1015 and $1000 in the coming two years. The bonds have an interest payment of $40 per year and are due in three years. The relevant statistics are:

TABLE 15–1

t	C_t	$B_t(r_i = .04)$	$B_t(r_i = .03)$
0	1030	1000	1028
1	1015	1000	1019
2	1000	1000	1010
3	1000	1000	1000

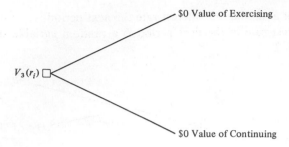

FIGURE 15-3

Figure 15-3 shows that at Time 3 the bonds reach maturity and the value of $V_3(r_i)$ is equal to zero. Figure 15-4 shows two values for V_2 reflecting the fact that the interest rate at Time 2 can be either .03 or .04.

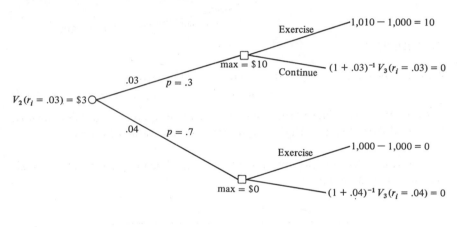

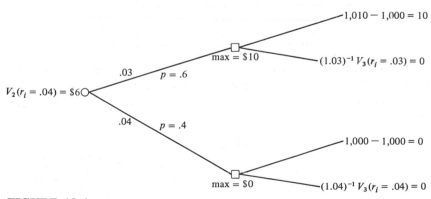

FIGURE 15-4

Figure 15-5 shows the determination of V_1.

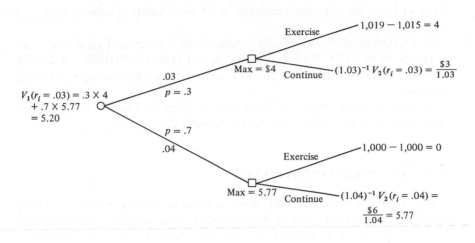

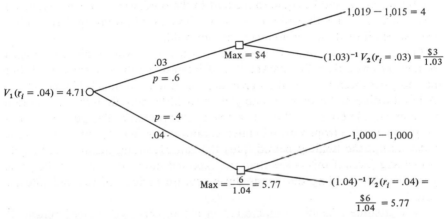

FIGURE 15-5

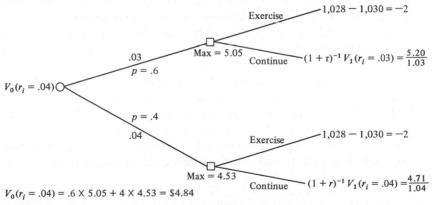

$V_0(r_i = .04) = .6 \times 5.05 + 4 \times 4.53 = \$4.84$

FIGURE 15-6

Since we know the current interest rate is .04 we will only determine $V_0(r_{i=.04})$ (Fig. 15–6).

In this simplified example we have determined the expected value of the call provision to be \$4.84. We will exercise the call option in Periods 1 or 2 if the interest rate is .03 otherwise we will stay with the present contract until maturity.

We cannot predict when the bonds will be called (unlike the certainty case) since we do not know the r's of each time period.

The Use of Call Provisions

If all decisions were rationally made and used expected monetary values, and if all decision makers had the same time value of money and the same matrix of transaction probabilities, then the value of the call provision to the borrowers would be equal to the cost to the borrower. There would be no advantage to having the call provision on a bond. Call provisions have usefulness since all of these requirements do not hold.

Let us assume a situation where there is a lender who is pleased to earn somewhat more than the market rate of interest for the current period, but has no great incentive to make a great deal more than the market in the future. A bond with a call provision, and yielding a little more than the market rate for comparable bonds, will be attractive to this investor. The possibility of a large gain arising from a drop in interest rates is eliminated, but the increased yield during the holding period, plus the call premium, insure that he gets something (even if this is less than the expected monetary value of the gains possible from holding the bonds during future periods of reduced interest rates).

Now assume a lender is interested in a long-term guaranteed return. If there is a call provision he may find himself having to reinvest in low-interest bearing securities if the interest rates decrease before the maturity date of his securities. The lender would prefer a sure return from noncallable securities where the return may be lower than that available from callable bonds, but the return is for his entire planning period.

The borrower has the advantage of being able to terminate an old debt contract that is less advantageous than new debt contracts. It is likely that he will have to pay less than the expected monetary value of the call for the privilege of being able to call the bonds.[8] Even if he had to pay more than the expected monetary value, there could be situations where the consequences of high-cost debt were so bad that the firm would be willing to pay "insur-

---

[8] See A. P. Hess, Jr., and W. J. Winn, *The Value of the Call Privilege* (University of Pennsylvania, 1962) for evidence that the cost of attaching call provisions has historically been low.

ance" to avoid this event. There will be a reluctance to use call provisions where these consequences are not severe, or where the financial officers think the market demands increased yields, increasing the expected cost of a call provision at least equal to the value of the call provision.

We have implied that the choice is between a call provision or no-call provision, but there are a wide range of middle choices. The right to call may be deferred for a given number of periods (thus decreasing the value of the call provisions) or the call provision can be made to be an initially large amount (again decreasing the value of the call).

Conclusions

The valuation of a call provision attached to a bond can be a complex task. On the other hand, there are techniques available for accomplishing the mathematical computations. In a perfect world the cost of a call and its value would be exactly equal. In an imperfect and uncertain world it is possible for managers (and investors) to take advantage of disequilibrium conditions. Thus it may be possible for a firm to issue a security with a call provision and benefit from this more than its cost (the cost is expressed in terms of an increased yield demanded by the market). The types of computations suggested here may be helpful in making the evaluation of cost and value.[9]

PROBLEMS

1. Assume a company issues $10 million of .08 four-year bonds at par. The bonds are callable at a price of $10,500,000. It is expected that the following interest rates will apply:

YEAR	INTEREST RATE
1	.08
2	.08
3	.08
4	.06

Required: Based on the information given, would you pay $10 million for the bonds?

[9] For estimates of the value of call provisions see Gordon Pye, "The Value of Call Deferment on a Bond: Some Empirical Results," and F. C. Jen and James E. Wert, "The Effect of Call Risk on Corporate Bond Yields," both in *The Journal of Finance* (December, 1967), pp. 623–636 and pp. 637–651, respectively.

2. Continue Problem 1. Assume the same situation except the following interest rates now apply:

YEAR	INTEREST RATE
1	.10
2	.04
3	.04
4	.04

Required: (a) Would you pay $10 million for the bonds?

              (b) What is the maximum amount the company should be willing to "pay" for having a call provision attached to the bond?

3. Continue Problem 1. Assume the same situation except the following interest rates now apply:

YEAR	INTEREST RATE
1	.10
2	.10
3	.04
4	.04

Required: (a) Would you pay $10 million for the bonds?

              (b) What is the maximum amount the company should be willing to pay for having a call provision attached to the bond?

4. The current interest rate for twenty-year bonds is .08. The ABC Company expects that interest rates in one year will drop to .05. The one-period interest rate is .09 for this general type of security. Assume the call price of the bond is $10,500,000 for a $10 million issue.

Required: (a) What would you pay for the issue with the call provision?

              (b) Without the call provision?

REFERENCES

Hess, A. P., and Winn, W. J. *The Value of the Call Privilege* (University of Pennsylvania, Philadelphia, 1962).

Jen, F. C., and Wert, James E. "The Effect of Call Risk on Corporate Bond Yields," *The Journal of Finance* (December), 1967.

Pye, G. "The Value of the Call Option of a Bond," *The Journal of Political Economy* (April), 1966.

————. "The Value of Call Deferment on a Bond: Some Empirical Results," *Journal of Finance* (December), 1967.

PART V

Stock Options, Warrants, and Stock Purchase Plans

A "call" gives the holder the right to buy a share (or shares) of stock in the future at a given price independent of the market price of the stock. Stock options, warrants, and convertible bonds all are types of calls, though their characteristics differ.

The stock options and stock purchase plans for employees are devices used to pay employees in a form that may have tax advantages. Warrants have recently become a popular means of making other securities more sweet to the market. These devices also affect the capital structure of the firm since they are a form of raising capital, thus their issuance is a financial policy decision. The convertible bond chapter is included in this part of the book because it builds on the understanding developed in the stock option–warrant chapter.

CHAPTER 16

The Valuation of Stock Options and. Warrants[1]

SYMBOLS

P	is the stock price at the end of the option period and $E(P)$ is the mean price	$F(C)$	is the probability of unfavorable outcomes (the left tail of the probability distribution) and
P_0	is the current stock price		$G(C) = 1 - F(C)$
$E_C^\infty(P)$	is the partial expectation of the favorable outcomes	$f(P)$	is the density function of P
C	is the option price (the exercise price)	S	is the number of shares per warrant
$E_{-\infty}^C(P)$	is the partial expectation of the unfavorable outcomes	$E(V_{1W})$	is the absolute expected value of one warrant
		$E(V_W)$	is the absolute expected value of P_0/K warrants
	$E(P) = \overset{C}{\underset{-\infty}{E}}(P) + \overset{\infty}{\underset{C}{E}}(P)$	$E(V_B)$	is the expected value of buying stock
		$E(V_{W-B})$	is the expected value of the P_0/K warrants compared to buying stock
K	is the cost of the option or warrant		

There is little question that stock options have value, but there is considerable question as to how much stock options should be valued. Persons studying the valuation question and writing in business periodicals have tied the value of the stock option to the expected or the actual appreciation in the value of the stock.[2]

---

[1] This chapter is partially based on an article by the author appearing in the September 1967 issue of *The Journal of Financial and Quantitative Analysis*. The author benefited from conversations with his colleague, Warren Hausman, and several of his suggestions have been interwoven into the chapter.

[2] For example, see E. D. Campbell, "Stock Options Should be Valued," *Harvard Business Review* (July–August, 1961), pp. 52–58; and D. M. Holland and Wilbur G. Lewellen, "Probing the Record of Stock Options," *Harvard Business Review* (March–April, 1962), pp. 132–150.

Recognizing the need for a theory of stock option value, A. James Boness in an important article developed a general theory.[3] While advancing the understanding of options his theory is incomplete and can lead to incorrect valuations of stock options if it is not applied carefully.

Boness states, "The investor in options, then, is concerned not with the entire probability distribution of future prices, but only with that portion consisting of future prices favorable to him."[4]

In a very important sense the probability distribution of unfavorable prices is relevant.

Boness computes the present value of the partial expectation of favorable outcomes less the product of the cost of the option and the probability that the option will be exercised. He then gives the following decision rule. "When this exceeds the market price of an option, investors will tend to purchase that option."[5]

This is a necessary, but not sufficient, condition for the option to have value. One must also consider the possibility of the investor taking a long position in the stock instead of acquiring the option.

Stock options have value because they

1. Reduce risk by giving the investor a look at the future before requiring him to commit himself (the expected decrease in price can be avoided).
2. Enable the investor to multiply his investment (there is leverage).
3. Enable the investor to participate in capital gains while still conserving his cash (on the other hand, one drawback of an option is that the holder of an option gives up the right to dividends until the option is exercised).
4. Enable a manager receiving an option to convert normal income into an expected capital gain (an advantage for tax purposes).
5. Move a manager to make an investment that he would otherwise not make.

An option must be compared to a straight purchase since they are both ways of going long. In the situation where purchasing of the stock is not desirable, a combination of selling short and acquiring an option may be desirable.

EXAMPLES: Assume the current market price and the option price are both $100 and there is a .9 probability that the terminal price will be $200 and .1 probability that the price will be $0. The option itself has zero cost. Assume the events occur within a short time period; thus time discounting is not necessary.

---

[3] A. James Boness, "Elements of a Theory of Stock–Option Value," *The Journal of Political Economy* (April, 1964), pp. 163–175.

[4] *Ibid.*, p. 169.

[5] *Ibid.*

If we consider buying the investment we find the investment has a net expected value of $80. Thus buying is a desirable alternative.

The decision tree for buying is:

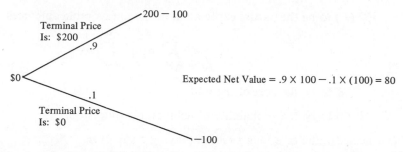

The decision tree for the situation where we have an option to buy at $100 is:

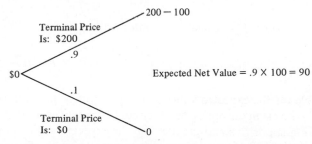

The option alternative has an absolute net expected value of $90. Thus using the option is more desirable than buying outright. The possibility of a $100 loss has been eliminated.

In this situation, the option to buy at $100 has a value of $10 compared to buying. Only if there were no buy alternatives (without the option) would the option have a value of $90. The relative value for the option compared to buying may also be obtained by multiplying the possible loss ($100) by the probability of it occurring (.1).

Now assume the probability of unfavorable prices is zero. The alternatives of buying and acquiring an option both have a net value of $100, and the value of the option compared to buying is zero. The product of the possible loss ($100) and the probability of loss (0) is zero.

The Mathematical Model

The last example illustrated how we might think of the value of a stock option. Let us now consider the mathematical expression of the model being presented.

Define: $E(P)$ to be the expected price at the end of the option price

$E_C^\infty (P)$ to be the partial expectation of the favorable outcomes

where C is the option price and the current market price

$E_C^\infty (P)$ to be the partial expectation of the unfavorable outcomes

$$E(P) = \mathop{E}_{C}^{\infty}(P) + \mathop{E}_{-\infty}^{C}(P)$$

K to be the cost of the option

$F(C)$ to be the probability of unfavorable outcomes.

The expected value of a long position (buying a share) is

$$\text{Expected value of buying} = \mathop{E}_{C}^{\infty}(P) + \mathop{E}_{-\infty}^{C}(P) - C.$$

The expected value of purchasing an option to buy is[6]

$$\text{Expected value of an option} = \mathop{E}_{C}^{\infty}(P) - C(1 - F(C)) - K.$$

It is possible for the expected value of an option to be positive and for the opportunity to invest in the option to be rejected. This will occur if the expected value of buying is positive and greater than the expected value of an option.[7] We can compute the two expectations and choose the larger of the two (if it is positive). However, it is illuminating to compute the relative benefits of an option compared to buying.[8]

$$\text{Relative Benefits of Option} = -C(1 - F(C)) - K - \mathop{E}_{-\infty}^{C}(P) + C$$

$$= CF(C) - \mathop{E}_{-\infty}^{C}(P) - K.$$

where $F(C)$ is the probability of an unfavorable price (thus we save the option price) and $E_\infty^C (P)$ is the expected price at the end of the option period (it is the partial expectation for unfavorable prices).

In this relationship the probability of unfavorable events is very evident.

[6] This expression for the absolute value is equivalent to the formulation of Boness.

[7] Several aspects of options are being neglected; for example, an option may offer leverage and is a type of loan. Also, dividends are foregone during the period of time before the option is exercised.

[8] If we are dealing with a corporation's stock option plan, K will be equal to zero. The relationship presented should be used only if the buy alternative has a positive expected value.

EXAMPLE: Assume the current price and the option conversion price is $100 and that the following prices may occur:

TERMINAL PRICE	PROBABILITY	EXPECTATION
$190	.6	114
50	.3	15
0	.1	0
		129

Relative value of option $= 100 \times .4 - (50 \times .3 + 0 \times .1)$
$$= 40 - 15 = 25.$$

Using the mathematical relationship derived above we have

Expected value of buying $= E(P) - C = 129 - 100 = 29$

Expected value of option $= \overset{\infty}{\underset{C}{E}}(P) - C(1 - F(C)) = 114 - .6 \times 100 = 54$

Relative value of option $= CF(C) - \overset{C}{\underset{-\infty}{E}}(P) = 40 - 15 = 25$

Assume we changed the possible outcomes so that they were now:

350	.6
50	.3
0	.1

The relative value of the option compared to buying would remain unchanged at $25.

The value of the option can also be expressed in terms of the expected loss that is avoided (let L be the conditional loss):

$$\text{Relative value of option} = \int_{-\infty}^{c} Lf(p)\, dp.$$

Continuing the example, there is a loss if the $50 or $0 price occurs:

PRICE	LOSS	PROBABILITY OF LOSS	EXPECTATION
50	50	.3	15
0	100	.1	10
Relative value of option (expectation of the loss)			25

The relative benefits of the option involve saving the expected difference in the purchase price and the terminal price if the event is unfavorable (by not exercising the option we avoid the expected decrease in price with unfavorable events), and the expected benefits are decreased by cost of the option. This procedure can be used to compute the value of the option if the buy alternative has a positive present value.

The mathematics is consistent with a logical approach to the valuation question. If, at the end of the option period, the price of the stock is higher than the option price, we can exercise the option and be as well off as the investor who went long. However, if the terminal price is less than the option price, the option holder, unlike the purchaser of the stock, avoids the loss by not exercising the option.

The entire probability distribution of future prices is relevant in determining whether going long and purchasing an option are both desirable alternatives. Also, the portion of the probability distribution of future unfavorable prices may be used to choose the more desirable of the two alternatives, and is certainly relevant to the valuation of options.

Only if the expected value of buying is positive (thus an acceptable alternative) can we compute the relative benefits of the option plan. If the expected benefits of buying are negative, the option plan may still be desirable, and this desirability may be tested using the absolute benefits of the option.

K not Zero

Let us now assume a situation where there is a known cost of the option. This cost may be in the form of wages foregone by accepting the option. We now must solve a problem that was previously left implicit. The size of the investment in purchasing the stock may be different than the cost of option for a share of stock. We have been comparing the benefits for purchasing one share or acquiring an option for one share. Now we will consider the desirability of purchasing stock at a cost of P_0 or acquiring options requiring the same total investment. The value of an option investment of P_0 is

$$EV(P_0 \text{ invested in options}) = \frac{P_0}{K}\left[\overset{\infty}{\underset{C}{E}}(P) - C + CF(C) - K\right].$$

Returning to the example when the relative value of the option is $25 and the terminal price is $190 or $50 or $0, we now assume the cost of an option (K) is $40. The option is now undesirable if we use the relationship:

$$\text{Relative value} = CF(C) - \overset{C}{\underset{-\infty}{E}}(P) - K$$

$$= 100(.4) - 15 - 40 = -15.$$

However, if we make the investment in options equal to the $100 investment in stock we have

$$EV(\$100 \text{ invested in options}) = \frac{P_0}{K} \left[\overset{\infty}{\underset{C}{E}}(P) - C + CF(C) - K \right]$$

$$= \frac{100}{40} [114 - 100 + 40 - 40]$$

$$= \$35.$$

The expected value of investing $100 in stock is only $29, thus the options at a cost of $40 per option has a higher expected monetary value for an investment of $100.[9]

This analysis incorporating the cost of the option applies to the situation where a manager is given an option to buy stock in his company, if there is a measurable cost of the option (such as when there are measurable wages that are foregone in order to obtain the option).

Utility Considerations

One important advantage of the option arrangement is that it is a relatively painless way to cause managers to invest in the firm.

In the above example we computed the relative value of the option for one share to be $25. Now assume that the manager is somewhat of a risk-averter and that he would not buy the stock on the open market at $100. He knows the expected monetary value of the $100 investment (buying) is $129 but he also knows there is .1 probability that his investment will become worthless and .3 probability that it will halve in value. If the manager would not buy at $100 then the option has an expected monetary value to the manager of $54 despite the fact that its relative value is only $25.

We can compute the expected monetary value of the option by comparing the absolute value of buying and the absolute value of the option. When the manager would not buy because of risk aversion the option may have value in excess of the relative value. The manager by using the option can avoid all events where the value of the stock falls below the option price during the option period, thus the option acts as a type of insurance. The manager may be willing to value the option at more than its expected value because of its insurance value (he is insuring against large losses that would result if he bought and if the stock went below the option price).

On the other hand, the manager accepting an option in lieu of wages is

---

[9] Mr. Leonard Borer, a graduate student at Cornell University, called this point to the author's attention.

not entirely forsaking risk. The option has a cost to the manager (he is for-saking incremental wages), and it may be that risk aversion leads him to value the option at less than its expected monetary value. He can reject the insur-ance if he does not have to buy.

Assume an option arrangement has a value relative to buying of $100,000 and buying itself is worth $500,000 (thus the absolute value of the option is $600,000). Assuming a .5 probability of complete disaster most of us would not forsake $100,000 of wages for this option arrangement.[10] A risk averter would neither buy the stock *nor* "pay" $100,000 for the option.

Thus the actual value of an option arrangement to a manager may be less or more than its expected monetary value.

When to Exercise

Assume the option is for n periods and that the stock, once obtained, will not be sold during that period of time. The option purchase price is equal to the market price at the time the option is granted. As long as the market price is less than the option price, the holder will not exercise his option. Figure 16–1 shows a situation where the market price is above the option price in one or more time periods.

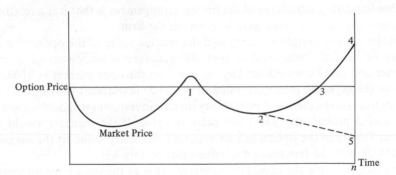

FIGURE 16–1

If the option is exercised at the time when the price first exceeds the conversion price, there is risk that the stock may reverse its price trend and the holder will suffer a loss (e.g., if the price curve follows the dashed curve from Point 2 to Point 5). It should be noted that the total gain accruing to the stockholder, whether he exercises his option at Time 1, 2, 3, or 4, will be the same. In addition, if he acquires the stock at Time 4, there is no probability of loss (assuming he sells at Time 4). If the stock is going to be held till the

[10] Assume the stock can be bought for $200,000 and then there is .5 probability of its price becoming $1,400,000 and .5 probability of its price being $0.

end of the option period, then loss (at least up to that point) can be avoided by not exercising the option until the end of the option period.

If the stock may be sold prior to the end of the option period, the holder of the option may buy prior to the end of the period, but he should buy only when he is ready to sell. This situation will occur if he is more pessimistic than the market is about the future.

We can point to the winner of the New York State Lottery and compare his winnings to the costs of his ticket. While the winner makes a large profit we cannot say that the value of his ticket at the time of purchase was greater than its cost. A manager may have an option for a share of stock selling for $1 and the stock may go up in value to $1000, but the maximum value of the option at the time the option was given is measured by the maximum possible loss of $1, not the actual gain that was realized.

Warrants

A warrant gives its holder the right to purchase a share(s) of common stock at a given price. Unlike the stock options awarded to managers there is generally a market for warrants and they can be bought and sold. Also, the warrant exercise price may be set higher than the current market price of the common stock (the option exercise price is generally set equal to or less than the current market price). There may have to be significant price appreciation before the warrant is worth exercising.

The analysis to follow will contain several simplifying assumptions so that we may concentrate on the basic nature of the value of a warrant. We will ignore the payment of dividends during the warrant period (including dividends would increase the value of buying relative to the value of a warrant). We will also ignore the fact that the warrant may be exercised any time during warrant period. We will be considering the value at only one point, and it should be recognized that the actual value of the warrant is higher than the value we will compute because of the flexibility of timing. The right to exercise at any time has value. The third simplification is that we will ignore the time value of money. With long-lived warrants this is unrealistic, but with warrants (or calls) with lives of less than a year, not considering time value, is a reasonable assumption.

Because of the importance of the limitations listed above, the material that follows must be looked at as guide to warrant valuation rather than as a prescription.

The Absolute Value of a Warrant

Let us consider a one-period situation where the current price is P_0 and the price one period from now is a random variable P with a density function

$f(P)$. The warrant which costs K gives us the right to purchase a share of common stock at a price of C. $E(V_{1w})$, the absolute expected value of one warrant, is

$$E(V_{1w}) = \int_C^\infty (P - C)f(P)\, dP - K$$

$$= \underset{C}{\overset{\infty}{E}}(P) - CG(C) - K,$$

where $G(C)$ = probability $(P > C)$.

The lower limit of integration is C since we will not exercise the warrant if P, the market price, is less than C, the exercise price. $CG(C)$ is subtracted since this is the expected cost (we buy if $P > C$).

To place the investment in warrants on the same basis as an investment in common stock we will make the amount invested in warrants equal to P_0, the current market price of the common stock. The expected value is

$$E(V_w) = \frac{P_0}{K} E(V_{1w})$$

$$= \frac{P_0}{K} \left[\underset{C}{\overset{\infty}{E}}(P) - CG(C) - K \right].$$

The Relative Value

We have computed the absolute value of an investment of K or P_0 in the warrant but have not considered the fact that the investor has an opportunity to buy the stock instead of purchasing the warrant. One of the factors contributing to the value of the warrant is the expected change in the price of the stock. But the value of this expected change can also be obtained from purchasing the stock.

If the stock is purchased the expected value of buying is

$$E(V_B) = \int_C^\infty (P - P_0)f(P)\, dP = E(P) - P_0.$$

Subtracting V_B from V_w, and taking the expectation, we obtain the relative expected value of the warrant compared to buying:

$$E(V_{w-B}) = E(V_w - V_B) = \frac{P_0}{K} \left[\underset{C}{\overset{\infty}{E}}(P) - CG(C) - K \right] - [E(P) - P_0].$$

We can break down the expected value of buying stock and buying one warrant:

$$E(V_B) = \underset{C}{\overset{\infty}{E}}(P) + \underset{-\infty}{\overset{C}{E}}(P) - P_0;$$

$$E(V_{1w}) = \overset{\infty}{\underset{C}{E}} (P) \qquad - CG(C) - K.$$

Note that to an extent the good consequences of a range of favorable events are common to both buying stock and buying the warrant (the E_C^{∞} (P) is a measure of favorable events and is common to both). The consequences if there are bad events $(P < C)$ or $P < P_0$) are greatly different.

EXAMPLE

$$P_0 = \$50$$

$$C = 75$$

Here P can be either \$100 with .6 probability or \$0 with .4 probability.

$$K = \$5$$

$$E(V_w) - \frac{50}{5} [100 \times .6 - 75 \times .6 - 5] - \frac{50}{5} \times 10 = 100$$

$$E(V_B) = E(P) - P_0$$

$$= 60 - 50 = 10$$

$$E(V_{W-B}) = 100 - 10 = 90.$$

If we computed the expected value of one warrant we will have

$$E(V_{1w}) = \overset{\infty}{\underset{C}{E}} (P) - CG(C) - K = 100 \times .6 - 75 \times .6 - 5$$

$$= 60 - 45 - 5 = 10.$$

In this example we find that $E(V_{1w}) = E(V_B)$, but $E(V_w)$ is \$90 higher than $E(V_B)$. If we assumed that the probability distribution of P is

.6 \$200

.4 \$0

the expected values for the one-warrant investment alternative and buying one share would be

$$E(V_{1w}) = 200 \times .6 - 75 \times .6 - 5 = 120 - 45 - 5 = 70$$

$$E(V_B) = 120 - 50 = 70$$

$$E(V_{1w-B}) = 0.$$

The increase in the expected value of P has not changed the relative value of the one warrant compared to buying one share. However if we adjust V_{1w} for the possibility of investing an amount equal to P_0 in P_0/K warrants, the expected values for the warrants and buying would be

$$E(V_W) = \frac{50}{5} [200 \times .6 - 75 \times .6 - 5] = 10[120 - 45 - 5] = 700$$

$$E(V_B) = [120 - 50] = 70$$

$$E(V_{W-B}) = 700 - 70 = 630.$$

The increase in the expectation of P has now drastically changed the relative value of buying the ten warrants compared to buying one share. The increase results because of the implicit leverage in a warrant.

Now assume that there is an increased probability of loss and the probability distribution of P is

$$.4 \quad \$200$$

$$.6 \quad \$0.$$

$$E(V_{1W}) = 200 \times .4 - 75 \times .4 - 5 = 80 - 30 - 5 = 45$$

$$E(V_B) = 200 \times .4 - 50 = 80 - 50 = 30$$

$$E(V_{1W-B}) = 50 - 30 - 0 - 5 = 15.$$

The increased probability of loss has increased the value of the one warrant compared to buying one share of stock. The warrant enables us to avoid buying if the stock is not a good buy thus the increase in the riskiness of the stock will increase the relative value of the one warrant.

This above analysis was for one time period. If we made the situation more realistic and considered a multiperiod situation the analysis would become more complex, but the basic elements of the analysis would remain the same. The absolute value of the warrant would depend on the expected price increase of the stock, and the relative value of the warrant would depend on the amount and likelihood of the losses that could be avoided.

We will now consider an example where the computations indicate the warrants have a positive value (in an absolute sense). Not only is the relative value of the warrant negative, but the absolute expected value of the warrant is misleading.

EXAMPLE

$$K = \$1.25$$

$$P_0 = \$1$$

$$C = \$76 \text{ (the option price)}$$

P has the following probability distribution:

P	PROBABILITY	EXPECTATION
$0	.1	$0
75	.8	60
100	.1	10
		$70

The absolute expected value of one warrant is

$$E(V_{1w}) = \overset{\infty}{\underset{C}{E}} (P) - G(C) - K$$

$$= 100 \times .10 - 76 \times .10 - 1.25 = 10 - 7.60 - 1.25 = 1.15.$$

However, we can buy the stock for $1 per share and would not pay $1.25 for a warrant to buy a share of stock that we can purchase for $1. We can see this by comparing buy and warrant alternatives. First we must adjust the amount of investment in warrants to equal P_0:

$$E(V_w) = \frac{P_0}{K} E(V_{1w}) = \frac{1}{1.25} \times 1.15 = .92.$$

The expected value of buying the stock is

$$E(V_B) = E(P) - P_0$$
$$= 70 - 1 = 69.$$

The relative expected value of the warrant is

$$E(V_{W-B}) = .92 - 69 = -68.08.$$

The negative relative expected value occurs since the common stock may rise from $1 to $75 without this benefiting the warrantholder. But this rise does benefit the purchaser of the stock. Whenever the warrant price (C) is above the current price (P_0), this possibility of negative relative value for the warrant exists. Also, the absolute value of the warrant cannot logically be larger than the current price of the stock (assuming we can buy the stock) since the investor would then purchase the stock.[11]

Analysis of Warrant Value Using Current Stock Price

We have attempted to relate the value of a warrant to the future price of the common stock. There are, however, several generalizations that can be made about the cost (K) of a warrant and the current price (P_0).

[11] The negative relative value results because of the comparison with the buy alternative. The minimum value of a warrant to an investor is zero.

1. The cost of the warrant (and the value V_{1w}) cannot logically be greater than the current market price of the common stock.
2. The value of a warrant may be equal to zero but cannot be less than zero.
3. The market price of a warrant must be at least as large as the difference between the stock's market price P_0 and the warrant exercise price C. (Otherwise investors would buy the warrant, exercise, and sell with an immediate no risk profit.)

We can graph these conclusions (see Fig. 16–2). The range of plausible values is between the two parallel 45° lines.[12]

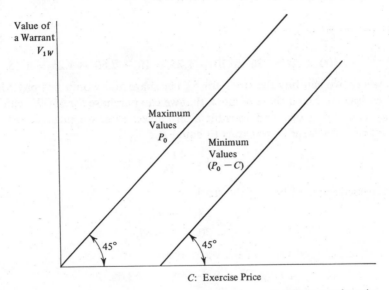

FIGURE 16–2

EXAMPLE

$$C = \$25$$

$$P_0 = 100$$

The value of the warrant cannot be greater than $100 (if it were greater an investor would buy the stock not the warrant) nor can it be less than $75. Assume we buy a warrant for $48. We could then pay $25 and exchange the warrant for a share of common stock that we can sell for $100 (the total cost was $73). Thus the warrant will not sell for less than $75 as long as the com-

---

[12] We will modify the plausible range later.

mon stock is selling for $100. We are assuming that risk preferences do not affect the value of the warrant or the share of stock.

Let us return to the equation for the value of one warrant (K is omitted since we are solving for the value of the warrant):

$$E(V_{1W}) = \mathop{E}_{C}^{\infty} (P) - CG(C).$$

We will assume that $E(P) = P_0$ and that P_0 is very much larger than C so that the probability of $P > C$ approaches 1; that is,

$$G(C) = 1 \quad \text{and} \quad \mathop{E}_{C}^{\infty} (P) = E(P) = P_0.$$

Therefore,

$$E(V_{1W}) = E(P) - C = P_0 - C.$$

Thus if P_0 is a large enough multiple of C so that the probability of not exercising is close to zero we would expect a warrant to be selling at a price close to the minimum value, $P_0 - C$. Shelton has found this relationship holds if $P_0 \geq 4C$.[13]

Let us assume the stock is selling for $100, the warrant exercise price is $25, and the warrant costs $75. If we "know" that the price of the stock is going to be $150 we can buy the stock and earn a 50% return $(150 - 100)/100$ and a $50 profit.

Alternatively, we can buy one warrant for $75 and earn a 75% return $(150 - 75 - 25)/75$ and a $50 profit. Or we can buy $1\frac{1}{3}$ warrants with the $100 and earn $67 profit. The warrant gives us leverage in that we do not have to pay the $25 exercise price until we do exercise (we are assuming we do not exercise until we are ready to sell). If there is certainty as to the outcome of the investment in common stock then the warrant is likely to be a better investment than the common stock because the investment of a given amount goes further. Thus we might expect the value of the warrant, with certainty, to be somewhat in excess of the difference $P_0 - C$. We would also expect that P_0 would tend to increase so that it was equal to the known future value of P (neglecting the time value of money). If $P = P_0 = C$, the value of the warrant would be zero, because we know the future with certainty, and there is no chance of profit or loss. In the real world there is not likely to be a situation where we know the future with certainty. P is not known but rather there is a probability distribution on the different values.

[13] For empirical evidence that the value of a warrant will be equal to $P_0 - C$, if P_0 is a large multiple of C, see J. P. Shelton, "The Relation of the Price of a Warrant to the Price of its Associated Stock," *Financial Analysts Journal* (May–June, 1967) and also (July–August, 1967). Another relevant source is P. Samuelson, "Rational Theory of Warrant Pricing," *Industrial Management Review* (Spring, 1965), pp. 13–32.

Dilution

The number of warrants outstanding and the difference between the market price and their exercise price greatly affect their value. We will assume K equals zero.

Let V_0, N_0, P_0 be the value of the common stock equity, the number of shares outstanding and the market price before the issuance of the warrants, where generally $V_0 = N_0P_0$.[14]

V_1, P_1 be the value of the common stock equity, and the market price after the issuance of the warrants and their exercise

N be the number of shares into which the warrants are convertible

We can solve for P_1 assuming exercise of the warrants:

$$V_1 = V_0 + NC,$$

$$P_1 = \frac{V_0 + NC}{N + N_0}.$$

EXAMPLE

$$P_0 = \$100 \qquad N_0 = 1000 \qquad V_0 = \$100,000$$

$$C = 25 \qquad N = 4000$$

$$P_1 = \frac{V_0 + NC}{N + N_0} = \frac{100,000 + 100,000}{5000} = \$40.$$

Previously we had computed the minimum value to be $P_0 - C = 100 - 25 = \$75$. This is a minimum for the first warrant. Each warrant issued decreases the value of future warrants; thus the size of the warrant offering as well as the presence of warrants outstanding greatly affects the value of the warrants being offered. When we consider the warrants currently outstanding or the issuance of more than one warrant we find that the value of a warrant can be below $P_0 - C$.

In the above example the minimum value of a warrant to be issued is: $40 - 25 = 15$. It is important for the analyst to incorporate the effect of the number of warrants (including stock options and convertible securities) that are outstanding or are likely to be issued. Once issued warrants of like characteristics would sell for identical prices.

---

[14] If P_0 reflects the anticipation of the market for the dilution of the stock, but does not reflect the expected benefits of the new securities, then V_0 may not be equal to N_0P_0.

Risk Considerations

To this point we have assumed that it was appropriate to make decisions using the expected monetary values of the alternatives. Now, we will consider measures that give some indication of the amount of risk.

The value of P_0/K warrants is

$$V_w = \frac{P_0}{K}[P - C - K] \quad \text{if} \quad P > C$$

$$= \frac{P_0}{K}[-K] \quad \text{if} \quad P < C.$$

The variance of an investment of P_0 in warrants is:

$$\text{var}(V_w) = \text{var}\left[\frac{P_0}{K}(P - C - K)\right]$$

$$= \left[\frac{P_0}{K}\right]^2 \text{var}(P).$$

Since P_0/K is greater than one, we are multiplying var (P) by a number that can be large. Thus we can expect the variance of outcomes with a warrant to be higher than the variance of outcomes with the same dollar investment in common stock. We shall illustrate the risk aspects of warrants with the following example.

EXAMPLE

$$P_0 = \$50 \quad K = 5$$

$$C = 80$$

$E(P) = 60$ when there is a .5 probability of $0 and .4 probability of $100 and .1 probability of $200.

The expected value of an investment of $50 in warrants is

$$E(V_w) = \frac{P_0}{K}\left[\overset{\infty}{\underset{C}{E}}(P) - CG(C) - K\right]$$

$$= \frac{50}{5}[(.4 \times 100 + .1 \times 200) - 80 \times .5 - 5] = 10[60 - 40 - 5]$$

$$= 10 \times 15 = \$150.$$

Figure 16–3 shows what happens if we buy ten warrants for $50.

$$E(V_w) = .1 \times 1150 + .4 \times 150 + .5(-50) = 115 + 60 - 25 = \$150.$$

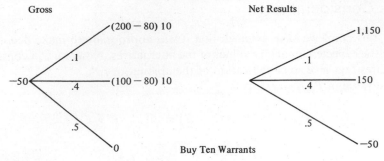

FIGURE 16–3

The expected value of buying stock is

$$E(V_B) = E(P) - P_0 = 60 - 50 = \$10.$$

Figure 16–4 shows the consequences of buying stock.

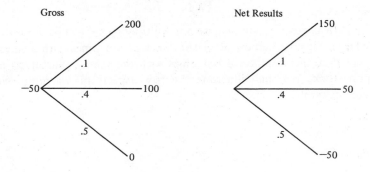

FIGURE 16–4

$$E(V_B) = .1 \times 150 + .4 \times 50 + .5 \times (-50) = 15 + 20 - 25 = \$10.$$

The variance of buying stock is:

X	$\bar{X}$	$(X - \bar{X})^2$	$P(X)$	$P(X)(X - \bar{X})^2$
150	10	19,600	.1	1960
50	10	1600	.4	640
− 50	10	3600	.5	1800
				var $(X) = 4400$ $\sigma_X = 66.3$

The variance of buying ten warrants is:

X	$\bar{X}$	$(X - \bar{X})^2$	$P(X)$	$P(X)(X - \bar{X})^2$
1150	150	1,000,000	.1	100,000
150	150	0	.4	0
−50	150	40,000	.5	20,000
				var (X) = 120,000 σ_X = 346

The variance of the investment in warrants is much larger than the variance in common stock.

Now consider the measure of skewness $(S = E(X - \bar{X})^3/\sigma^3)$.

For Buying Stock

X	$\bar{X}$	$(X - \bar{X})^3$	$P(X)$	$P(X)(X - \bar{X})^3$
150	10	2,744,000	.1	274,400
50	10	64,000	.4	35,600
−50	10	−216,000	.5	−108,000
				192,000

$$S = \frac{192,000}{\sigma^3} = \frac{192,000}{292,000} = .7$$

For Buying Ten Warrants

X	$\bar{X}$	$(X - \bar{X})^3$	$P(X)$	$P(X)(X - \bar{X})^3$
1150	150	10^9	.1	100×10^6
150	150	0	.4	0
−50	150	$−200^3$	.5	$−4 \times 10^6$
				96,000,000

$$S = \frac{96,000,000}{41,500,000} = 2.3$$

The skewness measure for the warrants is positive and larger than the skewness associated with buying stock. There is some evidence that some investors prefer positive skewness, thus would find warrants to be attractive despite the increased variance. (The presence of an active warrant market tends to substantiate this hypothesis.)

Time Value and Dividends

Let us consider a simplified version of the valuation problem where P_n (the price of time n) is known and n is the duration of time till exercise of the warrant. An investor in common stock buys that stock since he expects the present value of the future price (assuming no dividends) to be at least as large as the current price:

$$\frac{P_n}{(1 + r)^n} \geq P_0 \qquad P_n \geq P_0(1 + r)^n. \tag{16-1}$$

The investor in warrants believes the present value of the amount that the price of the common stock exceeds the exercise price will be as large or larger than the cost of the warrant:

$$\frac{P_n - C}{(1 + r)^n} \geq K \qquad P_n \geq K(1 + r)^n + C. \tag{16-2}$$

Assuming the equality exists, equating the values for P_n obtained from Equations 16–1 and 16–2, and solving for K:

$$P_0(1 + r)^n = K(1 + r)^n + C,$$

$$K = P_0 - \frac{C}{(1 + r)^n}. \tag{16-3}$$

If $n = 0$, we then have

$$K = P_0 - C. \tag{16-4}$$

Because of the assumption of equality, K now measures the value of a warrant as well as the cost.

Since the exercise will take place sometime between now and the expiration time, the value of K will be

$$P_0 - C \leq K \leq P_0 - \frac{C}{(1 + r)^n}. \tag{16-5}$$

If we assume the stock pays dividends, for the buy–stock alternative, we now have

$$\frac{P_n}{(1 + r)^n} + \sum_{i=0}^{n} D_i(1 + r)^{-i} \geq P_0,$$

$$P_n \geq \left[P_0 - \sum_{i=0}^{n} D_i(1 + r)^{-i} \right] (1 + r)^n. \qquad (16\text{--}6)$$

The warrant relationship remains:

$$P_n \geq K(1 + r)^n + C.$$

Assuming equality exists and solving for K:

$$K = \left[P_0 - \sum_{i=0}^{n} D_i(1 + r)^{-i} \right] - \frac{C}{(1 + r)^n}. \qquad (16\text{--}7)$$

Remember that we have assumed P_n is known and is larger than C and P_0. This results in relationships that are not valid if we allow uncertainty to exist, that is, if we allow P_n to be a random variable.

Conclusions

It is not reasonable to determine the expected value of a stock option using the ex post profitability of the stock option. The fact that a stock shot up in price and resulted in great riches for a manager holding a stock option does not prove that at the time of issuance the stock option had a great deal of value. The value of a stock option may be related to the possibility of the stock decreasing in value since the holding of the option enables the manager to avoid this risk. To use this relationship to compute the value of the stock option it is necessary that the purchase of the stock also have a positive expected value.

The analysis has been in terms of expected monetary value, thus omitting considerations of risk aversion and the accompanying problem of portfolio selection. At the level of decision making for the individual and for the firm, these considerations are relevant. They are not as relevant in considering the public policy question of whether managers have had tremendous opportunities for wealth by possessing the opportunity to receive stock options.[15]

The "call" either in the form of an option, warrant, or in some other form is an attractive type of security to a wide range of investors because it offers the possibility of large gains for relatively small investment. (The investment is small compared to buying shares of common stock.) We can expect to see these securities used extensively by corporations in the future, especially in combination with other safer securities, such as bonds.

---

[15] The tax treatment of qualified gains associated with stock options as capital gains does tend to make stock options a desirable form of compensation from the point of a manager in a high tax bracket. But since the firm cannot deduct an expense for the stock option, the granting of a stock option is not an unmixed blessing from a tax standpoint.

PROBLEMS

1. The common stock of the ABC Company is now selling at a price of $60 per share. There is a .5 probability that the stock will go up to $100 and .5 probability that it will go down to $40. You can buy an option to buy 100 shares of the stock at a price of $60 during the time period that the above probabilities apply. (The time period of this problem is short and it is not necessary to discount for time.)

Assume you are willing to use expected monetary value as the basis for your decisions.

Required: (a) What is the expected value of buying the stock?
  (b) If you could not buy the stock, what is the expected value of the option to buy?
  (c) Assuming you can buy the stock, what is the expected value of the option to buy?
  (d) Assume you could purchase the option described for $1500, would you buy it?
  (e) Assume you could purchase the option described for $1500, would you buy it if the common stock could not be purchased currently?

2. Continue Problem 1. Assume the option price and the market price of the stock at the time of the option is $80 (instead of $60).

Required: (a) What is the expected value of the option?
  (b) What would be the expected value of the option if the option exercise price is $55 when the market price is $80?

3. The RST Company has given warrants to purchase 50,000 shares of common stock to the brokers who handled a recent stock issue. The stock can be purchased at a price of $5 per share. There is a .2 probability that it will sell for a price of $20 and a .8 probability that it will be worthless.

The warrants allow the broker to purchase the stock at a price of $8. Assume you make decisions using expected monetary value.

Required: (a) What is the expected net value of buying 50,000 shares of stock at $5?
  (b) What is the absolute value of the warrants?
  (c) How much would you pay for the warrants?
  (d) If the warrants allowed the broker to buy the shares at $6, how much would the warrants be worth?

4. The XYZ Company has given warrants to purchase 50,000 shares of common stock to the brokers who handled a recent stock issue for the company. The stock can be purchased at a price of $12 per share. There is a .3 probability that the stock will become worthless and a .7 probability that it will sell for $20.

The warrants allow the broker to purchase the stock at $14 per share. Assume you make decisions using expected monetary value.

Required: (a) What is the expected net value of buying 50,000 shares of stock at $12?
   (b) What is the absolute expected value of the warrants?
   (c) What is the relative expected value of the warrants?
   (d) Assume the probability of the $20 price is .6 and a $0 price is .4. What is the relative expected value of the warrants with these probabilities?

5. In 1967 Ling–Temco–Vought (L–T–V) made a tender offer for the common stock of Greatamerica Corporation. For each share of common, L–T–V offered a 20-year, 5% debenture with a face value of $30 and one-tenth of a warrants for the purchase of a share of L–T–V common stock at $120 per share. The bonds could be used at par to finance the purchase the common stock warranted during the first five years. On the day of the tender announcement L–T–V closed at 154 and Greatamerica at 19.

The corporate income tax rate was .48 and industrial bonds were selling at between 6 and 7%. The earnings per share for L–T–V during 1966 were $4.02 and for Greatamerica were $.90 (the income was $15,000,000 and there were 16,600,000 shares outstanding.)

Required: Discuss the offer from the point of view of the two groups of stockholders concerned.

REFERENCES

Boness, James. "Elements of a Theory of Stock-Option Value," *The Journal of Political Economy* (April), 1964.

Campbell, E. D. "Stock Options Should be Valued," *Harvard Business Review* (July–August), 1961.

Cootner, P. *The Random Character of Stock Market Prices* (MIT Press, Cambridge, 1964).

Holland, D. M., and Lewellen, Wilbur G. "Probing the Record of Stock Options," *Harvard Business Review* (March–April), 1962.

Samuelson, P. "Ration Theory of Warrant Pricing," *Industrial Management Review* (Spring), 1965.

Shelton, J. P. "The Relation of the Price of a Warrant to the Price of its Associated Stock, "*Financial Analysts Journal* (May–June) and (July–August), 1967.

CHAPTER 17

The Valuation of Convertible Bonds

SYMBOLS

C_n — the market price of the convertible bond that matures at period n

C — the expected value of holding the convertible bond one period

B — the convertible bond's value as a bond

S — the number of shares of common stock into which a bond can be converted

P_n — price per share at time n

$\bar{P}_n$ — the expected value of P_n

P_c — the conversion price per share of common stock and we assume

$$P_c = \frac{B}{S}$$

$f(P_n)$ — the density function for the price per share of common stock at time period n

$F(B/S)$ — the probability that the price per share one period from now will be less than B/S

$E_{B/S}^{\infty}(P_1)$ — the partial expectation of P_1

V — the expected value of buying C_0/P_0 shares

B_t — the value as a bond at time t

$n - t$ — the number of periods until maturity

r — the time-value discount factor (rate of interest)

c — the coupon rate on the convertible bonds

M — the face value of the convertible bond

The use of convertible bonds to raise additional debt capital that is likely to be converted into common stock (thus creating a favorable situation for issuing more debt) has been a growing phenomenon.[1] These securities have many of

---

[1] See Robert R. McKenzie, "Convertible Securities, 1956–1965," *The Quarterly Review of Economics and Business* (Winter, 1966), pp. 41–51; Eugene F. Brigham, "An Analysis of Convertible Debentures: Theory and Some Empirical Evidence," *The Journal of Finance* (March, 1966), pp. 35–54; and, for an earlier study, James Pilcher, *Raising Capital with*

the characteristics of debt; thus they may appeal to the person who normally purchases debt. At the same time the security offers, by way of the conversion feature, the possibility of large gains, thus appealing to the person who normally buys common stock.

In addition to its broader appeal, a convertible security also has another characteristic, which may be an advantage or a disadvantage. The valuation of a convertible bond is more difficult than either the valuation of a bond or common stock. The difficulties arise from the fact that the security is part stock, part debt, with the holder having to devise a decision rule as to when he will convert to common stock. In general, the valuation problem cannot be solved until the problem of optimal conversion strategy has been solved.

We will only consider a simple one-period situation to illustrate the basic elements of valuing a convertible security. This model follows the valuation model presented by Baumol, Malkiel, and Quandt, though it differs by not accepting a preliminary model, which they offer,[2] and by adding a "sell short" alternative.

A Simplified Model of Valuation

We will attempt to determine the value of a convertible bond that matures in one time period. The value will be determined for an investor who currently holds the security.

Let C_n be the market price of the convertible bond at period n
  C be the expected value of holding the convertible bond one period
  B be the convertible bond's value as a bond if held to maturity (includes any interest earned but not collected)
  S be the number of shares of common stock into which the bond can be converted
  P_n be the price per share of common stock at period n
  $\bar{P}_n$ be the expected value of P_n
  P_c be the conversion price per share of common stock (we assume that $P_c = B/S$)
  $f(P_n)$ be the density function for the price per share of common stock at time period n

Convertible Securities (University of Michigan Press, Ann Arbor, 1955). Also see Otto H. Poensgen, "The Valuation of Convertible Bonds," *Industrial Management Review*, Vol. 7, Nos. 1 and 2 (Fall, 1965 and Spring, 1966).
  [2] W. J. Baumol, B. G. Malkiel, and R. E. Quandt, "The Valuation of Convertible Securities," *The Quarterly Journal of Economics* (February, 1966), pp. 48–59. We do not accept the model offered on page 50 (Equation 2). On page 54 the authors modify this model to a form that is acceptable.

The investor has three choices.

1. *Sell* the convertible bond (including the alternative of selling the bond and buying the common stock).
2. *Convert* into common stock.
3. *Hold* for one time period.[3]

If C_0 (the current market price of the convertible bond) is greater than C, P_0S, and $\bar{P}_1S$, the investor would be better off to sell the bond; if C_0 is greater than P_0S but $\bar{P}_1/P_0$ is greater than C/C_0, the investor would be better off to sell but he may immediately buy the common stock (the stock is a better investment than the bonds if $\bar{P}_1/P_0$ is greater than C/C_0); otherwise he will hold.[4]

If P_0S is greater than C_0, it would be more desirable to convert than to sell the bond. Again assuming zero transaction costs, we could convert to stock, sell the stock, buy more bonds, and continue the cycle until the market adjusted. It is unlikely that this situation would occur, and if it did occur the market forces would soon tend to make C_0 at least as large as P_0S.

Now consider the value C obtained from holding the security one period (to maturity). At Time one if we convert we will receive P_1S. If we do not convert we will receive B. Assume that collection of the bond's face value is certain at maturity, but that P_1 is a random variable with a density function $f(P_1)$. If $P_1 > B/S$ we will want to convert; if $P_1 < B/S$ we will want to sell the bond.

The expected value of the "hold" decision is

$$C = \int_0^{B/S} Bf(P_1)\, dP_1 + \int_{B/S}^\infty P_1 Sf(P_1)\, dP_1$$

$$= BF(B/S) + S \overset{\infty}{\underset{B/S}{E}} (P_1), \qquad (17\text{–}1)$$

where $F(B/S) = \text{prob}\,(P_1 \le B/S)$ and $E_{B/P}^\infty (P_1)$ is the partial expectation of P_1.

We can also express the value of the "hold" decision in a somewhat different manner. The value of holding the convertible bond one period is equal to its value as a bond (which we will assume is B) plus a value factor arising from the conversion feature. This can be expressed mathematically as

$$C = B + \int_{B/S}^\infty [P_1S - B]f(P_1)\, dP_1. \qquad (17\text{–}2)$$

---

[3] We are ignoring time value of money, different margin requirements, and transaction costs for stocks and convertible bonds and personal-income tax considerations that could affect the decision, and are assuming that we are willing to use expected monetary value as the guide to decision making.

[4] The expected value of holding is C; the expected value of selling is $C_0/P_0 \times \bar{P}_1$. Sell is better than hold if $C_0/P_0 \times \bar{P}_1 > C$ or $\bar{P}_1/P_0 > C/C_0$.

This approach can be shown to be equivalent to our former method of evaluating C:

$$C = B - B(1 - F(B/S)) + S\int_{B/S}^{\infty} P_1 f(P_1)\, dP_1$$

$$= BF(B/S) + S\sum_{B/S}^{\infty} (P_1). \tag{17-3}$$

The expression for C in Equation 17-2 (the value of the bond plus the integral) may be explained as follows. The convertible bond's value is equal to the basic value of the bond plus the expectation of a gain arising from price appreciation of the common stock. Appreciation only occurs if P_1 is greater than B/S; thus the limits of the integral from B/S to ∞. The amount of the gain is $(P_1 S - B)$, and the density function $f(P_1)$ is included to take into consideration the likelihood of the gain. Thus the term represented by the integral represents the expected increase in value arising from the conversion terms attached to the bond.[5]

EXAMPLE: Assume a convertible bond has the following characteristics:

$$C_0 = \$1200$$
$$B = \$1000$$
$$S = 4, B/S = \$250$$
$$P_0 = \$200$$

P_1 has the following probability distribution:

.1	$100
.5	200
.4	400

The expected value of the "hold" decision is

$$C = BF(B/S) + S\sum_{B/S}^{\infty}(P_1)$$

$$= 1000 \times .6 + 4(400 \times .4)$$

$$= 600 + 640 = 1240.$$

Since C_0 is larger than $P_0 S$ we would not convert now as compared to selling now ($1200 is larger than 4 times $200). Should we sell and receive $1200?

[5] From Equation 17-1 it can be shown that C will always be greater than $\bar{P}_1 S$.

Based on the analysis, the expected value of the "hold" decision is $1240 and the investor would continue to hold if he compares the $1240 with the current price of $1200 or with the $800 value from immediate conversion.

Considering a Buy Stock Alternative

The analysis in our example considered three alternatives available to the decision maker but failed to consider the possibility of selling the bonds and buying the common stock. Using the information from the example being examined we have an expected value for P_1 of $270:

$$
\begin{aligned}
.1 \times \$100 &= 10 \\
.5 \times 200 &= 100 \\
.4 \times 400 &= 160 \\
\hline
\bar{P}_1 &= \$270
\end{aligned}
$$

Since P_0 is $200, using expected monetary value, the stock is an attractive investment. We have computed the expected value of the bond to the investor to be $1240 and he can only sell the bonds for $1200 (this is the market price); thus we concluded that the investor should hold. Now consider what happens if he sells the convertible bond and invests his proceeds in the stock. He receives $1200 with which he can buy 6 shares of common stock. Each share of common stock has an expected value of $270. The expected value of selling the bonds and buying the six shares of common stock is $1620. Based on this analysis, it is better to sell the bonds at less than expected value and invest in the common stock than it would be to hold the bonds.

We have computed the expected value of the "hold" decision to be

$$
C = BF(B/S) + S \sum_{B/S}^{\infty} (P_1).
$$

V, the expected value of buying C_0/P_0 shares, is

$$
V = \frac{C_0}{P_0} \bar{P}_1. \tag{17–4}
$$

The relative value of holding the bond compared to selling it and buying the stock is

$$
C - V = BF(B/S) + S \sum_{B/S}^{\infty} (P_1) - \frac{C_0}{P_0} \bar{P}_1. \tag{17–5}
$$

For the example:

$$C - V = 1000 \times .6 + 4(160) - \frac{1200}{6} \times 270$$

$$= 1240 - 1620 = -\$380.$$

On a straight expected monetary value basis the stock is preferred to the convertible bond.

Let us now change the probability distribution of P_1 to

.3	$100
.6	200
.1	400

The expected value of the "hold" decision is now

$$C = BF(B/S) + S \mathop{E}_{B/S}^{\infty} (P_1)$$

$$= 1000 \times .9 + 4(400 \times .1) = 1060.$$

Now C is less than the current market value of the convertible bond, and the investor would now conclude that the bond should be sold for $1200. The investor would not hold the bond since the expected value of the "hold" decision is only $1060. He would not convert into common stock since four shares of the common stock are now worth only $800, with an expected value of $190 per share ($760 in total) for the next period. This disequilibrium situation may arise because the investor's view of the probability distribution for the P_1 differs from the market's view.

Selling Short: No Discounting (One Period)

We will first assume a situation where we buy (or sell) today and complete the transaction in the next period. To simplify the presentation we shall ignore the time value of money.

The net expected value of buying a convertible bond is

$$\text{Buy bond} = \int_0^{B/S} Bf(P_1)\, dP_1 + \int_{B/S}^{\infty} SP_1 f(P_1)\, dP_1 - C_0. \qquad (17\text{--}6)$$

The net expected value from selling S shares of the common stock short is

$$\text{Sell stock short} = P_0 S - \int_0^{\infty} SP_1 f(P_1)\, dP_1. \qquad (17\text{--}7)$$

If we buy bonds *and* sell short we have

$$\text{Buy bonds and sell short} = BF(B/S) - S \overset{B/S}{\underset{0}{\text{E}}} (P_1) + P_0 S - C_0. \quad (17\text{--}8)$$

EXAMPLE: Assume the following facts apply to the convertible bond and common stock of a company:

$$P_0 = 250 \qquad S = 4 \qquad B = 1000 \qquad C_0 = 1050.$$

P_1 has the following probability distribution:

$.8 \times \$200 = \$160$

$.2 \times \$350 = 70$

$E(P_1) = \bar{P}_1 = 230$

$$\text{Buy bond} = BF(B/S) + S \overset{\infty}{\underset{B/S}{\text{E}}} (P_1) - C_0$$

$$= 1000 \times .8 + 4 \times (.2 \times 350) - 1050 = 800 + 280 - 1050 = 30$$

Sell short 4 shares $= +1000 - 4(230) = 80$.

The expected value of doing both is:

$$\text{Buy bond and sell short} = BF(B/S) - S \overset{B/S}{\underset{0}{\text{E}}} (P_1) + P_0 S - C_0$$

$$= 1000 \times .8 - 4 \times 160 + 1000 - 1050$$

$$= 110 \text{ [also equal to the value of the bond (\$30)}$$
$$\text{plus the value of selling short 4 shares (\$80)].}$$

The decision trees for the three alternatives are of interest (Figs. 17–1 to 17–3).

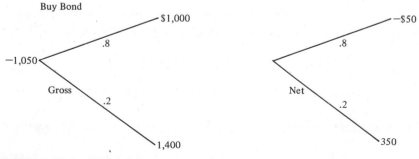

FIGURE 17–1. Buy bond.

If we just bought the convertible bond we would have a .8 probability of $50 loss. If we sold short the common stock we would have a .2 probability of a $400 loss. After buying the convertible bond and selling short the probability of a $50 loss is reduced to .2.[6]

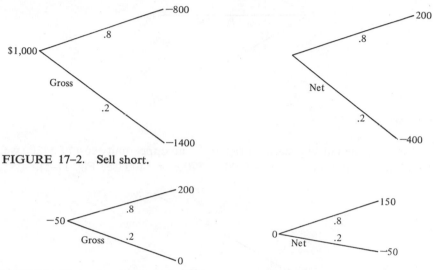

FIGURE 17–2. Sell short.

FIGURE 17–3. Buy bond and sell short.

Risk Considerations

Let us return to the original example where P_1 has the following probability distribution:

.1	$100
.5	200
.4	400

Up to this point we have considered expected monetary values. Risk attitudes are another factor that must be considered. We have looked at the expected values in our example and have concluded that it is possible to increase the expected value of our holdings by selling the bonds and buying the stock (neglecting transaction costs and personal taxes). Let us now consider the changes in risk that occur if the investor switches. Holding the bond, the investor faces the situation shown in Fig. 17–4.

[6] In reality the proceeds from selling short would not be received immediately. In fact, the investor would have to make an outlay at time zero equal to some percentage of the value of the stock sold short. Also, the change in risk will be a function of the number of shares sold short.

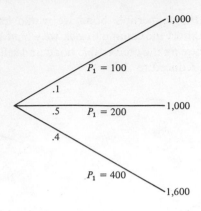

FIGURE 17-4

Considering the current market price to be an opportunity cost of $1200 we would have changes of either − $200, − $200, or $400 (see Fig. 17–5).

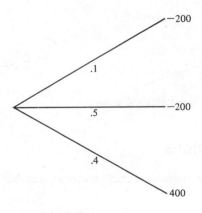

FIGURE 17-5

If we sell the bond for $1200 and invest the proceeds in stock, the investor now faces the situation shown in Fig. 17–6.

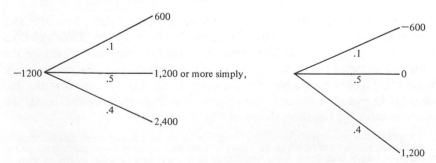

FIGURE 17-6

Let us compare the two relevant decision trees (Fig. 17–7) showing the net results:

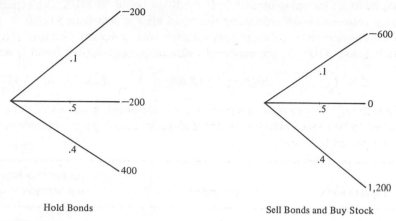

Hold Bonds   Sell Bonds and Buy Stock

FIGURE 17–7

The decision "Sell bonds and buy stock" has the higher expected value but there is also the .1 probability of losing $600 (compared to .6 probability of losing $200 if we hold the bonds). It is not obvious as to which decision is more desirable when we consider risk preferences or aversions of the investor.

It is important to recognize that one of the inputs into the valuation of the convertible bond is the expectation concerning future stock prices. If we are optimistic about the performance of the stock this may lead to a decision to buy the convertible bonds. However, before paying a premium for the bonds, the opportunity to buy the common stock must also be evaluated. The same optimism that leads to an accept decision for the bonds is likely to lead to an accept decision for the common stock. The choice will hinge in part on risk preferences of the investor.

Allowing the Bond Price to Change: One-Period Case

We will now consider a complication in the analysis. It is likely that the value of the convertible security *as a bond* will not be constant through time. There are several factors at work that will tend to cause the value to change. Among these factors are:

1. A change in value as the length of time till maturity changes.
2. Changing interest rates.
3. A change in risk arising from changes in the financial affairs of the corporation.

In our example we assumed that *B* measured the amount that would be received one period from now from the corporation. Thus P_1S had to be higher than B if the stock were to be converted. We will now assume that the bonds have a face value of $1000. If P_1 drops below $1000/S$, the expected amount recoverable on redeeming the bond may be less than $1,000.

If we consider B to be a random variable with a density function $g(B)$ if P_1 falls below $1000/S$, the expected value of the convertible bond is now[7]

$$C = \int_0^{1000/S} \int_0^{1000} Bf(P_1)g(B) \, dB \, dP_1 + \int_{1000/S}^{\infty} P_1Sf(P_1) \, dP_1. \quad (17\text{--}9)$$

Continuing this example, assume that the following amounts of debt are expected to be recoverable for the three respective stock prices that are possible one period from now.

PROBABILITY	STOCK PRICE	EXPECTED BOND REDEMPTION VALUE	
.1	100	980	$.90 \rbrace$ 1000 $.10 \rbrace$ 800
.5	200	1000	
.4	400	1000	

$C = .1 [.9 \times 1000 + .1 \times 800] + .5(1000) + .4(4) (400)$
$= 98 + 500 + 640 = \$1238$

When we assumed the redemption value of the bond was certain to be $1000, the expected value of the convertible bond was $1240. Because we are allowing the stock price to fall substantially, we should also allow the redemption value of the bonds to reflect the possibility of events that could result in bonds being redeemed at a lower value than $1000.

Bond Value Changes: Multiperiod Case with Discounting

We have stated that the value of a convertible bond in the one-period case is equal to its value as a bond plus the value of the conversion feature. We will now consider the determination of its value as a bond where there are $(n - t)$ periods to maturity.

Let B_t be the value as a bond at time t

$n - t$ be the number of periods until maturity

   r be the time value or discount factor used to evaluate comparable bonds without the conversion privilege

[7] Assuming B is always greater than P_1S when P_1 is less than $1000/S$.

c be the coupon rate on the convertible bond

M be the face value of the convertible bond

We will assume that interest is paid annually and that the first interest payment is due one period from now. The value today is

$$B_0 = \sum_{i=1}^{n} \frac{cM}{(1 + r)^i} + \frac{M}{(1 + r)^n}. \tag{17-10}$$

Comparing the values for two years, t and $t + 1$, we have

$$B_t = \sum_{i=1}^{n-t} \frac{cM}{(1 + r)^i} + \frac{M}{(1 + r)^{n-t}}. \tag{17-11}$$

$$B_{t+1} = \sum_{i=1}^{n-t-1} \frac{cM}{(1 + r)^i} + \frac{M}{(1 + r)^{n-t-1}}. \tag{17-12}$$

Subtracting Equation 17-11 from Equation 17-12, we obtain

$$B_{t+1} - B_t = \frac{M(r - c)}{(1 + r)^{n-t}}. \tag{17-13}$$

EXAMPLE: Assume we have a $1000 convertible bond ($1000 maturity value) that has a 4% coupon and twenty-year maturity ($n = 20$). The current interest rate on comparable (nonconvertible) bonds is 6%.

The values of the bond (as a bond) for different years (different values of t) are:

t	B_t	$B_{t+1} - B_t$	$\dfrac{M(r - c)}{(1 + r)^{n-t}}$
0	770.60	6.23	20(.3118) = 6.24
1	776.83	6.61	20(.3305) = 6.61
2	783.44		

B_t will increase by $M(r - c)/(1 + r)^{n-t}$ per year until B_t finally is equal to $1000 at $t = 20$.

Conclusions

We have investigated the valuation of convertible bonds when there is the alternative of holding for one period. We did not consider the situation in which the investor has to decide whether or not to convert or sell when there are many time periods. This would be a problem that lent itself to dynamic programming, the solution of which would be somewhat more difficult than the analysis of this chapter. For example, we would have to choose a probability distribution for future stock prices as well as for future interest rates.

Despite the limitations of the model considered, insights are offered as to the components of value obtained when a convertible bond is purchased. As in many other situations, perhaps the most valuable use of the analytical approach is that it enables us to break down the analysis into small enough pieces so that we can see the effect of alternative decisions and possible events.

PROBLEMS

1. The current market value of a convertible bond is $1260. The bonds have a maturity value of $1000. As a bond (without the conversion feature), the bonds have a value of $1000 (based on the market value of comparable bonds).

   Each bond is convertible into five shares of common stock.

   The current market price of the common stock is $210. It is expected that the price of the stock in the next time period will have the following probability distribution:

.1	$200
.8	250
.1	400

   Assume you are administering a portfolio that holds these bonds.

   Required: (a) Would you continue to hold the bonds or would you sell?
   (b) Assuming you had the cash would you buy the common stock?
   (c) Would you be better off selling the bonds and buying the stock?
   (d) Assuming the bond (as a bond) is perfectly safe, what are the risks of holding the bond compared to selling the bond and purchasing the common stock?

2. Continue Problem 1. Change the probabilities of the stock prices to be:

.1	$0
.8	250
.1	400

   Required: (a) Would you continue to hold the bonds or would you sell?
   (b) Assuming you had the cash, would you buy the common stock?

(c) Would you be better off selling the bonds and buying the common stock?

(d) Assuming the bond (as a bond) is perfectly safe, what are the risks of holding the bond compared to selling the bond and purchasing the common stock?

3. Continue Problem 2. Assume that it has been suggested that you continue to hold the bonds for one period and sell short immediately shares of common stock.

Required: (a) Prepare an analysis showing the risk of holding the bonds and selling short six shares.

(b) Repeat for selling short three shares.

(c) Assume the bond market price is $1050. Prepare a risk analysis for selling short five shares and holding a bond.

4. Continue Problem 1. Assume the probability of the stock price one period hence are

.3	$0
.6	250
.1	600

Required: (a) Would you want to hold the bonds?

(b) Would you buy the common stock?

(c) Prepare an analysis showing the risk of holding the bonds, selling short five shares, and doing both.

(d) Repeat (b) assuming you sell short four shares.

(e) Repeat (b) assuming you sell short two shares.

5. In 1966 Litton Industries issued a convertible preference stock to the stockholders of the company in exchange for shares of common stock and the outstanding convertible preferred stock.

Common holders could exchange $12\frac{1}{2}\%$ of their shares for the new convertible preference stock. The rate of exchange was one share of new convertible preference stock for one share of common.

The preference shares paid noncumulative cash dividends equal to the cash dividends declared on each share of common stock multiplied by the conversion rate then in effect.

The conversion rate starts at one for one and increases at a compound rate of 3.09% annually until 1989 when it becomes 2.014 shares of common for each share of preferred. The rate is adjusted for stock dividends paid on common stock exceeding $2\frac{1}{2}\%$.

All the shares are redeemable after January 1, 1976 at the option of the company at an initial price of $67.75 per share. However, each stockholder may ask the company to redeem up to 3% of his holdings annually (the company has the option of refusing). The initial redemption price is

$51.65 in 1967 with the redemption price increasing 3.09% annually until the redemption price reaches $100.95 per share in 1989.

In liquidation the preference shares receive $25 per share prior to any distribution on the common stock.

The company has been paying a $2\frac{1}{2}$% annual stock dividend.

Required: (a) If you held 1000 shares of common stock would you convert your holdings?

(b) Discuss the company's motivations in issuing this type of security in exchange for shares of common stock.

6. In 1966, Ling–Temco–Vought (L–T–V) tendered offers for shares of its own common stock in exchange for cash and convertible preferred stock. In exchange for ten shares of common the holder would receive $200 cash and five shares of convertible preferred stock paying $3 annual cumulative dividends. The company set a limit of 1 million shares to be the maximum number of shares tendered.

During 1966, the market price of the common shares ranged from 38 to 80. The earnings per share of the common stock were $6.03 and the dividends were $1 per share.

Required: Discuss some of the possible reasons for the tender offer.

REFERENCES

Baumol, W. J., Malkiel, B. G., and Quandt, R. E. "The Valuation of Convertible Securities," *The Quarterly Journal of Economics* (February), 1966.

Brigham, Eugene F. "An Analysis of Convertible Debentures: Theory and Some Empirical Evidence," *The Journal of Finance* (March), 1966.

Broman, K. L. "The Use of Convertible Subordinated Debentures by Industrial Firms, 1949–59," *Quarterly Review of Economics and Business* (Spring), 1963.

McKenzie, Robert R. "Convertible Securities, 1956–1965," *The Quarterly Review of Economics and Business* (Winter), 1966.

Pilcher, James. *Raising Capital with Convertible Securities* (University of Michigan Press, Ann Arbor, 1955).

Poensgen, O. H. "The Valuation of Convertible Bonds," *Industrial Management Review* (Fall), 1965 and (Spring), 1966.

CHAPTER 18

Stock Options and Other Employee Compensation Plans

SYMBOLS

t_c the marginal tax rate for corporations

t_p the marginal tax rate for the manager

t_g the tax rate on capital gains

P_e the market value of the common stock at the time of exercise

C the option price (exercise price)

W the amount of wages paid to the manager

K the value of options

The form of employee compensation is important to a firm for several reasons. One of the most important is the tax implications, but in addition there are different effects on the cash balance and the measurement of income.

We will consider four different types of employee compensation plans:

1. Wages
2. Ordinary stock options
3. Qualified stock options
4. Stock purchase plans

Prior to 1964 managers could be offered "restricted stock options," but since the 1964 change in the internal revenue code this type of stock option plan is no longer available to managers and thus will not be discussed here.

It should be noted that different tax relations will change the details of the analysis but not the basic form. The material that follows assumes the 1964 tax code is in effect.

Wages

Wages are the most straightforward method of employee compensation and the economic effects of wages are the easiest to analyze.

Assume a situation where a firm has cash and retained earnings equal to

$100,000 available for distribution as wages to a manager. It wants to determine the economic consequences of the alternatives.

Define t_c to be the corporate marginal tax rate and let it be equal to 48%. If the corporation paid $100,000 of wages to the manager, the net cost of the corporation would be $100,000 $(1 - t_c)$ or $52,000. The corporation would:

1. Disburse $100,000 of cash.
2. Taxes would be reduced by $48,000 or $100,000 t_c.
3. The net change in cash position would be:

wages paid	$100,000
taxes saved	48,000
Net changes in cash	$52,000

4. The decrease in the equity of the stockholders would be $52,000.

If we let W be the amount of the wages paid to the manager, the net cost to the present stockholders and net cash distributed is:

$$W(1 - t_c).$$

Let t_p be the manager's marginal tax rate. The manager would receive $100,000 cash but would have to pay $100,000 t_p taxes. With t_p equal to .48 his improvement is $52,000. The use of high personal tax rates cause "wages" to be relatively less desirable than some of the alternative plans of compensation.

Ordinary Stock Options

The issue of a stock option by a corporation to a manager serves three purposes. (1) It acts as a form of compensation for services rendered and to be rendered, (2) it conserves cash that would otherwise be paid, and (3) it brings in new equity capital, assuming that the receiver of the option has to pay some positive amount of cash on the exercise of his option.[1]

We will only consider the situation where the fair market value of an ordinary stock option is not readily ascertainable.[2] In this situation the person receiving the ordinary option has income in the year of exercising the option equal to:

$$\text{Ordinary income} = P_e - C,$$

[1] For discussions of how stock options should be valued see E. D. Campbell, "Stock Options Should be Valued," *Harvard Business Review* (July–August, 1961), pp. 52–58; D. M. Holland and Wilbur G. Lewellen, "Probing the Record of Stock Options," *Harvard Business Review* (March–April, 1962), pp. 132–150; and A. James Boness, "Elements of a Theory of Stock-Option Value," *The Journal of Political Economy* (April, 1964), pp. 163–175; see also Chapter 16.

[2] If it is ascertainable, the difference between the value of the option and the amount paid for it is income at the time the option is received.

where P_e is the market value of the common stock at the time of exercising and C is the option price.

The corporation in turn, can deduct an amount equal to $P_e - C$ from its income as a wage deduction in computing its taxable income.

Now assume a manager is offered stock that is currently selling for $600,000 for an option price of $500,000 and he has to exercise the option immediately.[3] The ordinary income is

$$\text{Ordinary income} = P_e - C,$$

$$= 600,000 - 500,000 = 100,000.$$

The $100,000 is taxed immediately (at time of exercise) as ordinary income and the corporation has a $100,000 expense deduction in computing its taxable income.

The corporation will:

1. Keep $100,000 of cash it would otherwise have disbursed as wages.
2. Reduce taxes by ($100,000 × t_c) where t_c is the corporate tax rate (assume it is .48). The tax saving is $48,000. The net cost to the firm is

$$100,000(1 - .48) = \$52,000.$$

3. The cash position is improved absolutely by $548,000, the $48,000 tax saving resulting from the $100,000 tax deduction plus $500,000 contributed by the manager exercising the option.
4. The option has been defined to have a value of $100,000. The decrease in the equity of the old stockholders (the classification "old stockholders" is exclusive of the holders of the new option) is

Total decrease	$100,000
less tax saving	48,000
Net decrease in old equity	$52,000

The manager will have $100,000 taxed as ordinary income. At a rate of t_p (where $t_p = .48$ in this example), the manager will

1. Receive options of $100,000 value.
2. Have to pay $100,000 × t_p of personal income tax at the time of the exercise of the grant. Let t_p be 48%. He will have to pay $48,000 of income tax and will have $52,000 of net improvement in his position.

The corporation's net cost is again $K(1 - t_c)$ where K is the value of the

---

[3] If the manager did not have to exercise immediately the value of the option would not be $100,000 but is likely to be something higher. At the time of exercise of the option the ordinary taxable income would be equal to the difference between the fair market value of the stock and the amount paid for it.

ordinary option. The individual's after-tax benefit is $K(1 - t_p)$. Equating these two amounts we can find a break-even value for t_p:

$$K(1 - t_c) = K(1 - t_p),$$

$$t_p = t_c.$$

If $t_c = 48\%$ then the break-even value for t_p is 48%. Thus if the manager's tax on ordinary income is in excess of 48% he would net out *less* than the net cost to the corporation. If t_p is less than 48% the manager would net out *more* than the net cost to the company.

The ordinary stock option may be combined with "restricted stock." The company can impose restrictions on the stock (e.g., prohibiting the sale of the stock for a period of time) which will delay the taxation of the income arising from the option until the restrictions lapse. There is an obvious gain to the individual of being able to delay payment of income taxes. The decrease in the value of the stock arising from the restrictions is much more difficult to measure. Nevertheless, unless there is a change in the tax law (or regulations) accelerating the moment of taxation, one can expect to see an expanded use of restricted stock as a means of deferring personal income taxes.

One artificial advantage of options arises from the accounting treatment. It is general practice not to record any expense at the time of the issuance of the option. Thus if $100,000 of value (in the form of an option) is given a manager there is no expense entry recorded. If the $100,000 had been paid in the form of dollar wages the after-tax income would be decreased by $100,000(1 - t_c)$.

Qualified Stock Option

The term "qualified stock option" refers to a stock option that meets the requirements set forth by the internal revenue code to qualify for special tax treatment. To be a qualified stock option certain conditions must be met. Included in these conditions are

1. The option price must be set equal to the fair market value of the stock at the time of the grant.
2. The option plan must be approved by the stockholders.
3. The option must be exercisable within five years of the grant.
4. The option is not transferable.
5. The employee must own less than 5% of the voting power of the company.
6. The person receiving the option must hold the stock he buys for three years after the stock is transferred to him, and he must be an employee up to within three months of the exercise of the option.

If these conditions are satisfied, then unlike the ordinary stock option the employee is not taxed when he exercises the option. He is only taxed if he sells the stock, and then only at capital gains rates for the difference between the selling price and the option price (assuming the selling price is greater than the option price).

The corporation has no business expense deduction unless the employee is taxed at ordinary rates because he has sold the stock within the three-year holding period.

Let us continue the example where the company has $100,000 to distribute. If it grants a qualified stock option worth $100,000 the following changes take place:

1. The firm keeps the $100,000 of cash it would have paid in wages.
2. Taxes are not reduced since the $100,000 is not a tax deduction.
3. The cash position of the company is not changed by the granting of the option (it will be increased when the options are exercised).
4. There is a $100,000 decrease in the equity of the stockholders (the equity will be increased when the options are exercised).

One of the necessary conditions for a qualified option is that the grant price be equal to the market price at the time of grant. Thus the option derives its value from possible changes in stock value during the five-year period from the date of grant to the end of the option period.

The individual's wealth is increased by an expected value of $100,000 but this increase is subject to taxation only if the gain actually occurs *and* if he sells. Let us ignore the problem of time value of money.[4] *If* the employee sold immediately upon exercise and if the increase in the market value over the option price is $100,000, he would have a change in wealth of

$$(1 - t_g)100,000,$$

where t_g is the capital gain rate. If we assume a .25 capital gain tax rate, the manager would have his wealth increased by $75,000. If he chose to hold the investment until death and thus avoid the income tax completely, we would not have to reduce the $100,000 by the full $25,000 (the lack of flexibility has some cost). He could also defer or avoid an income tax by making a gift of the stock.

Comparison of the Three Methods

With all three methods of compensation $100,000 was given to the manager. A summary of how the corporation was affected follows:

---

[4] Since the option period may be as long as five years and the holding period is three years, the time-value problem is nontrivial. We will assume the $100,000 is the present value of the option.

	WAGES	ORDINARY OPTION	QUALIFIED OPTION
Total amount of value given	100,000	100,000	100,000
Cash outlay	− 100,000	0	0
Tax saving	48,000	48,000	0
Change in cash	− 52,000	48,000	0
Change in the equity of the old stockholders	− 52,000	− 52,000	− 100,000

Several items should be noted. The total amount distributed to the manager is the same for all three situations. The changes in cash are different (the ordinary option being superior to the other two) and the changes in the equity of the old stockholders are different (the qualified option being inferior to the other two). Before making any conclusions about the relative desirability of three alternatives we have to consider the position of the manager.

	WAGES	ORDINARY OPTION	QUALIFIED OPTION
Value received by manager	100,000	100,000	100,000
Immediate tax (assume 48% tax rate)	48,000	48,000	0
	52,000	52,000	100,000
Future tax (assume 25%)			25,000
Benefits	52,000	52,000	75,000
Ratio of the benefits to the net cost to the corporation	$\frac{52,000}{52,000} = 1$	$\frac{52,000}{52,000} = 1$	$\frac{75,000}{100,000} = .75$ if we assume the future tax should be included or $\frac{100,000}{100,000}$ without the future tax

If we change the ordinary tax rate from 48% we can increase or decrease the relative desirability of wages and the ordinary stock options compared to the qualified option plan, but the benefit-cost rates for the qualified plan can never be greater than 1.

Assuming the benefit-cost ratios of all three plans are equal to one, we can then inspect the changes in the corporate cash position. If the firm is in need of cash, the ordinary stock option plan is better than the other two plans.[5]

From the point of view of the manager the fact that the benefit-cost ratios are equal does not mean that from his standpoint the three plans are equally desirable. The qualified option plan has more risk since the option price and market price are set equal at the time of grant. An increase in the price of the stock is necessary for the manager to realize his gains. In addition, to realize the gain the manager must hold the stock for a period of time (three years) to qualify for special tax treatment.

Instead of making the total value distributed equal for all three alternatives, we will make the change in the stock equity equal for the three alternatives. This would be the situation where the stockholders have agreed to give up a given amount of their equity; the question is how it should be done. In the following table the changes in stock equity of the old stockholders will be equal for the three alternatives.

	WAGES	ORDINARY OPTION	QUALIFIED OPTION
Total amount of value given	192,300	192,300	100,000
Cash outlay	− 192,300	0	0
Tax saving	92,300	92,300	0
Change in cash	− 100,000	92,300	0
Change in the equity of the old stockholders	− 100,000	− 100,000	− 100,000

The manager will receive the following:

	WAGES	ORDINARY OPTION	QUALIFIED OPTION
Value received by manager	192,300	192,300	100,000
Immediate tax (.48)	92,300	92,300	0
	100,000	100,000	100,000
Future tax (.25)			25,000
	100,000	100,000	75,000

[5] In addition to the 48,000 cash shown for the ordinary option there would also be the amount of cash paid in by the manager when he purchases the shares. This would increase the advantage of the ordinary option plan compared to cash wage payments even more. Stock may also be issued if wages are paid, but this procedure would result in higher transaction costs.

Again if we omit the future capital gains tax (which can be avoided) we find the ratio of benefits to costs to be identical for the three methods.[6] However, again the ordinary option conserves more cash of the corporation than the other methods.

We have not yet considered stock purchase plans, but it should be noted that at the level of the analysis being conducted, the results of using stock purchase plans would be identical with the qualified option plan as long as the option price was set equal to the market price of the stock at the time of the grant.

Risk Considerations

Before reaching a conclusion we should consider the risks as well as the expected benefits to the manager. With a wage payment the manager knows what he is receiving in the period in which the payment is made. Under the several options plans the manager may estimate the expected value of the option, but he will not know the actual value for some period of time in the future.

Let us investigate somewhat more closely the situation in which the qualified option has an expected value of $100,000. Assume the stock has an option price and present market value of $40,000, and there is a .5 probability of its value becoming $240,000 and .5 probability of its value becoming $0 during the option period. The expected value of buying is

$$E(\text{Buy}) = (.5 \times 240,000 + .5 \times 0) - 40,000 = \$80,000$$

The expected absolute value of an option to buy at $40,000 is

$$E(\text{Absolute value of option}) = .5 \times (240,000 - 40,000) = \$100,000$$

The relative value of the option compared to buying is $20,000. Since the manager can buy the stock at $40,000 without the option, it is not clear that the value of the option is $100,000 (the relative value compared to buying is only $20,000). We will tighten the example by eliminating the possiblity of buying the stock without the option. Now the expected monetary value of the option is $100,000.

If we assume an ordinary option, at the end of the option period the manager will have gained $104,000 (net of taxes) or nothing.

$$(240,000 - 40,000)(1 - .48) = 104,000.$$

---

[6] If the personal income tax were less than 48% the benefit-cost ratios of "wages" and "ordinary option" would both be greater than one and clearly somewhat larger than the qualified option plan. With the personal tax rates above 48% the qualified plan's position improves relative to the other two alternatives.

The after-tax expected value of this is .5 × 104,000 = $52,000. This is the same expected value as he would receive from $100,000 of wages taxed at 48%, but note the .5 probability of his receiving nothing of value.

Stock Purchase Plans

An alternative (or supplement) to stock options are employee stock purchase plans. The following conditions are required for special tax treatment:

1. Only employees are granted options and the plan must be approved by the stockholders.
2. The option price may not be less than the smaller of[7]
   (a) 85% of market value at the time of grant.
   (b) 85% of market value at the time of exercise.
3. The option must be exercised within a five year period of grant (if the price is less than 85% of market value at time of exercise the option must be exercised with 27 months) and the employee must be employed by the firm three months before the date of exercise.
4. Full-time employees employed in excess of two years must be eligible, with their participation proportional to salaries (a maximum participation may be set).
5. A person possessing in excess of 5% of the voting power cannot participate.
6. The options are not transferable.

A prime advantage of an employee stock purchase plan is that the employee has no tax liability at the time of grant or at the time of exercise (unlike the ordinary option.[8] Unlike the qualified stock option plan, the price at the time of grant may be less than the fair market value. Another advantage of a stock purchase plan over the qualified stock plan is that some risk is removed from the manager.

Let us assume the manager is being given an opportunity to purchase an amount of stock under a stock purchase plan. The method of evaluating the costs to the firm and the benefits to the manager would be essentially the same as we previously used in evaluating the benefits and costs of the qualified stock option plan (the tax rate on sale by the employee would be different). There would be a difference in describing and computing the value of the option. Assume that with a qualified option plan the value to the manager is $10,000, and that he is able to buy at $20,000 (the current market value) stock

---

[7] For example, if the market value at time of grant is $100 and at time of exercise is $200, the option price could be as low as $85.

[8] The corporation has no deduction.

that has a .5 probability of increasing to $40,000 and a .5 probability of becoming worthless. The expected monetary value of this option is $10,000.

Now consider a stock purchase plan with the same stock (expected to go to zero or to double in value). We will adjust the number of shares available to the manager at a price of 85% of current market value. The manager can now buy stock with a market value of $17,391 at a cost of $14,782 (this is 85% of market value).[9]

This option again has an expected value of $10,000 but the risks are less. The value of the option is equal to the $2609 gain we can realize now (17,391 − 14,782) plus the expected loss of .5 (14,782) we avoid by not exercising the option if the price goes down. Assume that all prices are possible rather than only two possibilities. Under the qualified plan if the stock went down from $20,000 (even as little a decrease as $1) the manager would have no incentive to exercise the option. With the stock purchase plan the stock price could decrease in value up to 15% and the manager would still receive something of value and would exercise the option. In fact, with stock purchase plan the option price may be variable, tending to insure the manager some benefit.

It is clear that the individual manager accepts less risk (less variance of returns) with a stock purchase plan (with option price set at 85% of market) than with a qualified stock option plan. He may have even less risk with an ordinary stock option plan since there are no restrictions on option price or holding period in that situation. A qualified stock option and a stock purchase plan can be made to give equivalent results from the point of view of a decrease in the stockholders' equity and the before tax benefits to the manager. In neither case would the corporation have a tax deduction. The effects to the corporation are very similar (the number of shares and the cash received on the exercise of the options would be different).

There are several drawbacks to the stock purchase plans.

1. Because they are given to a wide range of employees it is not possible to reward merit.
2. If the stock is sold after the required holding period (or at time of death) there is ordinary income to the employee equal to the lesser of the difference between the:
    (a) fair market value at the time of grant and the price paid
    (b) fair market value at time of selling and the option price.[10]

---

[9] If the market value doubles the value of the stock will be $34,782. The stock cost $14,782, therefore the conditional gain is $20,000 and the expected gain is $10,000. We can solve for the $17,391 as follows:

$$\tfrac{1}{2}(X - .85\ X/2) = 10,000$$
$$X = 17,391$$

[10] Assume that the option price was $85 and the fair market value at the time of grant was $100 and the stock was finally sold for $220 after the required holding period. The $15 would be ordinary income and the $120 would be taxed as a capital gain.

The tax advantage of a stock purchase plan over a qualified stock option (being able to set the grant option price at time of grant below the market price) is a way of deferring taxes, not avoiding them.

A prime advantage of the stock purchase plan, where the stock is newly issued stock, is that it is a means of raising capital. A second advantage is that it causes the workers to increase their interest in the well being of the corporation as they become owners.

Conclusions

In the absence of personal income taxes would workers (including managers) want stock options? Even without income tax considerations an employee may welcome the opportunity to become a stockholder via the exercise of a stock option. Stock options have value even without income tax considerations. Thus we can expect to see ordinary stock options used even though they do not give the individual any tax advantage compared to ordinary wages.

Despite the above concession, it becomes evident that a large function of a qualified stock option or a stock purchase plan is to gain a form of tax advantage for the employees of a firm. The merits of encouraging this sort of activity should be weighed carefully against the costs associated with one portion of the economy being able to earn income that is treated differently under the tax code than the same amount of income paid in a different form.

PROBLEMS

1. The ABC Company wants an analysis of the costs and other effects of three different forms of compensation to its employees. It is considering either paying dollar wages, using ordinary stock options, or qualified stock options. The decisions will affect $1 million marginal compensation (the basic wage bill is $50 million). The corporate tax rate is 40% and the time value of money is assumed to be zero.

   For all the alternatives there will be $1 million value given to the employees. Assume stock with a market value of $11 million will be issued immediately for $10 million with the ordinary stock option. Assume stock will be issued for $11 million with the qualified plan, but the option will be for a larger period of time and has a value of $1 million now.

   Required: For each plan alternative compute:

      (a) the direct gross cash disbursement.
      (b) the net change in cash position considering all factors. Assume all options are exercised.

   (c) the change in the stock equity arising from the effect on costs or expenses.
   (d) the change in the stock equity arising from the contribution of new capital.
   (e) Assume all workers are in the 20% ordinary income and 10% capital gains tax rate brackets. How much of the compensation will the workers retain? Assume the acquired stock is not sold.
   (f) Assume all workers are in 70% ordinary income and 25% capital gains tax rate brackets. How much of the compensation will the workers retain? Assume the acquired stock is not sold.

2. Continue Problem 1. For the three methods of compensation prepare an analysis showing:
   (a) how the cash position of the corporation was affected (include the cash contributions associated with the issue of stock).
   (b) how the equity of the present stockholders was affected (the cost or expense of the policy).
   (c) the before and after tax value received by the workers (without sale of stock) with both the 20% and 70% tax rates.
   (d) the ratio of the benefit received by the worker to the net cost to the corporation (the cost to the old stockholders).

3. Continue Problem 2. Repeat Problem 2(d) for wages and the qualified option plan but assume the persons receiving the stock options sell the stock thus have to pay capital gains tax on the $1 million benefits.

4. (a) Evaluate the risk from the point of view of the employees for wages, ordinary stock options, and qualified stock options.
   (b) Assume the common stock now selling for $11 million has the following probability distribution for prices in the future:

   .75 $20,000,000

   .25   7,000,000

   What would be the value of an option to buy this stock at a price of $11 million assuming the stock can be purchased on the open market for $11 million?

5. Repeat the calculations for Problem 1 assuming the tax rate of the employees is 40%.
   Required: Assume the stock acquired by option is not sold.

6. Continue Problems 1 and 2. Instead of distributing 1 million of value to the employees assume the stockholders decide to distribute $600,000 of after corporate income tax value.

Required: Recompute the items listed in Problem 2. Assume the employees all pay 40% income tax on marginal income and that stock acquired via option plans is retained by the investors. Do not include in the analysis the cash received by the corporation on the issue of stock for the stock option plans.

7. The ABC Company (see Problem 1) is considering an employee stock purchase plan.

Required: (a) Prepare an analysis of the costs to the firm and the benefits of the employees including a ratio of benefits to cost. Assume a 40% personal tax rate.

(b) Assume that the probability of the stock currently selling at $11 per share going to $20 is 75% and the probability of it going to $1 is 25%. How many shares of stock have to be optioned in order for the value of the option to be $1 million?

Under the qualified stock option plan options for 1 million shares were issued. Under a stock purchase plan where the purchase price is $10 how many shares would have to be submitted for purchase in order for the value of the rights to be 1 million? The employees do not have to decide whether or not to exercise the options until the above prices are determined.

REFERENCES

Boness, A. James. "Elements of a Theory of Stock–Option Value," *The Journal of Political Economy* (April), 1964.

Campbell, E. D. "Stock Options Should be Valued," *Harvard Business Review* (July–August), 1961.

Holland, D. M., and Lewellen, Wilbur G. "Probing the Record of Stock Options," *Harvard Business Review* (March–April), 1962.

National Industrial Conference Board, *Employee Stock Purchase Plans*, Personnel Policy Study No. 206, 1967.

———. *Top Executive Compensation*, Personnel Policy No. 204, 1966.

Index